Why Have They Taken Our Children?

*Chowchilla,
July 15, 1976*

Why Have They Taken Our Children?

Chowchilla, July 15, 1976

JACK W. BAUGH · JEFFERSON MORGAN

DELACORTE PRESS/NEW YORK

Published by
Delacorte Press
1 Dag Hammarskjold Plaza
New York, New York 10017

Manufactured in the United States of America

First printing

LIBRARY OF CONGRESS CATALOGING IN PUBLICATION DATA

Baugh, Jack W.
   Why have they taken our children? : Chowchilla,
July 15, 1976.

   1. Kidnapping—California—Chowchilla.
I. Morgan, Jefferson, joint author. II. Title.
HV6602.C48B38   364.1′54′0979481   77–26811

ISBN: 0–440–09463–1

For Marcia and Jinx

Preface

One of the first things a reader of this work might notice is that although one of the authors was at the center of the investigation into the Chowchilla kidnapping, the narrative is cast in the third person. There are a number of reasons for this.

The first is that Jack Baugh claims little credit for solving what may have been the most emotionally charged crime of a generation. Instead, he attributes the success of the investigation to the dedication of hundreds of people in a dozen different agencies who worked on the case. In that sense it is more a book by, rather than about, him. It is not his story alone.

Second, we decided that since so many of the events recorded here occurred outside of his presence most of the book would have been written in the third person anyway.

Finally, I have learned that Jack is an unnecessarily modest man, who has become a good friend.

For my part, after nearly twenty years as a journalist, much of the time devoted to covering law enforcement at different levels in several parts of the country, I was struck by the intelligence, determination, and cooperation displayed by almost everyone involved in the case, in particular all of those employed by Jack's department. He and I dedicated the book to our wives because of their heroic patience during its preparation. It could as easily have been dedicated to the men and women of the Alameda County Sheriff's Department.

—Jefferson Morgan

Acknowledgments

If I attempted to express my gratitude to all the people who deserve it for their part in the investigation or for their help on this book, the list would be longer than most of the chapters. However, some individuals and agencies must be singled out for special thanks. They include all of the professional men and women in law enforcement who worked on the case, particularly:

Lieutenant Ed Volpe and the entire Alameda County Sheriff's Department, including the best crime lab crew in the country;

Charles Bates, special agent in charge of the Federal Bureau of Investigation in San Francisco, now retired, since without the FBI we would probably still be looking for two of the three kidnappers;

The California Department of Justice, especially Sam Erwin, the expert on latent fingerprints, and John Lilly and Norm Gard for their unflagging cooperation and suggestions;

Everyone in the Hayward office of the California Highway Patrol;

The Federal Bureau of Alcohol, Tobacco, and Firearms;

The San Mateo County Sheriff's Department;

The San Jose Police Department;

The Atherton Police Department;

The Tuolumne County Sheriff's Department;
The Marin County Sheriff's Department;
The California Air National Guard;
The Royal Canadian Mounted Police.

Finally, I would like to thank Jack Keith for suggesting the book in the first place and for his perseverance, and Robert Gutwillig for his enthusiasm and encouragement, and for introducing me to Jeff Morgan.

—Jack Baugh

Prologue

In the beginning California's great San Joaquin Valley was a forbidding place, inhospitable to those who came from the south to plunder in the name of their king and the Church. They were repelled both by the land and its inhabitants, Indians descended from the ancient and forgotten race who built the buried cities of the Southwest that have perplexed and confounded European man since Coronado sought fruitlessly his El Dorado.

The huge valley that would one day be tamed into a sun-baked garden producing a quarter of the nation's food was then a wild, marshy swale made virtually impenetrable by the *tulares* and the endless sloughs that covered the valley floor at high water. The Indians, called Chauciles, were aggressive and stole horses from the first Mexican explorers who finally ventured into what is now Madera County in 1825.

The Mexicans were followed by Englishmen and Americans, like Kit Carson, who came to trap the beaver in the alpine streams of the Sierra Nevada in the eastern end of Madera County. They found herds of elk and wild horses and giant trees they called sequoia, and high in the mountains they came upon a spectacular mass of basaltic columns, monoliths left over from the Creation, carved by glaciers from volcanic lava, as wide as a man and standing up to sixty feet high. Sure that such a mindless jumble could not be the work of God, they called it the Devil's Postpile.

Later they would find gold in the Sierra foothills, and virgin stands of sugar pine, fir, and cedar would yield up millions of board feet of lumber after the railroad reached the valley in the 1870s. In fact they would name the county and its seat Madera after the Spanish word for wood.

But it was on the broad, fertile bottomland that the real riches lay, not necessarily for those who worked the rich black soil after the meandering waterways fed by the mountain creeks and rivers were reordered into irrigation canals, but for those who owned it. In 1914 a man named O. A. Robertson founded the United States Farm Land Company, and a town was incorporated on the south side of the Chowchilla River about halfway between Madera and the seat of adjacent Merced County. It would become one of dozens of agricultural hamlets in the great valley fenced by the Sierra on the east and California's Coast Range on the west. Chowchilla has twenty-two churches and 4,600 residents. The adults have an average of 9.8 years of public-school education.

Chowchilla was christened innocently after the river, which took its name from an anglicized corruption of Chauciles, the name of the Indians.

No one remembered that Chauciles meant "killers."

Part
One

Chapter 1

It was already warm when Ed Ray woke up Thursday morning, July 15. The air held the promise of another hot, dry day. California's unusual winter drought had given way to the normal dusty summer in the valley. Although there still was plenty of irrigation water for Madera County's farms and orchards, people were already speaking of shortages in the next growing season if there was to be another dry winter.

Ray was feeling chipper as he shaved that morning, getting ready to drive to the garage where his schoolbus was parked. The next day would be the last of the six-week summer session at Dairyland School, and then he would have seven weeks to tend his thirty-three acres of cotton, hay, and alfalfa before classes started again after Labor Day. His job as a schoolbus driver dovetailed nicely with his secondary occupation as a farmer. During the summer session he drove in the morning and late afternoon, leaving the middle hours of the day free for work around his place, work well suited to his solid five-foot-six, 190-pound frame. Despite his fifty-five years his friends said, "He's still a grizzly."

The farm where Ray lives with his wife, Odessa, is on Avenue

18, a section road that runs due east and west about seven miles south of Chowchilla proper. As is most of the big valley, Madera County is crisscrossed by a gridwork of roads that follow the primary points of the compass at one-mile intervals, every four corners enclosing a square mile of 640 acres. The numbered highways running north and south are called roads; east and west, avenues. Those in between are numbered in fractions. So, the one-story beige brick school that is part of the tiny collection of buildings called Dairyland is located on the northwest corner of Avenue 18 1/2 and Road 13. The only real exception to the rule around Chowchilla is Robertson Boulevard, the palm-lined, seven-mile-long main stem that runs southwest from Highway 99 across the railroad tracks and through the center of town before it intersects Highway 152 going west.

It's a simple system, one that makes it virtually impossible to get lost.

As he had most mornings for the twenty-three years he had worked for the school district, Ray said good-bye to Odessa, who was preparing to go into town to her job as a bank teller, and made his way to the school in time to start his normal run at 7:30 A.M. The route took his big yellow International bus over twenty miles, along the rural lanes between Dairyland and Wilson School in the town of Chowchilla and back again in time for school to start at 8:45 A.M. Ray's last chore in the morning before he left the garage was to fuel his own and the other four buses owned by the district. He finished about 9:00 A.M.

Summer school is popular with the kids of Chowchilla because it is as much recreational as it is educational and it helps fill up the long hot summer days. More than 125 were signed up for the 1976 session conducted at Dairyland. The few academic classes are held in the relative cool of the morning, and after lunch the kindergarten and eight grades are divided in half, either to be taken to the big swimming pool at the fairgrounds on the southeast edge of town or to remain at school for arts and crafts.

The afternoon of July 15 had that festive, frenetic atmosphere children generate when school is winding down and they are trying to complete favorite projects at the same time they are

8

enjoying the delicious anticipation of freedom. At 1:00 P.M. the youngest kids, kindergarten through the third grade, were loaded onto two schoolbuses driven by Louise Rickert and Mildred Birch, and transported the ten miles to the swimming pool. The older kids, grades four through eight, stayed behind. Most of the boys worked in the shop while the girls went to home economics class to bake cakes and make ice cream for the next day's picnic and "whacky olympics."

One of the girls, ten-year-old Darla Sue Daniels, was eager to get home and show her parents a certificate of achievement she got from her cooking teacher.

By about 2:30 the classroom routine at Dairyland had turned into something of a party, while the older children waited for the others to return from the pool. At 3:30 the two buses driven by Mrs. Rickert and Mrs. Birch let off their loads of damp, chattering youngsters, many of them still wearing swimming suits, in front of the school. They trooped inside noisily.

Ray returned to the school around the same time to put his bus and a second one "on the line," to get them ready for the homeward runs. He is particular about the cumbersome vehicles and repairs his own. The Dairyland Union School District has five buses and five drivers, including Ray.

Promptly at 3:45 P.M. the dismissal bell rang and the kids poured out to their waiting buses. Ray's gang was animated and happy. Ray is a native of Le Grand, eight miles from Chowchilla, and over the years his passengers have included the grandchildren of his own classmates and even the children of some of his charges from his early days as a bus driver. Some of the kids called him Edward, some Ed. Very few called him Mr. Ray.

But even though he's friendly with them all, Ray runs a tight ship. If a kid cuts up too much on his bus the parents get told about it, and the miscreant has to bring a note from home. Ray had picked up a couple of such notes that day and had clasped them to the little clipboard he hangs near the driver's seat.

In all, thirty-one children climbed on his bus that afternoon, twenty-two girls and nine boys, some still carrying their wet towels from the pool. Ray had been a little troubled by a petition many of the kids had signed asking for an extension of the summer session. The farm needed his attention. Today, however, he was good-natured about it.

"I bet you fifty cents we won't have three more weeks of summer school," he called. Half-heartedly some of the children took up the wager, knowing he was probably right.

"Okay, you're on," one replied.

It was ten minutes to four when Ray wheeled the bus through the Dairyland intersection and ran it up through the gears going east on Avenue 18 1/2. His first stop was to let off a kindergartener, five-year-old Edward Gregorio. A few minutes later, still on the same narrow road, he dropped off Nancy Tripp, eleven, and her brother and sister, Miles and Debbie.

Nancy watched as the bus ground off toward Road 16 a half mile away. She later said she noticed a white van pass the bus but thought nothing of it.

Ray turned left on Road 16 and stopped to let out Susan Zylstra, seven, in front of her house. Her parents were in the yard waiting for her. The bus rolled on past corn and wheat fields, orchards and grazing cattle, and Ray flicked on his left-turn signal again at Road 21. He swung around the corner exactly five and one-half road miles from the school. His next stop would have been to drop off twelve-year-old Lisa Nanette Barletta.

Lisa wasn't wearing a watch, but she knew it was a little after four as she gathered up her things to get off at her stepfather's ranch. She looked up and saw a white van parked on the roadway and felt the bus slowing down. Funny, she thought. We're not at my stop yet.

Chapter 2

Ray stared in disbelief. At first he wasn't so much frightened as he was confused. The apparition peering up at him through the windshield of the bus was holding two guns, for God's sake. At least he thought the man was looking at him. It was hard to tell with the nylon stocking pulled over his head. And the guns. One of the guns was so little it looked like a toy. But the other one had two barrels and a heavy wooden stock. Ray had never seen a sawed-off shotgun before, but he was pretty sure he was looking at one now.

After he had turned left on to Avenue 21 Ray started the mile drive to the corner of Road 15, where Lisa lived. As soon as he passed Road 15 1/2 he saw a white 1971 Dodge van parked close to the center of the road. The door was opened over the white line. He glanced into the adjacent almond orchard to see if someone had stopped to go to the bathroom. There didn't seem to be anyone around.

If he had been alone, Ray might have stopped to learn if a motorist was in trouble and needed help. But he wasn't alone, and Edward Ray was a man who obeys the rules. People said they could set their clocks by his schedule. He slowed to a crawl and pulled far to the left, his front wheels just off the edge of the road, to get by the van.

The bus lurched to a halt. A man wearing a stocking mask and what looked like khaki overalls and white gloves had jumped out from behind the front of the van. Ray couldn't take his eyes off that shiny little revolver. It *must* be a toy, he thought.

The gunman stepped over to the driver's window. "Would you open the door, please?" he asked quietly, politely.

"What?"

"Open your door."

Ray pushed the button that operated the automatic front door of the bus and watched, stunned, as two other men, masked and dressed like the first, came from nowhere and jumped aboard. One had a rifle. "Get to the back of the bus and keep quiet," he said. Ray did what he was told.

Ten-year-old Jeff Brown thought the whole thing was a joke. "We didn't do it!" he yelled, raising his hands. The man with the gun said nothing, simply pointed it at Ray, who had retreated down the aisle. There was no mistaking the menace.

"Real funny, Jeff," his sister, Jennifer, nine, murmured from her seat in the back.

The gunman ordered the children in the front rows to move toward the rear. Judy Reynolds, thirteen, watched as her little sister, Becky, nine, edged past her. "Can I go back too?" she asked.

"Stay where you are," the man with the gun said.

The man who had originally forced Ray to stop still was outside. The gunman inside sat down on one of the front passenger seats and kept his rifle pointed at Ray. The third man slipped into the driver's seat. Jeff Brown thought it was funny that he wore prescription glasses over his pantyhose mask.

Ray saw the man who had remained outside get into the driver's side of the van. Then the bus started to move, and the van fell in behind. Ray didn't look back again. He just stared up the aisle at the gun.

"What do they want, Edward?" a little girl whined.

12

"Be quiet and do what they say," he said. The two kidnappers said nothing.

Realization came slowly to some of the kids, almost instantly to others. A couple giggled nervously, still convinced it was a prank. Not so Angela Robison, nine. She was terrified. For some reason she knew these men were going to kill her. She started to sob.

By now fear had replaced Ray's bewilderment. A stolid man, the bus driver had not at first grasped what was happening. Now he began to think about terrorists and airplane hijackers. But people didn't hijack schoolbuses. Where could they take them? He regarded his job as a sacred responsibility. He knew the parents of these children soon would be calling the school. He wondered what the superintendent, Mr. Tatom, would think. He worried fleetingly whether he would get into trouble for letting this happen.

He thought of Odessa. She wouldn't miss him until dinner time. He usually didn't finish up at the bus barn until about five. He was afraid and frustrated because he didn't know what to do. At the bank they gave tellers like Odessa instructions about how to handle people with guns, but nobody ever told bus drivers what to do.

The bus rolled at a normal rate of speed west on Avenue 21. At Road 15 Lisa's sister, Pamela Barletta, watched from her house as the bus passed without stopping. Lisa must not be on it, she thought.

Ray glanced out the window and saw Clarence Musick on a tractor, plowing his cotton field. Maybe he'll see me in the back, he thought. Maybe he'll know something's wrong.

The farmer finished the row and turned the tractor the other way as the bus went by. He didn't look up.

Ray had never ridden in the back of his bus before. He felt strange watching someone else drive it, even a little jealous. The man obviously knew what he was doing. He had driven some sort of big rig before.

About a mile west of where it had been stopped, the bus suddenly slowed and made a left turn. Judy Reynolds noticed they were almost at the bridge over Berenda Slough, a dry creek bed.

13

The bus was too long to negotiate the turn. The driver stopped, and—expertly, Ray thought—whipped it into reverse, backed once, and then eased the bus over the margin of the road. "Hold on," he warned. "We're going over some bumps." The bus bucked and teetered, and for a second Ray thought it would tip over.

The bus came to a stop in a bamboo thicket that concealed it from the road a short distance away. Ray and the children saw another van, a green one, parked about seventy feet away. Then they felt a bump and heard a grinding noise. The white van had followed them into the slough and had scraped the bus getting by.

The kidnappers worked rapidly. The driver of the white van opened its rear doors and backed it up to the door of the bus. The gunman motioned for the children in front to get into the van. Jodie Heffington, ten, heard one of the men say, "Don't worry. Be calm."

Twelve of the children stepped directly from the bus into the rear of the white van. They were not allowed to put their feet on the ground, to leave footprints. The floor of the van was carpeted, the walls had heavy wood paneling, the ceiling looked as if it were covered with burlap. A wooden partition had been erected completely separating the front seat from the cargo area. The rear windows were painted over. The interior smelled strongly of gasoline. It reminded Lisa Barletta of the odor of weed killer her stepfather used on the ranch.

Mike Marshall, fourteen, was the oldest child on the bus. He got into the white van along with Lisa, Jeff and Jennifer Brown, Darla Sue Daniels, and Judy Reynolds; and Monica Ardery, five; Linda Carrejo, ten; Robert Gonzales, ten; Sheryll Hinesley, seven; Jody Matheny, ten; and Michelle Robison, eleven. The children, without thinking about it or being asked to do so, carried their personal belongings with them, as if they were transferring from one public conveyance to another. Darla Daniels clutched her certificate of achievement.

Ray watched as the white van pulled away and the green one was backed up to the bus door. He gazed at the license plate, trying desperately to memorize the number. He repeated it over and over in his mind, but it simply wouldn't take hold. All he would remember a few minutes later were the last three digits: 414.

Ray stood as the rest of the children climbed from the bus into the van: Lisa Ardery, nine, who had been separated from her sister, Monica; Irene Carrejo, twelve, and her sisters, Julia, seven, and Stella, six, all separated from their other sister, Linda; John Estabrook, eight; Andres Gonzales, eight, whose older brother, Robert, had left in the white van; Jodie Heffington, ten; Andrea Park, eight, and her little brother, Larry, six; Barbara Parker, eight; Becky Reynolds and Angela Robison, both separated from their older sisters, Judy and Michelle; Cindy Vanhoff, eight; and Laura Yazzi, five.

Ray was the last person to get into the back of the green van. Like the white one, it had been sealed off from the front, and when the rear door was slammed and locked Ray and the children found themselves in total darkness. As his eyes dilated he discerned a faint light leak flickering around what he guessed to be the gas tank spout. For the next several hours it would be his only gauge of day and night, since he couldn't see his watch in the dark.

The prisoners in the green van heard and felt the engine start, and the machine rolled forward, started upward, then stopped, rear wheels spinning. Ray felt momentary elation. Maybe they'll be afraid they'll get caught here and run, he thought. He heard the driver's door being thrown open. It banged against the side of something metal—the bus, he thought. Then he heard the engine roar and felt the van being rocked back and forth. After a few minutes it pulled free.

Sitting a few feet from Ray in the darkness, little Julie Carrejo began to cry. "They are going to take us somewhere else and we'll never see our moms and dads ever again," she said to herself.

The dozen kids packed into the rear of the white van didn't know what to think. Jeff Brown still insisted it was an elaborate hoax. The others knew better. It was hot, stiflingly so, and dark. One of the children felt some holes near the rear wheels that had been filled with putty. They poked it out and could see the pavement passing below them. They watched the holes until it got dark outside.

15

By now fatigue had started to replace fear, and the children tried to sleep. Some of the younger ones, perhaps more resilient, or sure of immortality, were successful. After a while the older ones managed to doze fitfully. Sometimes they sang.

In the green van Ray sat with his back propped against the locked rear door. He could hear a fan cycling on and off, and occasionally felt fresh air. But the atmosphere quickly became fetid.

"Edward, I have to go to the bathroom."

"You just have to go, then," he said.

"I don't want to go in my pants."

"You just have to."

People in the farm communities of the valley are used to having dinner early, and Ray and the children soon became hungry.

"Are we going to stop for dinner?" a child asked from the darkness.

"I don't know."

The heat grew more oppressive, accentuating the gasoline fumes and the stench of urine and excrement in both vans. Some of the children got carsick. The nausea fed on itself, and most of them followed suit. Dry heaves led to dehydration and exhaustion. Jennifer Brown fainted. Jodie Heffington's nose started to bleed profusely. Then her ears popped. "We must be in the mountains," she told the others.

Ray and the children began to lose all sense of time. They did not know how long they rode in the vans, or in fact if the two vehicles were even together. After several hours—some children who had slept said one, Ray thought six—the green van stopped. The captives jumped up. Was the ordeal over? They heard the clatter of cans and smelled gasoline. The van was being refueled with the motor running.

The white van stopped too. Mike Marshall was trying to keep track of the sounds he heard from the outside during the ride. He felt the van going up and down hills and around curves. At one point he thought he felt it being buffeted by high winds. Now he heard the scrape of a gasoline can against the sidewall. He was startled by a voice from the outside.

16

"How are you kids doing back there?"

"Fine," someone replied sarcastically.

"Okay," the voice answered. "Be quiet."

Both vans stopped several times. No one could remember how many. During one pause Judy Reynolds overheard voices. She pressed her ear against the side and thought she heard something about going to Reno to get some money. She was sure she heard the names Fred and James, and maybe Jerry.

Finally the vans turned on to a rutted track, slowed down, and halted. Ray felt the green one bulling its way through a clump of vegetation and heard brush scratching against the sides and floorboards. The engine was turned off, and the fan stopped. The door slammed. Then there was silence.

The white van also halted. It sure has squeaky brakes, Jody Matheny thought.

In the green van Ray waited expectantly for something to happen. Nothing did. As the heat rose even higher he began to panic. They were going to suffocate. Frantically he tore at the carpet and pulled it up. He could feel a wispy draft of fresh air from below.

Chapter 3

They sat in silence for at least an hour. Ray, his brain dulled by fear and sleeplessness, started when he heard someone call from outside.

"Are you ready to get out now?" A chorus of juvenile assent. "Okay, you'll come out one at a time. Where's the driver?"

"Right here by the door," Ray replied. "Right here."

"I want you out first," the other said. Then, for the first time in eleven hours, the door was opened.

Ray expected fresh air to wash over him, but as he swung his cramped legs around and stood up outside the tailgate he found he was in a tarped, green enclosure, almost a tent, that had been thrown up to conceal the vans. He saw two men. One had a flashlight. He saw the glint of the little gun.

"What's your name?" one of them demanded.

"Edward Ray."

"How old are you?"

"Fifty-five."

"All right, take off your pants and boots," the kidnapper said. Embarrassed, Ray did so awkwardly, his legs still sore from inactivity. He dropped the trousers and cowboy boots on the ground.

He felt foolish, with the kids getting out of the van and looking at him in his jockey shorts.

"Here," the masked man said, handing Ray a flashlight and two extra batteries. Then he pointed to a hole in the ground with a ladder protruding from it. "Go down," he ordered.

Ray hesitated. "I have grandkids, and I want to see them again," he pleaded. No answer. Ray climbed down the ladder. Above him he could hear Barbara Parker.

"What do you want?" she demanded.

"Be quiet."

Ray got to the bottom of the ladder and flashed the light around. There also was a candle guttering. He found himself standing on the forward end, over the wagon tongue, of what he quickly recognized as a truck trailer or freight van. The walls were covered with wire mesh, and the sides and ceiling were bowed in from the weight of the earth. A timber braced the sides and a slanted post was jammed against the roof, secured only by an eighteen-inch kick block. There were two holes cut in the ceiling, one in the left front, the other in the right rear. He could hear fans, but couldn't see the two white plastic tubes that were air shafts or the thirty-five-foot, four-inch flexible hose extending from one battery-powered exhaust fan into a tree where it was concealed from view.

There were fourteen mattresses and box springs stacked on the floor, and some old bedspreads and what looked like used drapery material. At the far end he saw two loaves of sliced bread, a jar of peanut butter, a box of Cheerios, a couple of bags of potato chips, and some five-gallon water containers. The two rear-wheel wells had holes cut in them with a torch for use as toilets.

Ray suddenly remembered to look at his watch. It was past 3:30 A.M.

Above ground the children were being asked their names and ages and then ordered to go down the ladder. The first to go was John Estabrook.

"Empty your pockets," a kidnapper said. The boy dropped a crushed model of Evel Knievel on a motorcycle in the dirt. Then they took his green sweater and his Little League baseball shirt

19

with the number 12 and the name of the team sponsor, Jewel Arts, stenciled on it and told him to climb down with Ray.

"They had the gun, and I didn't want my head blasted off," he told his companions later.

Next came Angela Robison. They asked her name and age and took her bathing-suit cover-up before she scrambled down the ladder. She, like Ray and the others, never saw anyone writing down their names and ages. They didn't see the man who was recording the information in a childish scrawl on the outside of a grease-stained Jack-in-the-Box hamburger bag.

Little Larry Park was next. They took his swimming towel, and also took one from Cindy Vanhoff, who followed him down the ladder. Andrea Park surrendered her purse and a towel and started down to join her brother.

"How old are you?" the man asked before she got on the ladder.

"Eight," she said. "I just had a birthday." In the darkness the unseen hand wrote that down.

Lisa Ardery was next. They took her shirt. Modestly, the nine-year-old thought how grateful she was that she was still wearing her swimming suit top.

Barbara Parker also had on her bathing suit. The men took the clothes she was carrying as well as her lunch pail and towel. Stella Carrejo offered a towel when her turn came. "It ain't mine, it's my other sister's," she said, as if to admonish them to take good care of it.

Stella's sister Irene handed over a skirt and blouse she was carrying. Her little sister Julia tried to stay close to her. The kidnappers asked for Julia's tennis shoes. "They're my best ones," she protested tearfully.

One by one they made their way down the ladder. Laura Yazzi gave the men her lunch pail and her towel and her bathing suit haphazardly stuffed in a beach bag. Becky Reynolds followed Laura. "They didn't take anything from me," she whispered to the others in the trailer body.

Jodie Heffington had been in a skit at school the day before and was carrying her costume: a pair of knee-length cutoff pants, a red corduroy vest, and a pink butterfly-sleeved blouse. They took the clothes, as well as a fruitcake can full of pencils and some bits of ceramic she had made in class.

The last child out of the green van was Andres Gonzales. They took nothing from him, or from Sheryll Hinesley or Darla Daniels, who followed her.

Darla left her cooking certificate behind in the white van.

Linda Carrejo was not as frightened as the others. Armed with the easy sophistication of a ten-year-old, she thought her kidnappers were "kinda cute." She was annoyed when they took her purse, because it had her boyfriend's picture in it.

They took nothing from Judy Reynolds, or from Lisa Barletta or from Michelle Robison, who followed in succession down the hole. Mike Marshall emptied his pockets of six cents and a book of matches, and they took his hat.

Jeff Brown gave up his tennis shoes, and Jody Matheny lost his glasses and his shoes. He was mad. The shoes were only a week old.

They told Robert Gonzales to empty his pockets, and all he could find was some string he had been saving. They took it, along with a book he had carried on the long ride.

Monica Ardery, five, was the youngest of the victims by exactly a month.

"What's your name?" they asked her.

"Monica."

"Monica what?"

"Monica Ardery." The hidden writer heard the name as "Ronica Andre."

"How old are you?"

"I want to go home," she sobbed.

"She's five," a voice said from the hole. The number went next to her name on the hamburger bag with a question mark.

Jennifer Brown was the last one down. They took a shoe from her and a pair of pants she was carrying, and then one of the men took her arm—gently, she thought—and helped her onto the ladder. Once she was down, it was pulled up. One of the kidnappers tossed down a roll of toilet paper.

"How long are we going to stay here, Edward?" a child asked.

21

Others took up the question and began to cry. He had no answer.

"Until tomorrow," one of the kidnappers called through the hole. Ray heard another voice.

"Make that twenty-four to forty-eight hours. We'll be back."

A steel plate three eighths of an inch thick clanged down over the hole in the roof of the truck body. Ray and the children heard two metallic clunks. They didn't know that two heavy-duty industrial batteries, weighing over a hundred pounds each, had just been dropped on the plate.

The children heard what sounded like wires being cut, and they recoiled as dirt sifted down around the steel plate. The roof groaned and seemed to sag. In a sudden, hysterical babble they begged to be released. They couldn't see the thirty-inch-high wooden shaft over the batteries being covered with a plywood box filled with graveled soil to a depth of eight inches, or the dirt and twigs mounded up to conceal the box. Ray began to cry and pray aloud.

The activity above them went on for about an hour. Then it was quiet again. The only noise was the frail-sounding whirr of the fans.

Part
Two

Chapter 4

"Aw, shit."

The young man stood up and watched the black-and-white patrol car pull to a stop. He could see the Seal of the County of Sierra on the door as it opened and a sheriff's deputy got out.

"What's the matter?" asked one of his two companions, both boys about his own age.

"It's a smoky," the first replied.

The deputy approached the three, watching them closely. "What you boys doing?" he asked.

"Just looking over this old wreck," one said, pointing to the rusting hulk of an automobile overturned alongside the road.

"What's that?" The deputy was pointing to a piece of metal in one young man's hand.

"It's a carburetor."

"You weren't planning on stealing it, now, were you?"

"Aw, come on. This car is abandoned for sure. Look at it. It has bullet holes in it and everything."

"Where you from?" the deputy asked.

"The Bay Area."

"You're a long way from home."

"My folks have an old mine up here," one of them said.

"Where's that?"

"Up off Henness Pass Road," he replied.

"I think you boys better come with me."

"You gotta be kidding," one protested.

"Get in the back seat," the deputy ordered. "I'm gonna tell you once."

"What about our car?"

"We'll bring you back for it, unless you get charged. If you do we'll have it brought to town."

"Town" turned out to be Downieville, seat of Sierra County and an unincorporated collection of Gold Rush era buildings that forms a wide spot along State Highway 49 north of Lake Tahoe. Three thousand feet above sea level on the western escarpment of the Sierra Nevada, the village was named after "Major" Bill Downie, a wild-eyed Scot who came to dig for gold in 1849, accompanied by ten black sailors, an Indian, an Irish boy, and a Kanaka with the unlikely name of Jim Crow. Boomtowns were born overnight along the rivers and creeks of Sierra County, and by 1851 Downieville had a roistering population of 5,000. Today all of Sierra County has only 2,500 residents.

The sheriff decided to charge the three with grand theft auto, a serious felony. They argued, but a check of the license number had revealed the car still had a registered owner, a man named Johnson.

While the unhappy young men wrote out holographic statements telling their side of the story, the deputy wrote the date on his report, October 6, 1974, and filled in the booking information about the three alleged thieves:

Name:	FREDERICK NEWHALL WOODS
Race:	WMA
DOB:	October 18, 1951 (22)
Height:	6'
Weight:	145 pounds
Eyes:	Brown
Hair:	Light Brown

26

Scars and marks:	Scar, left arm
Address:	The Hawthornes, Portola Valley, California
Parents:	Mr. and Mrs. Fred N. Woods III Same address as above

Name:	JAMES LEONARD SCHOENFELD
Race:	WMA
DOB:	October 15, 1951 (22)
Height:	6'
Weight:	170 pounds
Eyes:	Blue
Hair:	Red
Scars and marks:	None
Address	273 Stockbridge Avenue, Atherton, California
Parents:	Dr. and Mrs. John B. Schoenfeld Same address as above

Name:	RICHARD ALLEN SCHOENFELD
Race:	WMA
DOB:	June 30, 1954 (20)
Height:	5' 11"
Weight:	155 pounds
Eyes:	Blue
Hair:	Blond
Scars and marks:	None
Address:	273 Stockbridge Avenue, Atherton, California
Parents:	Dr. and Mrs. John B. Schoenfeld Same address as above

"Okay," the deputy said as they signed their statements, "we'll get the judge to fix bail, then you can call your folks."

People from the city call it "Mother Lode Justice" and complain that in the mountain towns judges and sheriffs try to make examples of outsiders. Whether there is any truth in the

27

stereotype or not, Richard Campbell, the local attorney the Woods and Schoenfeld families hired to defend their sons, said his clients were "very clean-cut, nice kids. They definitely weren't criminal types."

Early that year Jim Schoenfeld had started keeping a journal in a light-green shorthand notebook he'd originally bought to take notes in a junior college mathematics class. He did it almost as a game, inventing an arcane code that would make it impossible for others to read his innermost thoughts. He obtained tables of the Arabic and Russian alphabets, and substituted the letters for their Roman counterparts. He made long lists of words and names, family members and friends, and practiced "translating" until he could write in English, using the foreign ciphers almost as fast as he could print normally. Anyone looking at his diary would think it was gibberish.

The case in Sierra County was set for trial on Monday, January 20, 1975. The lawyer told the three defendants the district attorney had agreed to reduce the charge to petty theft, since the entire automobile was not worth enough to justify the felony count.

Before their court appearance Jim expressed apprehension in his journal over whether the three could convince people they didn't know, that they had not intended to steal anything.

The day after the hearing he wrote that he was dissatisfied with the outcome. He was angry with himself for not having had the courage to speak out in his own defense.

The charge was changed to tampering with an automobile. All three pleaded guilty, and the judge fined them $125 each and ordered them to serve a year's unsupervised probation.

Their booking records, photographs, and fingerprints routinely were sent to the Criminal Identification and Investigation Archives in Sacramento, there to gather dust for the next year and a half.

Chapter 5

When Henry Mayo Newhall took leave of his native Massachusetts in 1850 to follow the other gold-hungry prospectors to California, he left behind a rock-ribbed New England heritage. Most Americans of the period would have taken pride in a single ancestor among the *Mayflower* company of Pilgrims. He could count half a dozen, including Governor William Bradford and John Alden. For the most part their descendants had settled not far from Plymouth Rock and had stayed there. But at twenty-five Henry Newhall was restless. He wanted to possess the world and the riches in it.

He got off to a slow start. By the time he landed in San Francisco, he was broke. To raise enough money to eat he was forced to auction off all of the belongings he had brought with him. But it quickly dawned on him that he was not the only immigrant with financial difficulties, that others also often found themselves in need of ready cash. Having learned how it was done in his own case, he went into business as an auctioneer.

Newhall gradually prospered in the heady atmosphere of the Gold Rush, and he began speculating in land and, later, railroads. He built a fine house on San Francisco's Rincon Hill, where one

29

of his neighbors was General William Tecumseh Sherman. His holdings spread to Southern California. Railroad towns were founded near Los Angeles named Newhall and Saugus, the latter after his birthplace north of Boston. One of his locomotives set a speed record between San Francisco and San Jose—sixty-seven miles per hour.

Newhall amassed enough for his five sons to form the Newhall Land and Farming Company, a corporation now listed on the New York Stock Exchange. The Newhall company today owns nearly 148,000 acres in California and enjoys annual revenues upward of $80 million from sources as diverse as ranching, oil, shopping centers, and the Magic Mountain resort and amusement park north of Los Angeles. Among its agricultural ventures the company farms 12,000 acres near Chowchilla.

One of Henry Newhall's granddaughters, Frances Newhall, married Frederick Nickerson Woods, Jr., a San Francisco businessman whose interests included sand and gravel. They had three children, Frederick Nickerson Woods III, Edwin Newhall Woods, and Virginia Newhall Woods, and settled into a life of country elegance at The Hawthornes, a seventy-eight-acre estate in Portola Valley, an affluent rural enclave near where the widow of Governor Leland Stanford had endowed a university in her late son's name on the family ranch. Frances Woods became known as a gracious hostess, and invitations to her casual outdoor parties were cherished by those lucky enough to receive them. She and her husband shared the widespread local fancy for horses, and for years she pastured the animals retired from the San Francisco Police Department mounted patrol to save them from the glue factory.

Her son, Fred III, went to Stanford, where he became an avid basketball fan. The wonder teams of the 1930s often were invited to The Hawthornes for postgame celebrations, and Hank Luisetti, the Stanford All-American who helped revolutionize the modern game, became Fred's friend.

At the outbreak of World War II Fred Woods joined the navy and saw duty in the South Pacific before being tapped for officers' training school. While he was home on leave in 1943, his engagement was announced to Harriet Wright of Palo Alto, an honor student at the University of California in Berkeley. After the war Fred and his new wife settled into a house on his parents' estate, and eventually he took over the family firm, the California Rock and Gravel Company. The couple had two children. Frederick Newhall Woods was born in 1951. Six years later they had a daughter, a retarded child, who was eventually institutionalized after it became certain that her emotional and mental age never would surpass five. Their daughter's plight had a profound effect on Mr. and Mrs. Woods, and they sought comfort in each other.

Young Fred never revealed to anyone that he had a sister. He told everyone he was an only child.

As Fred Woods grew up, The Hawthornes by degrees lost its luster as a center of Peninsula society. His widowed grandmother became an invalid, dependent on twenty-four-hour nursing care. His parents preferred to live quietly, out of the public eye. In 1968, in fact, they requested that their names be dropped from the San Francisco social register.

Fred never was a good student. Although he had a quick mind when it came to the subjects that interested him, such as auto mechanics and making deals, he was indifferent to most things scholastic, and his teachers never were able to inspire him to achieve much beyond a grammar school level.

He attended Woodside High School, where his fellow pupils were the sons and daughters of affluent families similar to his own. It was difficult for him to make friends, and he was something of a loner. Many of his peers found him abrasive, and it was not uncommon for them to ape his vulgar speech. In *The Wildcat,* the Woodside High annual, the only activity noted under Fred's senior picture was "track."

Oddly enough, he did make friends with one high school classmate, Jim Schoenfeld. The two could not have been less alike. Jim, on the surface at least, was articulate, gregarious, easygoing, and an intelligent student. He was a member of the chess club. Both boys shared a passion for machinery, particularly cars and trucks and motorcycles.

Fred betrayed no real convictions of any kind. He and Jim were

31

solidly of the generation that matured in the late sixties and early seventies, divorced from the activists of a decade earlier who had spawned the civil rights and antiwar movements. The children of the pre-Watergate upper middle class, not driven by the social concerns of the sixties or by the competitive work ethic that began to reemerge on the college campuses of the late seventies, drifted comfortably, and Fred and Jim drifted with them.

In the wealthy suburbs of the San Francisco Peninsula, owning The First Car at or near the legal age threshold of sixteen is almost a birthright, like braces, or tennis and riding lessons, or pre-enrollment in the college one's parents attended, or the summer tan. The tree-lined roads and boulevards of places such as Atherton, Portola Valley, or Hillsborough, where Patty Hearst lived with her sisters and parents, carry the traffic of indulgence, cars bought as birthday presents or with the proceeds from allowances and odd jobs.

Fred didn't know Patty Hearst, although his father's first cousin, Scott Newhall, the flamboyant former editor of the San Francisco *Chronicle,* was well acquainted with her father, San Francisco *Examiner* president Randolph Hearst. Fred didn't follow the story of the girl's abduction and transmogrification as closely as some of his friends did.

Fred inherited his interest in old cars from his father, a serious collector of antiques and classics. As a teenager he started buying battered cars, fixing them up and selling them. He showed neither aptitude for nor interest in the family businesses, and his lack of ambition often provoked arguments with his father. He got along better with his mother, but sometimes resented her devotion to her husband. The parents and son traveled a good deal, to Europe, Hawaii, New Zealand, Baja California, and Martha's Vineyard, where the Newhall family has extensive property. Until 1976 they hardly missed a summer Olympic Games.

As Fred's grandmother's health deteriorated, contacts between the Woods and Newhall families became fewer. The only member of the Newhall branch Fred grew to know well was his grandmother's niece, Jane Newhall, an unmarried woman in her sixties who lived in San Francisco's Pacific Heights district.

Mr. and Mrs. Woods took trips by themselves sometimes, leaving Fred with relatives when he was young and by himself when he was older. Although he could not articulate it to them, he resented their absences and often felt shut out. He became a young man almost incapable of showing emotion. Then, uncharacteristically, he spoke of his loneliness to Songel Faye, a girl he met in 1969 when he was a senior in high school and she was a junior. She had run away from home and was living with a foster family. He dated her after they left high school, and although he had a veneer of self-assurance, the two secretly shared their mutual insecurity. They were married February 28, 1971, in Redwood City, and moved into an apartment in Mountain View. He worked for a while in a paint store, and he hated it.

"I was left alone, and he took me in," Songel would say later. "It was a mistake. I didn't love him. I was just grateful."

Fred soon became dominated by the fear that Songel had married him because of the family wealth. The young husband owned only 1,385 of the 5.5 million shares of Newhall Land and Farming Company outstanding, a stock position worth about $40,000 at the time and returning less than $1,000 a year in earnings, but he reportedly stood to inherit a thirty-sixth of the family's interest in the company. Songel recalled later that he began going shopping with her to prevent the smallest extravagance. "It upset him every time I asked him for money," she said. "I got tired of asking, so I got a job." She worked for a cleaning shop in Palo Alto for $1.75 an hour.

A year after their wedding Woods filed for separation. He worried that she would seek a large settlement, and was openly relieved when she took only the $1,000 her in-laws had given her as a wedding present, used it to buy a car, and drove east. Later Fred got a divorce and moved back to his parents' estate.

"He was very strange, a different type of man," Songel said.

In the summer of 1969, just after his graduation from high school, Fred was at his parents' place one day when a young man approached him. His name was David Boston, then twenty-one, a student majoring in filmmaking at San Jose State College. He was

33

looking for a location to shoot a movie as a term project, and wondered whether the family that owned the estate would mind if he used it. The old and abandoned vehicles would fit in with the mood he was trying to create.

Fred willingly gave permission, and during the next few days he watched as Boston and other students worked on the film. He was fascinated by the technology and asked a lot of questions. He and Boston became friends. Like Jim Schoenfeld, Boston was an opposite of Fred, intelligent, fluent, and ambitious. He was shorter but heavier than Woods, with dark hair and somewhat fleshy good looks. He was flattered by Fred's interest in his craft.

Later, Boston began earning money by selling some of the surplus cars and trucks Fred restored. What he wanted most of all was to raise enough capital to produce a motion picture from one of his own scripts. Woods liked the idea of going into the movie business, and on August 7, 1972, the two formed a legal partnership, Townhouse Enterprises. The company would buy and sell old cars and trucks and other surplus items to raise money for films.

About two years later Jim Schoenfeld, following a half-hearted try at college, would join them in their informal business. Boston would become vaguely jealous as Jim's role in the venture grew and his diminished.

The salvage business did not always provide a reliable living, and occasionally Fred took on odd jobs or part-time work. For a while he drove a shuttle bus for the Hewlett-Packard Corporation in Palo Alto. In 1973 he got a job as a driver for the Fields Ambulance Service in Palo Alto. Jerry Thompson, the dispatcher, rode with him sometimes, but they never became friendly. Fred isn't much of a talker, Thompson concluded.

One fall afternoon, while Fred was at the Stanford Medical Center, he met a seventeen-year-old patient, Mary Egeberg. After she was released they dated for a few months.

Fred told the girl of his family's fortune and background. He took her to the estate and showed her some of his favorite cars, and told her one day he would be a film producer. As they got to know each other better she got mad at him from time to time about the ease with which he would lapse into profanity.

He told her that he had been married, but was divorced. She asked him why and he said it was because he was unable to have children. When she asked him what the problem was, he answered only that his condition would require surgery and that he didn't want to have an operation.

She thought it all sounded a little strange.

In April of 1975 Fred walked up to the teller's window of Irene Bolzowski at the Wells Fargo Bank branch in the Stanford Industrial Park, where he had a couple of accounts. They chatted for a few minutes, and he asked her for a date. Eventually she agreed.

Irene, a solidly built blonde about five foot three, was twenty-three when she met Woods. A native of Willimantic, Connecticut, she now shared an apartment in Mountain View with her twenty-one-year-old sister, Stephanie, who was going to San Jose State College. She was taken by the taciturn, skinny young man whose principal form of expression was saying, "Aw, yeah." She fell in love with him. Woods, perhaps for the first time in his short adult life, returned the affection.

Irene found Fred reserved but undemanding. He had a small vocabulary and, on long drives, his favorite recreation, he would sit behind the wheel for hours and say almost nothing. She appreciated the fact that he didn't drink or use drugs. In fact his only vice seemed to be smoking an Old Gold cigarette once in a while while he was driving.

Fred was not a handsome man, but, then, Irene knew she was not a beautiful woman. His light-brown hair, clipped unfashionably short, was thinning a little in front. His clean-shaven face bore the light scars of adolescent acne, and he still was troubled by scattered pimples on his back. Even though he was outdoors most of the time and his face and neck were bronzed by the sun, the rest of his body was white, since he always wore long pants and long-sleeved shirts. Sometimes he wore a cowboy hat. His only jewelry was a wristwatch with a built-in alarm.

For a man whose surroundings were usually messy, Fred himself was curiously fastidious, she thought. He showered at least

35

once a day. He told her he didn't like camping because he preferred indoor plumbing, that he hated crawling insects, and he couldn't stand sleeping on the ground. He didn't even like picnics. He had a sleeping bag, but he used it only as a comforter on his bed in an apartment over a garage on the opposite side of The Hawthornes from his parents' house.

Irene tried to share Fred's fascination with cars, but he didn't insist on it. She met some of his friends, Dave Boston, Jim Schoenfeld, and his younger brother, Rick, and Craig Hunt, the young man they had hired to help work on the old cars and trucks they overhauled for resale. She knew they were interested in making movies, but it seemed unlikely that they ever would, unlikely except to Boston, who wanted to be a scriptwriter. A more attainable goal, she thought, was their idea of buying a dilapidated old mansion in Mountain View, moving it to a city-owned lot they hoped to purchase, and then refurbishing and remodeling it. Fred said he always wanted to live in a mansion, and it would be big enough for all of them. It was a funny coincidence that the mansion they wanted was called the Rengstorff House. The street where Irene's apartment was had the same name, Rengstorff Avenue.

Irene knew they had other dreams, but they never discussed them when she was around. Fred seldom talked about his business other than to brag about a particularly slick car deal now and then. Although it seemed to her he really enjoyed making money, he never appeared to worry about not having it.

Once when they were both visiting his parents' home, Irene saw a picture of a little girl and a dog on his mother's bedstand. She asked Fred if the child were a relative.

"It's just a friend of the family," he said abruptly. "Forget about it." He never told Irene that he had a sister.

Five months after they met, Irene took a week's vacation from the bank and she and Fred went on a trip in his green station wagon. They drove to Los Angeles and stopped at Magic Mountain, using Fred's free passes, and then visited Universal Studios and Knott's Berry Farm, where they stayed in a motel. From there they took a marathon drive to the Grand Canyon in Arizona,

36

north to Zion National Park in Utah, south to Las Vegas in Nevada, and north again through Yosemite National Park. The only other trip they shared was a drive to Reno on Easter Sunday, April 18, 1976. They stopped at a small town on the California side of the border, where they met Fred's parents. He and his father had arranged to look at an old car Fred was thinking of buying.

Fred had installed a CB radio in his station wagon, but seldom used the microphone. He said he got a kick out of listening to the broadcast conversations of other people.

On both trips to Nevada Fred didn't bet at the gaming tables, although he did self-consciously drop a few nickels into a slot machine. Once, when Irene had suggested they go to the races, he told her it was not worth the money.

Nothing, he said, was worth gambling on.

For her twenty-fourth birthday, on June 18, 1976, Fred gave Irene a puppy, a six-week-old border collie. She was delighted, and deeply touched. Tears welled in her eyes as she hugged him. She said she would call the dog Shelley.

Irene loved animals. After Fred had moved back to The Hawthornes, he had taken over the job of feeding the few horses and other stock his parents still kept. On weekends Irene would drive out to help him. One Saturday in the apartment over the garage she noticed something totally out of place, a Russian typewriter.

"Aw, yeah, you speak Russian, don't you?" he said.

"No, Ukrainian. I learned from my parents," she reminded him. "Why do you have a Russian typewriter?"

"It's not really for me," he said. "It's for Jim. He knows a little Russian."

Chapter 6

The life of John Bruce Schoenfeld was one of striving and quiet achievement, without a trace of eccentricity. He was almost the stereotype of a man in pursuit of the American Dream. In the summer of 1976, after a quarter century of hard work, his dream would become a nightmare.

It was a tough summer, and some of Schoenfeld's troubles were unrelated to the deeds of his two youngest sons.

In contrast to Frederick Nickerson Woods III, John Schoenfeld was born into a world where very little was easy. He grew up in the greenery of Oregon, but moved to California, where his parents settled in Palo Alto. He worked his way through the California College of Podiatric Medicine in San Francisco partly as a collector for a credit company, an experience that left him with a keen sense of fiscal propriety and thrift. He married Merry Masterson, a member of a prominent farming family from the Sacramento Valley. After his graduation in 1949 they moved to Palo Alto, and she had three sons fairly soon after that—John, Jim, and Rick.

Podiatry is not among the glamorous branches of medicine, and it was fifteen years before Dr. Schoenfeld made the move from the middle to the upper middle class, geographically the short distance from Donald Drive in San Jose to Stockbridge Avenue in Atherton, a community of walled estates, paddocks, and private tennis courts. The symbol of his success was a comfortable home with a swimming pool at the end of a block-long drive. Sometime after they moved in 1964, he would take the family on a camera safari to Africa.

The Schoenfelds were popular almost immediately, and the family established close ties with their neighbors, especially the family of Joe Muldown, a teacher in the San Mateo School District who lived next door. Their children—John, Jim, and Rick Schoenfeld and the seven Muldown sons and daughters—grew up as if they were brothers and sisters. Jim and Rick stabled their horses at the Muldowns' place, and the boys took turns taking care of them, along with feeding the Schoenfelds' German short-haired pointer.

As he watched his sons grow strong and healthy, John Schoenfeld was content.

John, the eldest, graduated from college, became a butcher, married, and moved to Menlo Park. He hoped that one day Jim, who was a good student and had a quick mind, or Rick, who went through Woodside High School in only three years, would follow him into podiatry. Both had taken courses at local colleges, but nothing seemed to capture their serious interest. He sometimes was troubled by the fact that Jim's teenage preoccupation with cars and motorcycles seemed to be becoming an obsession, so much so that he even sold his horse. But there was plenty of time. He could afford to give both his younger sons all the time they needed to decide what they wanted to do with their lives.

He was particularly proud of Jim's forthrightness and honesty. When Mrs. Muldown had offered him $1,000 for an old Cadillac he was working on, for example, he had told her he had already promised it to someone else for $800, and that he couldn't go back on his word. Dr. Schoenfeld also was thankful his sons had avoided the hard drugs and promiscuity he regarded as endemic among members of their casual generation, although there is evidence Rick may have tried marijuana. Jim didn't even smoke,

39

seldom dated, and never used strong language. Outside of tinkering with cars, his main recreation was playing chess, or playing hearts with Rick, the Muldown boys, and Jim Luthi, another friend, who lived in Redwood City. His aesthetic tastes ran to the Beach Boys, *Wild Kingdom* on television, and Walt Disney movies. He had a habit of creating nicknames for his friends, either calling them "Uncle" or, in the case of Luthi, "The Wimp." Somehow this further endeared him to his buddies.

Jim and Rick were closer to each other than either was to their older brother. They shared their friends, and Rick was among the few people in Jim's world who could stand Fred Woods's arrogance. The others who met him from time to time after Jim and Fred began seeing a lot of each other again in 1974 tolerated Woods for Jim's sake.

Rick's life revolved around his two horses, Stella and Honcho. He liked to trailer them to the Sierra on pack trips, fishing and hunting. He got occasional jobs through a Palo Alto employment agency, but his horses came first. Often, while he was working part time in the mailroom of the Stanford Linear Accelerator, he would call up and say he could not come to work because he was going to the mountains. They put up with it because he was an extremely good mail clerk. Rick was friendly, but during his school years he always was the quietest boy in his classes.

Jim also enjoyed the outdoors, but unlike Rick he was a meticulous planner. John Muldown marveled at the way Jim would prepare for a trip backpacking or river rafting, planning the routes and making lists of every item he would need down to the last package of dehydrated food.

Jim was an Eagle Scout.

Rick had a number of girlfriends over the years. In 1975 he started going with Julie Ciochetti, a pretty girl four years his junior from Menlo Park. Jim appeared to be far less concerned about women, although he went to school proms with the girl next door, and went out for a while with Lestari Tirtoprodjo, a pretty Indonesian girl from Redwood City he had met while taking some classes with John Muldown at Cañada College.

It was only in his diary—the secret inventory of his drives, fantasies, and insecurities—that Jim Schoenfeld bared his fear of women and longing for what he saw as ideal love.

Outwardly, as a neighbor would say later, he was like the rest of his family: "Norman Rockwell normal."

In 1971 a friend of Dr. Schoenfeld's, Dr. Robert D. Lewis, came to him with what he thought might be a good business proposition. Dr. Shoenfeld was happy to listen.

An acquaintance had introduced Dr. Lewis, who also had his office in Menlo Park, to an Oakland man named Max H. Mortensen, who told him of a golden opportunity. An old-line Contra Costa County family had decided to sell Quimby Island, 830 acres of below-sea-level farm and marshland surrounded by levees in the delta east of San Francisco Bay. Mortensen's idea was to put together a consortium to convert the island into a fish farm and recreational development. Instead of raising barley and milo as the previous owners had, he said, they would flood the island and raise fish in tanks in the holds of ships, mainly navy surplus vessels. It would be as revolutionary to the seafood industry as incubators had been to poultry farming. They would even have a "hospital" where live lobsters on the way from Maine to the Far East could recover from the rigors of air travel while they awaited final shipment. The lagoons created by flooding the island would become a haven for water skiers and pleasure boats. They would sell houseboat slips on the island as "aquaminiums."

Dr. Lewis, Dr. Schoenfeld, and a number of other Peninsula doctors, dentists, and friends in a dental supply firm pooled $145,000 as a down payment on the $395,000 purchase price and agreed to let Mortensen oversee their investment. Then began a series of events as bizarre as Mortensen's sales pitch.

First, using a little-known state law, they created a reclamation district, a taxing agency unique to California. The districts exist, mainly in the delta, to build and maintain levees. Any property they own is tax-free and exempt from county zoning regulations, Mortensen said.

The investors sold all but a small portion of the land to Reclamation District 2090 for $790,000, a paper profit of 100 percent.

41

They kept a few acres of marshland, because the reclamation law mandates that only property owners can vote in district elections. The investors elected three of their number, including Dr. Schoenfeld and Dr. Lewis, to the board of trustees, and the board officially named Mortensen district general manager.

The next step was to authorize the issuance of $96 million in municipal bonds.

From that point on the investors gave rubber-stamp approval to the work done by Mortensen and the bond counsel he hired, Urban J. Schreiner of Palo Alto. Soon the district was distributing an attractive blue-and-white brochure. "If you've ever dreamed of your own island paradise," it enthused, ". . . a world of sparkling waters and warm sun . . . of complete relaxation. A special place. Where you can get away without going too far. Or spending too much.

"From the moment you enter the ferry that transports you to Quimby Island, you're in another world," the brochure said. "You'll be getting a bargain under any plan because charges are infinitely less than the purchase of a recreational second home— and you won't have to pay any property taxes."

The brochure failed to mention that nothing had yet been built in this dream world.

Dr. Schoenfeld agreed to serve as president of the board. "It was probably because I wasn't present at the meeting," he would recall later, "and the one who wasn't present became the president. . . . It's just as if we were sitting here and someone is elected to go get a Coke. You just pick somebody to get the Coke."

In January of 1975 Mortensen came to the board with the happy news that a fine old company named Capital Trust, S.A., of Panama, had agreed to buy $50 million worth of bond anticipation notes. These types of obligations generally are sold with one-year maturity dates by municipalities which have delayed the actual sale of bonds in the hope of getting lower interest rates in the future. The notes were printed, and on February 1, 1975, the first $5 million worth were delivered to Capital Trust. The district never saw any cash.

Mortensen neglected to tell the investors that the two key employees of the Panamanian corporation were James H. Dondich and Louis M. Mayo. Dondich was convicted of conspiracy and mail fraud in Toledo in 1972, of interstate transportation of stolen securities in Tampa in 1974, of wire fraud and conspiracy in Los Angeles in 1975, and was enjoined from violating the securities registration laws in yet another case in Maryland in 1969. Mayo's Pennsylvania brokerage firm had its registration revoked for violations of securities fraud laws in 1964. He also had been convicted of interstate transportation of stolen securities in New York in 1964, and pleaded guilty to conspiracy in Pennsylvania in 1967.

Mortensen himself was an unsuccessful promoter who had been involved in a series of lawsuits over the ownership of the historic *Delta Queen* riverboat and had failed in a wax museum at Jack London Square in Oakland.

Both the Securities and Exchange Commission and the Justice Department, alerted by news reports about the unusual little municipality, began to take an interest in Quimby Island.

Toward the end of February 1975, Mortensen and Dr. Lewis flew to Chicago, ostensibly to deposit the other $45 million in bond anticipation notes in a bank there. They were met by federal agents who seized the paper. Later the agents picked up the $5 million worth of notes Dondich already had, returned the entire $50 million issue to the district, and warned Schreiner, the bond counsel, about the backgrounds of Dondich and Mayo. He and Mortensen continued to do business with them, however, with hardly an interruption.

The investors began to worry whether they would ever get their money out of the project, much less make a profit. Although one financial statement predicted $2 million in income for 1975, another reflected income would be only $42,822, with losses of $154,209 for the fiscal year ending that June. At the March 6, 1975, trustees meeting Mortensen told the board that Capital Trust had arranged for someone, he never said who, to donate a 350,000-acre ranch and mine in Columbia to the district. It could be carried on the tiny governmental agency's books as an asset to back the notes they were selling and help to get financing to make payments on dredges, barges, and a 300-foot retired navy trans-

43

port complete with auditorium that would serve as the development's "clubhouse." The trustees voted to accept the patently absurd "gift," and to give Capital Trust another $5 million in notes in gratitude for arranging it.

"It is odd indeed," Dr. Lewis admitted later, "but I certainly didn't question it. If somebody wants to give you a ranch, that's fine. Would you turn it down?"

The trustees apparently did not know at the time that $1.2 million in notes already had been sold through Dondich and Mayo, because the district never received any money.

Because they were getting desperate for cash to cover interest payments, the trustees agreed to sell $1 million worth of what were in reality promissory notes to a securities dealer in Florida for $890,000—an 11 percent discount, compared with the 1 to 2.5 percent usually granted to underwriters. Virtually all the investors in Florida, as had those in other parts of the country, thought the notes actually were municipal bonds backed by the county and state governments, "as sound as the U.S. dollar," one salesman said. In fact they were worthless green-and-white certificates secured only by Mortensen's pipe dream.

Inevitably, the district was driven into bankruptcy.

On June 17, 1976, just a month before the world would be electrified by the news of the Chowchilla kidnapping, the SEC filed a federal court complaint to stop what it said was a mammoth fraud. Dr. Schoenfeld, as president of Quimby Island Reclamation District 2090, was among twenty-one defendants in the civil suit, which alleged that one hundred sixty-one investors in twelve states had purchased $2.2 million in the district's notes. A criminal investigation into where the money had gone also had been started by the Justice Department's Organized Crime and Racketeering Strike Force. The case received national attention, in part because of its implications. There are about $220 billion worth of municipal bonds outstanding in the United States, and apparently it was perfectly legal for a public district in California with assets worth less than $1 million to float a $96 million bond issue.

Dr. Schoenfeld and his associates said they had simply let their advisers handle all the details. He didn't even read all the plans and papers he signed as president.

"I glanced through them," he said, ". . . but they were changed time after time, like the plans of a house, and every day somebody adds a new doorknob or subtracts a door. You know the gist of it, but you don't pay any attention to them."

Dr. Schoenfeld hoped his sons, who abhorred dishonesty, would not believe that he would knowingly do anything shady.

In February of 1974, a year before his father would realize his dilemma in the Quimby Island scheme, Jim sat at the desk in his bedroom, practicing the code he had worked out with Russian and Arabic letters and ruminating on the value and meaning of money, and on his future.

He had first come across Russian characters when he worked for the U.S. Geological Survey at its Peninsula headquarters. Sometimes the cartographers would use foreign maps for comparison, and one of Jim's jobs was to consult an alphabet chart and transliterate letters such as "USSR" from Russian to Roman characters. The Arabic letters he used were taken from Urdu, the main language of Moslem Pakistan after the Arab invasions. When he was a child, Jim had a friend who had lived in Pakistan, and they made up a code so they could write notes to each other in class which their teacher couldn't read if they were caught. His diary was further disguised by its cover, which said it was a workbook for "Math 1320." Indeed it had been, and the first twenty-two pages of the tablet were devoted to mathematical problems.

He dated most of his entries, entrusting his fantasies and deepest concerns to the code he believed no one would ever decipher. From the beginning the journal expressed his impatience with what he regarded as a life without focus—and a fear of leaving it without anyone noticing.

It was in his diary that he laid bare his overriding obsession with wealth.

Chapter 7

After David Boston earned his bachelor's degree in filmmaking, he continued to live in San Jose, taking postgraduate courses toward a goal of a master's. At the same time he wrote story treatments and scripts, trying, always unsuccessfully, to sell them to Hollywood producers.

Boston and Woods grew to be close friends. The aspiring scenarist visited the Woods estate often, and he traveled with Fred to see other family properties, including a quarry at Livermore in Alameda County south of Oakland, and the abandoned mine shafts in Sierra County. In 1974 the two took a twelve-day European vacation together.

Both young men were convinced that the key to their breaking into motion pictures lay in Boston's getting the opportunity to write, produce, and direct a screenplay, but Townhouse Enterprises never was successful enough to provide the capital they needed. They haunted government and private surplus auctions, buying cars and trucks and selling them. The profits made a modest living for them, but they were unable to accumulate the stake necessary to finance an independent production.

In 1974 Woods introduced Boston to a friend from his high

school days, Jim Schoenfeld. Soon, Jim had joined them infor-
mally in the salvage business. Boston liked Schoenfeld, but he
harbored a nebulous resentment over his intrusion into his partnership with Woods. Although the three might make more
money, their profits would have to be shared. On the other hand,
Jim and his younger brother, Rick, were talented mechanics and
knew as much as Woods did about fixing cars. And Jim, even
though he was no leader, had an incredibly orderly mind and a
genius for planning and organization. He complemented Woods
in that respect. Fred was a sloppy thinker but an aggressive leader.

Boston often talked about his script ideas with them, and sometimes took their advice.

He found his inspiration for plots from several sources, mainly
news stories and movies. He liked action films and tried to imitate
them in his own work. He was particularly impressed with the
films of actor-director Clint Eastwood, especially *Dirty Harry,* a
violent story of an improbable San Francisco police inspector
inclined toward meting out summary justice with a .44 magnum.
Boston saw the movie several times. In one scene a schoolbus full
of children is taken hostage, with a resulting chase across the
Golden Gate Bridge into Marin County.

In the summer of 1974, after Patty Hearst's kidnapping by a
handful of people calling themselves the Symbionese Liberation
Army and the subsequent spectacle of the botched mass-feeding
of the poor ordered by her captors, Boston began writing a story
he hoped to sell to Eastwood. He would call it "Chain Reaction."
The screenplay, which was never finished, became a curious amal-
gam of the Hearst case, an earlier escape attempt and shoot-out
at the Marin County Courthouse that left a judge and several
others dead, an even earlier television play about the nuclear
extortion of a city, and *The French Connection.*

In the first draft "Dirty Harry" Calahan probes the kidnapping
of the daughter of a prominent financier and politician by a shadowy cabal called the Cantonese Liberation Militia. He is plagued
by an assertive female television reporter whose investigative suc-
cesses prompt one of Harry's partners to remark, "I wish that I
had that broad's connections," a misquoted line once attributed

to a San Francisco law enforcement official in connection with Marilyn Baker's reporting of the Hearst case. In the script the CLM raids the San Francisco National Guard Armory to get weapons, and steals some plutonium from a radiation laboratory in Palo Alto. The kidnapped girl eventually joins her kidnappers, and they plot to hold the entire city of San Francisco for ransom by concealing a homemade atomic bomb in the TransAmerica pyramid. The demand for millions of dollars is left for the police to find attached to a small workable nuclear device to convince the authorities the terrorists possess the technical skill to build the bomb. The climax of the film, ending in the death of the debutante-turned-revolutionary, revolves around a spectacular chase in which the detective pursues a Bay Area Rapid Transit train in a commandeered car.

Earlier in the script Boston describes a courtroom raid to rescue two members of the CLM who are on trial.

They are accused of dynamiting a schoolbus full of children.

Boston worked on the script through August, September, and October, talking out his ideas for the plot with Woods and Jim Schoenfeld. One day, one of them said something like, "Do you think anyone could really pull something like that off and get away with it?"

As Boston worked on his script, Jim kept up his encrypted journal. His entries were irregular that summer and fall, but he tried to write something at least once a week. Sometimes he used other pads of paper if a notion struck him while he was away from home, but most of the diary was inscribed in the shorthand notebook.

His last entry in it would be dated July 13, 1976.

As the months stretched into over two years, the writing in the dog-eared tablet would change in tone. At first it revealed intelligence, even wit. The journal was his escape, not from reality but into a kind of self-examination, almost as if he were submitting himself to amateur psychoanalysis. He asked and tried to answer the questions he couldn't bring himself to explore with his parents, his brothers, or his friends. In the beginning, he would confide to his diary his obsession with success and money, an impatience with his own lack of direction and ambition, and his sexual frustrations.

In March 1974, while he was attending part-time college classes, he wrote that he was depressed because he had no immediate prospect of a career, or of achieving independence from his parents. In May and June he wrote of his fear of and fascination with women. He wanted to travel, perhaps to Asia, where he could stand out because everyone else would be shorter than he.

For a while he considered writing stories for teen-aged readers.

In July he addressed himself to the subject of marriage in an abstract way, cataloging his stiff moral, physical, and intellectual requirements for a wife, along with his own probable shortcomings as a husband. He wrote of his need for emotional and financial stability, but wondered where the money would come from.

In August and September he was bedeviled by loneliness and a frustrated desire to earn a living, to join the mainstream of society. On September 7, a Saturday night, he watched the Miss America Pageant on television as Shirley Cothran, a 21-year-old flute player from Texas with a *bouffant* pageboy, received the crown from her predecessor, Phyllis George. He was impressed by the smiling women he saw on the flickering screen, and puzzled over what qualities would make a man desirable to them.

It saddened him when he sold his horse late in September. He likened the animal to a reliable car.

From September through November Jim used his diary to try and sort out his confused image of himself and his desire for importance.

Always, he wrote about needing money.

In December of 1974, Fred and Jim saw the Rengstorff house, a vandalized Victorian mansion off Stierlin Road in Mountain View. It had been built in 1887 by Henry Rengstorff, a German immigrant and one of the founders of the Peninsula community just south of Palo Alto. It had been vacant since 1972, and was for sale.

The house seized Woods's imagination and, to a lesser extent, Jim's. They wanted to move the battered hulk to a lot they could

49

buy from the city, restore it to its nineteenth-century elegance, and move in, living there as well as making it the headquarters for the various businesses they hoped would include films, real estate, and other ventures.

Woods went to the city planning commission and inquired about the house. The staff there encouraged him. "They were very serious, very sincere, and they worked hard," city planner Ken Alsman recalled later. "What they wanted to do took imagination—it wasn't a normal thing for someone of that age to do."

Ironically, the house was owned by the Newhall Land and Farming Company. In January of 1975 Woods called Roger Jones, a Newhall executive, to find out if the building was for sale. He didn't identify himself as a member of the Newhall family, but said simply that he was interested in the property. The company was willing to sell the wreck cheap, since it was to be moved and the land was not part of the deal.

Woods and Schoenfeld got city approval for the purchase of the lot, but the total cost, with the bond the city required for moving the house, amounted to $39,500. The most they could come up with, tapping all their available resources including Woods's savings account and those of Townhouse Enterprises, was $32,000. To make up the rest they had an aerial photograph taken of the antique and junked vehicles on the Woods estate and offered them all to the city as collateral for the bond. The city refused, and the deal fell through.

Woods was crushed. He desperately wanted that house. It was the first time in his life he had been badly disappointed because of a lack of money.

They would just have to find a way to get it, he told the others.

Over the Christmas and New Year holidays Jim continued to speculate in his journal about his future. He was considering following his father into podiatry, although he had vague feelings that betrayed a higher, yet unformed ambition.

For the first time he mentioned his partnership with Fred Woods. With Fred encouraging him, anything was possible.

50

During the late winter and early spring, while they were trying to put together the deal for the Rengstorff House, including an attempt by Woods to borrow money from relatives, Jim made fewer entries in his diary.

In January he questioned the financial rewards of honesty, and remonstrated with himself for not fulfilling his domestic responsibilities as a member of his family. On the last day of the month he wrote that he had decided against podiatry, committing himself to his partnership with Woods and concluding that, with audacity, he could become a millionaire.

During the next four months Jim wrote only a few lines. But in June of 1975, in a guarded passage, he hinted that he was following Fred toward a big score. He set out his priorities for using the millions they would get: first to enrich himself, second to help ameliorate the human condition.

The seeds of his own destruction had been sown.

Chapter 8

Individually, none of the three would have dared to go through with it. Jim Schoenfeld himself would admit later: "It was just a crazy idea—just a wild idea, and I never thought we'd do anything."

In retrospect it is difficult to assess David Boston's role in the plot. Later he would insist to authorities that he knew nothing of what Fred, Jim, and Rick were planning to do, but, unwittingly perhaps, he helped them in their preparations and discussed some of the details with them as they all brainstormed ideas for "movie scripts."

At first that's all it was, a sort of literary challenge, to see if they could contrive the perfect crime. None of the three could honestly say when fantasy became reality, when they finally reached the point of commitment, when they actually *knew* they were going to do it.

The motives evolved just as haphazardly. For Fred it was simple, as most moral questions were. He wanted money to realize his dream of living in a grand, fully restored and modernized Victorian mansion. Since they promised themselves that no one would be hurt, it was no different from cutting corners a little too close on a sharp deal on a car.

For his part, Jim was driven by an almost manic desire to make something of himself as his father had. With real wealth, not just a comfortable income but a fortune, he could make a significant contribution to the society that had been kind to him, but to which he had contributed nothing.

Rick, as he had in the past, just went along. Fred was the leader. Jim was the planner. All three told themselves over and over again: "We'll never really do it; we'll just see if it could be done."

Almost whimsically, considering the form the adventure would take, they decided they would demand a ransom as a "fine" levied in retaliation for court-ordered busing of school children to achieve integration.

They hatched and discarded several plots. Meticulously Jim, using his code, set out each idea, each problem, each solution, not in his personal journal but in a Cañada College examination book. Above all, they agreed, they would not spend the money, except what they needed for the Rengstorff house, until the seven-year statute of limitations had expired. That is, unless something went wrong and they had to flee. They did not know that there is no time limit for the prosecution of kidnappers in California.

They decided the bus they would capture would have to be loaded with grammar school children. Older students were bigger and might resist.

Although Boston's setting for his script was the area in and around San Francisco, the three decided that urban congestion would pose too many problems. They would have a better chance for success in a rural area. Because he had worked for the geological survey, Jim knew that government section maps indicated not only landmarks but public buildings, such as country schools. He collected all the charts for central California.

At first they thought they would hold the children hostage in the Woods's Sierra County mine, but they rejected the idea because it was too remote, too hard to reach, and did not offer enough avenues for escape. After deciding to use a trailer buried at the quarry in Livermore, they narrowed their search for a likely school to the Central Valley.

During late 1975 and the early months of 1976, they drove hundreds of miles, casing grammar schools in secluded locations, noting their pluses or minuses on the maps. By March they had settled on Dairyland. That month they even attended Chowchilla's Western Stampede, the town's annual rodeo, to get a feeling for the people.

They followed the schoolbuses to and from Dairyland School during the regular session in the spring. The buses were full then, carrying up to forty-five pupils. That would be too many to handle safely, so they decided to wait until summer school started, when fewer students would be attending classes. In June they followed Ray's bus again, writing down its route and counting the children who got on and off. There were fewer than thirty, a manageable number.

Early on they decided they would have to get false identifications. They visited the vital statistics bureaus in the courthouses of several Bay Area counties, searching for records of people about their ages who were dead. Among other names they found Ralph Lester Snider, born April 5, 1954, in San Jose, who died before his sixth birthday. If he had lived he would have been in his early twenties.

Although the bull sessions that led to the plot started early in 1975, it was late fall before they took the first actual steps toward preparation. Those would take money, and Jim and Rick had none. To them it was still a mental exercise, but Fred wanted to go forward, to see if it could be done, he said. He offered to use his savings.

Firearms would be no problem. They all owned them.

On October 17, 1975, Fred bought a heavily used 1956 International truck trailer from Palo Alto Transfer and Storage Company for $750. A little over a month later, after some hard bargaining, he paid $500 to the same company for a 1956 Fruehauf moving van. He towed it away with the tractor, and took it first to his parents' estate to sit beside another van he had purchased earlier.

On November 24, using a pseudonym, they bought the three surplus shore patrol vans for a total of $3,750 in cash from the navy base in Alameda. They needed a place to hide them while they refitted the interiors, installed CB radios, and repainted them.

They had decided they would wait until just before the kidnapping to register them. That way, they reasoned, the license information would be lost in the bureaucracy for several days if the police somehow got the plate numbers. Fred told Boston he was looking for a garage to store some of the surplus he was buying. Boston took him to the real estate office of his uncle, Dominic Gigliardi, in San Jose. Gigliardi owned a warehouse on Knox Avenue in San Jose, and would rent space in it to Woods for $350 a month. Woods said the price was too steep. Gigliardi agreed to drop the rent to $300. Woods signed a fifteen-month lease, took possession of the warehouse December 1, and they moved the vans into it.

He always paid the rent on time.

Burying the moving van would be a major undertaking. Fred had worked briefly at his father's quarry a couple of years earlier and knew that it normally was closed on weekends. They could use one of the bulldozers at the quarry, but they would need a dump truck to remove and hide the displaced dirt. They bought one at an auction near Sacramento.

On the weekend of November 29–30 they assembled the dump truck and the two moving vans at the quarry and selected a dry lake bed as the place to bury one of them. It is unclear why they took both trailers to the quarry, whether they planned to bury both of them originally. But none of the quarry workers found it unusual that they were left there during the week. The following Sunday, December 7, they began the excavation, working quickly but carefully. With an acetylene torch they cut holes in the wheel wells of the white moving van for toilets, and cut the entry and vent holes. By Saturday, December 13, the hole in the ground was big enough. Using the truck tractor, they backed the trailer down and in. But when they started bulldozing the heavy, rocky earth back on top of it, the roof began to collapse. With lumber Fred brought from home and the warehouse, they shored up the ceiling from inside. They laid metal plates over the top for additional reinforcement before covering it.

By the third week of December the job was done, including the air vents and the concealed scuttle hole. All they would have to do when the time came to put their prisoners inside was to clear the dirt away from the entrance, lift the steel-plate trap door, and

55

connect the batteries to the fans. They had tested them and figured out they would go forty-eight hours without recharging.

They hauled the second van back to the estate. Maybe somebody would buy it someday, Woods said.

None of them noticed that a man had been watching them dig the hole.

They talked for a long time about how much of a ransom to demand. If it was too little, they were afraid the authorities would not take them seriously, too much and they would be unable to raise it quickly. They had decided to seek the money from the state treasury. Five million had a nice ring to it, and they hit on that amount. Remembering a series of luggage commercials they had seen on television, they decided to demand that the money be delivered in two suitcases dropped from a small airplane flying over a predetermined route. They stole some flashing hazard lights from the parking lot at the Cow Palace south of San Francisco to use to signal the pilot when he was over the drop zone in the Santa Cruz Mountains.

They knew they would have to be cunning to avoid a trap by the police and FBI. Perhaps the suitcases would be bugged or booby-trapped. That sort of thing happened all the time in the movies. The answer would be to x-ray them before they were opened.

On January 22, 1976, they returned to the navy's surplus disposal station at Alameda. Again using a false name, Norm Phillips, they paid $900 in cash for a used medical corps x-ray machine, which they hauled to the warehouse in San Jose.

Jim would have to go to the library to learn how to use it.

No matter how cautious they were, they knew they would have to prepare for an ambush, perhaps even a shoot-out. Their planning was almost antic in that regard. None of them had any military training, and though they all knew how to handle hunting weapons, none, with the exception of Woods, who had pointed pistols at teenage trespassers at the estate to scare them away, had ever dreamed of aiming a gun at another human being. In the spring of 1976 they sewed together homemade bulletproof vests, using lead and scrap metal.

The three decided they would need a "safe house," a hideout

where they could wait out the search for the kidnappers. If their identities were not discovered by the investigators, they would return to the Peninsula and resume their normal lives. If their covers were blown, they would leave the country and wait out the statute of limitations.

On April 23, 1976, Woods drove to Reno carrying a certified copy of Ralph Lester Snider's birth certificate. First he went to the Arrowhead Trailer Lodge at 4175 West Fourth Street and rented a vacant house trailer. He gave the manager, Angelina Schaible, $125.71 in cash to cover the first month's rent. She asked if he would need the space beyond August 1. He said he wasn't sure.

Then he drove to the Nevada Motor Vehicles Department office and applied for a driver's license, using Snider's birth certificate and the address of the trailer park. He scored 100 percent on the road sign test, 87 percent on his written examination, but only 82 percent on his driving test. The examiner said he tended to follow other cars too closely. Woods signed an affidavit that Ralph Lester Snider did not have a social security number, and the license was issued.

Next, Woods went to the main post office in Reno and rented Box 11532 in the name of Ralph Snider. Later he would use that address when he applied for Snider's passport.

The others would get passports also, but in their own names.

They debated how to get away after they picked up the money. They planned to hide or destroy the vans after the children were released (a detail they never fully worked out). The only evidence they wanted to leave behind was a bag with their victims' personal possessions and the ransom note in it. They would hijack a small plane and a pilot, they decided, perhaps even drop dummy parachutes to confuse any pursuers. Whoever picked up the suitcases would have to drive to a prearranged airfield to meet the commandeered aircraft. They had to find a fast car that they could paint an unreflecting black, even the chrome, so it would be difficult to see at night. In May, Jim answered a classified ad in the San Jose *Mercury* for the sale of a 1965 Cadillac. The price was $275. He told the owner, Pasquale Rizzo of Sunnyvale, that his name was James Reiker. He said he really wanted to buy the car, but that all he had was $236. Rizzo, who had bought the car for only $250, thought it over and agreed to accept $236 in cash. Schoenfeld counted it out for him, and then asked Rizzo to make out a bill of sale showing a purchase price of $50. That way, "Reiker" said, he could save a little money on the license fee.

On June 17, Jim Schoenfeld went to Picker Medical Products in South San Francisco and paid $39.90 plus tax for an x-ray film holder. He asked about buying a couple of lead screens to put behind the film. The clerk referred him to Sicular Associates, an x-ray service company in nearby Brisbane.

At Sicular, office manager Ron Ford was a little concerned that the young man who wanted to buy two film screens didn't seem to know much about radiography. He asked him a couple of questions, and when he said he didn't know what a radiation survey meter was, Ford asked him if he had the state license required to operate x-ray equipment. Schoenfeld said that he didn't know he needed one.

After Schoenfeld assured Ford he had a lead-lined apron to protect himself, and that all he was using the unit for was to x-ray pieces of structural aluminum in a warehouse, Ford cut him two lead screens to fit ten-by-twelve-inch film. Schoenfeld asked if Sicular had any Polaroid x-ray plates, but Ford said they were out of stock.

A week later Fred returned to the navy disposal yard in Alameda and bought twenty-five mattresses, ten chairs, a paint spray tank, and a printing calculator to help count the money.

They were almost ready.

Jim concealed the notebook detailing their plans at the warehouse in San Jose for safekeeping. Many of their ideas were incredibly farfetched, and most never would be worked out. The plot for their movie-turned-real-life changed constantly, and they never got around to writing the ending.

> Location? Bus and plane, [the first page began].
> Three vans used for transportation of kids.
> Two vans parked at predetermined hidden location. The third is used to transport Fred and Rick to the hijacking location.
> Rick and Fred will board the bus. Rick will disable the driver

with chloroform and Fred will drive the bus to the hidden location where Fred keeps an eye on the bus. Rick will escort the kids two by two to the vans where Jim is waiting. Watch for kids making a run for it. Count the kids!

The bus is left. The kids are taken to their receptacle and concealed.

The vans are taken and abandoned in strategic locations, to thwart any deductions of the kids' whereabouts.

We go to another area to receive the money.

Rick charters a plane to take Jim to a small airport like Lodi. On the way Rick has to meet a friend, Fred, who will meet the plane at an uncontrolled airport.

The plane lands at the airport and Fred is waiting with a gun. The pilot is abducted and the plane is put away. Beware FCC [*sic*] preflight and time arrival report. Maybe Rick should hijack the plane without the pilot's previous knowledge of the uncontrolled airport. Also, make sure to get a six passenger plane with a high wing, with autopilot.

Rick and Fred load the dummies into the plane with parachutes, and an extra parachute of course!

Jim is taking possession of the money thus; a state employed secretary will be appointed to bring the money in three brown paper parcels and instructed to . . .

That portion of the plan ended there and never was resumed. They would go ahead and use three vans because they had three drivers, but one would have to carry gasoline so they could drive aimlessly almost all night, so their victims would think they had traveled a great distance. The kidnappers would keep in touch with one another with short, cryptic CB radio messages. The procedure would be reversed when the victims were released, far from the quarry. The three gave up the idea of a face-to-face delivery of the ransom in favor of an aerial drop. They wanted to steal a high-wing escape plane to facilitate parachuting. It must also be equipped with an automatic pilot, in part because none of them knew how to fly, although one would have to learn to take off. After Fred or Rick, whichever took up the plane, dropped the dummy kidnappers with parachutes to throw the investigators off the trail, he would jump over a spot where the others would pick him up. The plane, flying automatically, would be followed by the

FAA radar until it ran out of fuel and crashed. They would be on their way to Reno.

The rest of the notebook, filled in over a period of months, listed things to remember and admonitions:

> Burn this book.
> Burn maps.
> Discard gray corduroy pants and blue and white shirt . . .
> Put valued possessions out of bedroom.
> Discard all items worn on job including watches.
> Must release hostages one at a time.
> Help disguise vans. Put on new bumper stickers after heist, keep a spare to cover first one if necessary (like "Vote for Regan [sic]"). Also install A.M. radio to keep on top of public knowledge.
> They have infrared to see at night.
> They also have heat seeking vision. Find out principles.
> Check Hayward for bullet proof vests.
> Assume aerial photograph during all phases.
> Last will and bankruptcy proceedings.
> Don't spend money for seven years.
> If caught—keep mouth shut (Brink's robbery).
> Demand used bills.
> Observe new laws giving young criminals shorter sentences.
> Have one kid in van when money is picked up for protection against trigger happy police?
> Make sure kid can't give information of any significance.
> Have money delivered about one hour before daybreak. If getaway is from a field then I need some indicator where tunnel is exp. [sic] a tree or pole, and I must be able to see it!
> Tear gas?—Police might use.
> Watch for SWAT.
> Safe deposit box.
> Concentrate on succeeding.
> Consider a double cross where they don't give the full amount.
> Big worry—aerial photography.
> Demand used bills to help guard against counterfeit.
> Figure what information is on file for each person, i.e., Fed. Gov't., state, school, personal files, public knowledge, etc.
> What might the Feds have on private files, i.e. Rick's dope, my income tax, Fred's registered guns.

Try to contemplate police observations and watch out for consistencies. Two plus two plus two plus two equals eight.

Rick is fouling up. He came from Jim and Kat's with his hair dye on, he got a moving permit with his real name and a copy was sent to DMV.

I don't know what to do about Jim and Kat, and maybe even Andria.

DMV will have to be tested.

Go in with the 53 dunebuggy and say it was moved but you forgot the permit that they gave you (but they really didn't). They will require a statement of facts. Argue that a statement is not necessary because they have a copy on file! Put up a fight about it and if they still require a statement then one might assume that DMV disposes of the duplicates.

(The entry above refers to the California law requiring that the owners of unregistered vehicles obtain permits to move them on public streets or highways, either to transfer them from one place of storage to another, or to drive them to a registration office. The Dodge vans, with government bills of sale dated November 24, 1975, would have needed such permits. Rick forgot to get one in the false identity and used his genuine name instead.)

From Rick's error [his brother wrote] we must make sure that the vans are not found. Crush them with the loader bucket full of gravel?

Put them in a storage van for future disposal?

Haul them to the mine and bury them?

Virtually all of the ideas and warnings in the last three pages of the book never would be needed:

Whoever is told to drive the van should wear headphones so that if they are bugged, the bug won't pick up any instructions.

When crooks get away with a crime, the law sets a trap. Beware!

Scent. FBI uses dogs as trackers so watch out for sweat, fingerprints or scent. (Scent: on bus, in vans, number two van, money case.)

X-ray truck needs a dark room, gas mask, lead vest, radios.

Think of possibilities of FBI intervention with the truck.

Consider microwave oven to foul the bug device. Melt any plastic.

Be prepared for gas in the money box.

Sea plane drop off?

Take some hundred dollar bills to the (money) pickup site to check against counterfeit.

Pick up the money using an illusion (like magic).

Take money out of case (wearing a gas mask), use a mini metal detector to find bug.

Using dummies in an airplane is risky. Because the dummies are traceable and the airplane has to be stolen.

Make sure money van has rifle holes on six sides in case of being followed. One on each side and two in the top in case of aerieal [sic] surveillance.

Dual control van. Steering, gas, shift etc. controlled from behind wall. Once money is delivered, the girl can be made to think van is radio controlled.

The entry above refers to the original plan to have the ransom delivered by a "state employed secretary."

The money will be requested as being a fine for mandatory busing. Besides just the money we will demand the repeal of mandatory busing.

Be careful of heat sensing photography.

Fake ID in case we're stopped in the vans after or before dropping off kids.

They made other lists, some in plain language, others in Jim's cipher, reminders of things to do and things to buy, such as material for disguises. One brief list was headed:

Set down planning like a business
1. Objectives
2. No killing (policies)
3. Everybody checks others work (disposal of evidence)
4. See business book.

They were sure they had thought of everything.

Chapter 9

The journal that Jim Schoenfeld kept at home referred only obliquely to the incredible act he and the others would undertake. Instead it examined his indecision. He was never sure he and Fred and Rick were doing the correct thing, but at least they were doing *something*. In the end, in the back seat of a police car, he would tell an incredulous detective: "Well, I wasn't doing anything at home, and I wasn't going anywhere, so I thought, well, I might learn something by this experience."

But in the summer of 1975, before he had committed any overt act, he still was considering his options.

He continued to be preoccupied with women and the idea of marriage, and to dwell on his fear of making an irrevocable decision. He wondered whether he was too much of a follower, incapable of asserting himself. But when he tabulated his prospects, he decided that if he went along with Woods, his life would be more exciting—even if it meant the risk of going to prison.

When it was all over, he thought, he might even run for public office.

Jim Schoenfeld did not write in his diary again until October 28. That Friday evening he went to the movies, an experience that affected him mightily. For the next month his journal would reveal his fear of spiritual retribution, as well as his vulnerability to dramatic images.

The motion picture he saw was "The Exorcist."

For two nights he barely slept. He was afraid now, not only of divine punishment but also of diabolical possession, something that had never occurred to him before. He wasn't sure he believed in evil spirits but, suddenly, he wasn't certain that he didn't.

"The Exorcist" would plague him for weeks.

On Friday, November 21, Jim strained his back helping Fred Woods's uncle move a piano. For two days he could hardly move. On Monday, while Rick was closing the deal to buy the vans at the naval disposal center, Jim wheeled himself through a city park in a wheelchair. By Tuesday he was able to drive.

That Friday, the night before their first weekend of labor at the quarry, he wrote that "The Exorcist" had caused him to question his grip on his sanity. His back hurt, and he was afraid of the devil.

But there was a lot of work that had to be done.

Three days before Christmas Fred, Jim, and Rick congratulated themselves for having managed to bury a moving van without being detected. It was as if they had won the first round of a game, with the odds on the other side. They still told themselves they wouldn't really go through with a criminal act, but Jim began to dream about what he could do with a great deal of money.

That night he used his diary to list some of the contributions he might make with his share of the ransom to make the world a better place. He considered transportation innovations to ease the energy crisis, cleaning up the environment, birth control and medical research.

In some twisted way, perhaps convinced by "The Exorcist" that he must atone in advance, Jim persuaded himself that what he was about to do was for the good of mankind.

The Schoenfelds, parents and sons, spent Christmas together that year, not knowing it would be for the last time. Jim felt mellow

64

in the warmth of his family, but the next day, after the presents had been shared, he observed in his journal that possessions obtained by labor are valued higher than gifts.

Starting on New Year's Eve, the traditional time for taking stock, he wrote a number of entries chiding himself for impatience, procrastination, lying, allowing himself to be pushed around by other people (including Woods), letting fear of the devil get the best of him, and turning his back on the moral injunctions he learned from his mother and father.

But he would show the world he was a man of action.

In January of 1976 Jim fell in love. The girl's name was Eileen Kelty, a nursing student from Louisville, who came to California to spend a brief vacation with her cousin, Irene Lile of Portola Valley. Mrs. Lile and her husband, Shannon, were close friends of the Schoenfelds', and shortly after Eileen arrived they took her over to Atherton to ride one of Rick's horses. The next day Jim took her for a ride on his motorcycle. Then he drove her up to San Francisco to see the sights, and they went out every night for the next week. He was truly smitten, and as the time approached for her to return to school in Kentucky, he wrote about her with an almost childlike enthusiasm.

She went back to Louisville on January 18. From that time on, whenever anyone asked him if he had a girlfriend, he replied, "Yes, Eileen." They corresponded, and their relationship seemed to magnify his yearning to be independent, to have a base upon which he could build a marriage and a home.

All he needed was the money.

Chapter 10

By the spring of 1976 David Boston was very nervous about his relationship with Fred Woods and the Schoenfelds. He believed they were up to something, although he would deny later that he ever knew what it was. In addition he was getting angry.

As Boston became more and more involved in scriptwriting, Woods kept after him to sell cars. Boston told him it wasn't as easy as Woods thought it was. Fred replied it was a simple matter of placing an ad in the newspaper and answering the phone. They argued on several occasions.

Early in May Boston went to see Carol Ann Geary, a friend who worked in his uncle's real estate office. He asked if she would help him prepare the legal papers to dissolve his partnership with Fred Woods. It just wasn't working out, he said.

On June 2, 1976, Boston filed a formal partnership dissolution with the San Mateo County Clerk in Redwood City. A week later he drove to Los Angeles, where he rented a small apartment on Clark Street in West Hollywood. He stayed for a month.

While he was in Southern California Boston arranged with an acquaintance, a writer who had worked on the story, to watch the

shooting of a scene of Clint Eastwood's latest movie, *The Enforcer,*
on location in San Francisco. Boston returned to San Jose and
called Fred. He invited him to watch the filming on Sunday morning, July 10. Then Boston called a sometime girlfriend, Indra
Romanis, and asked her to go along.

David and Indra arrived at the location about 10:00 A.M. The
scene would be a difficult one involving a car crash. Boston looked
on with great interest as the technicians and actors busily prepared
for the moment when the cameras would roll.

About 12:30 a.m. Fred arrived with Irene. They all chatted for
a while, and Fred told Boston he had a good car he wanted him
to sell, a 1972 Chevrolet Impala. Boston told him he would have
to think about it and that he would call him later.

Fred wandered over to the grip trailer and examined the props.
He studied the weapons carefully. He didn't even look up when
the director called for action and a car slewed into the set, rolled,
and exploded. He just fondled the guns.

Indra Romanis thought that was very strange.

Fred and Irene left the cordoned production site about 1:30 P.M.
Boston said later that it was the last time he ever saw him and that
he never saw the Schoenfeld brothers again.

Eventually he would tell investigators that he returned to Los
Angeles by July 13. When the detectives would ask him where he
was on the day of the kidnapping, he would pull out a notebook
and give them the names and addresses of two friends with whom
he had lunch that day. They spent the afternoon and evening
together, he would say, and went to see a movie called *Future-
world.*

In his journal that spring, Jim set forth some of the conflicts that
tormented him during the final months of planning and preparation for the kidnapping. He continued to try to convince himself
that his ultimate motive was the betterment of mankind—and he
worried about getting killed.

In the four months before he became one of the most wanted
fugitives in history, he wrote a dozen entries.

It was as if he were two people. By day he was plotting a

67

potentially deadly crime, using his self-taught letter substitution code to keep track of the details in a second notebook. By night, in the room he grew up in, he filled his journal with formless questions about girls, God, wickedness, ignorance, death, filial obedience, getting a job, marriage, becoming an inventor, having childern, trust, becoming a junior-high-school teacher, and his future in general.

It almost appeared that at home he was trying to ignore what he was really doing.

On July 13, 1976, the night before he and Woods would register the vans, and ferry one down to Los Banos to park it overnight to await the next day's work, Jim wrote that many things were troubling him, but that he couldn't define them.

He finally decided he was "apprehensive."

This man-child, so immature, so divided against himself intellectually and emotionally, had reached a point where he could not turn back.

He would not someday wonder: "What if I had done it after all?"

Part
Three

Chapter 11

When Joan Brown arrived that Thursday afternoon, July 15, 1976, at her house on Avenue 23 1/2 from her part-time job at an insurance agency in Chowchilla she sighed in mild exasperation. Jeff and Jennifer were hiding from her, a game they often played when she got home. For several minutes she walked from room to room. "Come on out, you guys," she called. "I know you're fooling."

Then Mrs. Brown noticed the peanut butter was not out, as it usually was a few minutes after the two got home from school, nor were there chairs in front of the television set. She called Ed Ray's house. Odessa, just home from work herself, didn't know where he was. Worried now, Joan Brown called the school.

She had not been the first.

When Lee Roy Tatom had left his office about 3:00 P.M. he told his secretary he would be at the county school's office in Madera all afternoon. If she needed him for some reason she could reach him there. At 4:35 he was called to the telephone. The secretary told him a parent had called to complain that Ed Ray's bus had not arrived.

Tatom could think of a lot of things that might have happened.

The most likely was that the bus had broken down, and the rules say the driver is never to leave a disabled vehicle or the children in it. He said as much to his secretary, and she began passing that theory along to other parents, including Mrs. Brown, as the calls multiplied.

Tatom set off in his car from Madera toward Chowchilla, sixteen miles to the northwest on Highway 99. He had headed the Dairyland Union School District for twenty-two years, and he knew all the bus routes just as well as the drivers did.

He swung off Highway 99 south of town and looked across the fields and orchards for the bus. Puzzled when he didn't see it marooned alongside one of the roads, he drove to the end of the run and reversed it to the school. The only other possibility was that Ray had managed to drive the bus to the shop in Chowchilla for repairs. He drove there, bending the speed limit now.

At the sheriff's office in Madera, Bill Cooley had expected a quiet evening. He had been helping keep the peace in the county for seventeen years, eight of them as a sergeant, and experience told him Thursday nights were usually not busy. Besides, there wasn't a full moon.

He checked the duty roster for the shift and saw he had three patrol cars working, two out of the main office and one out of the Chowchilla substation. The latter was manned by Charlie Reiring, a one-year rookie. Although Madera County is large geographically, 2,145 square miles, it has a population of only 42,000, half of it concentrated in the incorporated towns of Madera and Chowchilla, both of which have their own police departments. The sheriff's office has a total of seventy-six deputies. Three cars on the evening shift is adequate.

According to his log Cooley got the first call at 5:40 P.M. A schoolbus was overdue. It had dropped off some children but hadn't finished its run. He turned to the dispatcher. "Get 4412 on the air," he said.

Tatom was getting scared. After he failed to find the bus at the shop, he raced back to the school. He knew most of the families in the district, and he decided to check Ray's route again, house by house.

At the Gregorio place on Avenue 18 1/2 he was relieved to learn that little Edward had been dropped off right on time. Down the road the three Tripp children were all at home. He started toward the Zylstras's dairy farm on Road 16.

Around 6:00 P.M. Sergeant Cooley heard from the police department in Chowchilla. They had been getting a lot of calls from worried parents. Since most of the bus route was in the county's jurisdiction, did Cooley know what had happened? He decided he had better find out.

"Whitney, get a car and see if you can find Lee Roy Tatom," he ordered. "Radio Reiring to get over to the Chowchilla P.D. I'm going out there."

When Cooley arrived at the intersection of Avenue 18 1/2 and Road 16 he saw a man waving frantically. It was Tatom.

"I've gone over most of the route," the superintendent said. "The bus is two hours late now. I've checked the first two houses and the kids got home okay."

Cooley radioed Deputy Whitney to join them, and the three men went to the next place on Tatom's list. They found Susan Zylstra at home. Mrs. Tina Zylstra told them her older daughter, Eveline, had not gone to school that day, but Susan had. The mother had been standing in the front yard when Ed Ray let her off the bus. Nothing seemed to be wrong, she said.

Tatom and the officers next drove to the Williams Ranch. Lisa Barletta and her sister, Pam, lived there with their mother, Frances, who had been divorced and was remarried to Denver Williams. Only Lisa wasn't home.

"She never came home from school," Mrs. Williams said. "I called. Is something wrong?" By now Tatom was trembling.

"I don't know," he said.

The three men were truly baffled. "Something's got to be wrong," they agreed. "Something happened."

Whitney suggested they try to get a search plane up while it was still light, but Cooley demurred momentarily. Whatever had happened to the bus had taken place in the mile between Road 16 and Road 15 on Avenue 21. They would search that area first. They found nothing.

At 6:39 P.M. Cooley keyed the microphone on his car radio. "Call Sergeant Ring at home and see if he can get a plane from the sheriff's aero squadron to look for the bus," he said. The dispatcher radioed back that the Chowchilla police said they knew where they could get a plane if Dennis Ring were unsuccessful.

Twenty minutes later the dispatcher called Cooley to say that Ring and a local squadron volunteer were in the air, and that the other sergeant had a walkie-talkie that worked on channel 3. Cooley tried to raise Ring on that frequency and two others without success. He cursed.

At 7:00 P.M. Whitney went with Tatom to the school to compile a list of the missing children. After a quick check the superintendent told the deputy he thought the number who had not returned home was fifteen.

Edward B. Bates, Madera County's elected sheriff, had been listening to events unfold on his radio. After Ring started looking for an airplane, Bates drove toward the Chowchilla substation. At 7:10 P.M. Cooley radioed the sheriff that Tatom had upped the estimate to twenty-one kids.

The first radio bulletin resulted in a call from Fresno, twenty-two miles to the southeast. A yellow schoolbus had been seen there at Highway 99 and Central. Cooley had learned that Ring was receiving on his walkie-talkie but could not transmit. He radioed him to ask the pilot to fly over Fresno.

At 7:24 P.M. Cooley broadcast an all-points teletype to other law-enforcement agencies describing the bus, the driver, and the children. By now all of his patrol cars, several from the California highway patrol and the Chowchilla police, parents, school employees, and just about everybody in the neighborhood who had a citizens' band radio was scouring the countryside.

They didn't know about the kidnappers' vans, nor that they had CB transceivers installed in them.

Charlie Reiring had rejoined the search, and was driving his patrol car slowly near Berenda Slough. He was watching the airplane Ring was in, by now returned to the air over Chowchilla from the fruitless mission to Fresno. A little before 8:00 P.M. he saw the small craft wheel over the slough and waggle its wings. He drove to the bridge, parked his car, and walked down the bank into the bamboo.

At 8:11 P.M. Reiring radioed Cooley that he had found the bus. It was empty.

Cooley told him to keep people away from the place until he could get there. Bates overheard the radio traffic as he drove toward Chowchilla and turned instead toward the slough. Jim Hickman, a lieutenant, had started over from Madera with a couple of detectives.

Cooley found Reiring waiting for him alongside the road. "It's down there," the deputy said.

"Don't let anybody off the road," the sergeant said as he went down the bank. He stepped aboard the bus. The ignition was turned off and the key had been taken. He got out. There were tire tracks leading back toward the road. Cooley looked around and was startled to find no footprints. It was getting dark.

He trotted back up to the roadway. "Call Jim Angus," he said, referring to the department's identification and evidence specialist.

"What do we call it?" Angus asked when he arrived at 9:10 P.M.

"207 PC," Cooley replied.

"Kidnapping?"

"You got any better ideas?"

Chapter 12

By the time the bus had been found some of the parents had gathered in the basalt block building that is Chowchilla's police station, firehouse, courtroom, and sheriff's substation. Others waited at home by their telephones.

Bates had Tom Walsh, resident agent of the FBI in Merced, notified that his department was working on what looked like a mass abduction. The bureau accepted concurrent jurisdiction, and that night fifty agents from all over California descended on Chowchilla and booked all the available rooms in the town's two motels, the Star and the Safari. They commandeered the one-story city hall a block from the police station, and drew the blinds.

Slowly, the attention of the outside world focused on the little valley town. Alerted by Director Clarence Kelley at the FBI, President Ford called Attorney General Edward Levi and told him to use all the resources of the Justice Department and any other federal agency he needed to help in the search, including Defense. He asked Levi to keep him informed. Much the same was going on in Sacramento. Governor Edmund G. Brown, Jr., diverted momentarily from the Democratic convention just concluding in New York that had ended his quixotic skirmish with

Jimmy Carter for the Presidential nomination, ordered the full machinery of the state into motion, including the highway patrol and the national guard. The State Department of Justice, headed by Attorney General Evelle Younger, sent agents to Chowchilla. Lieutenant Governor Mervyn Dymally rushed to the little police station, along with Wilson Riles, the state superintendent of public instruction.

"I am here," Dymally intoned with a vestigial accent of his native Trinidad, "to give assurances to the parents and the community that all law-enforcement and supportive services of the state and federal governments are employed to do what is necessary."

"I thought this was the best place to be," added Riles. "My main hope is for the safety of these youngsters and the driver. We now have to make an assessment as to whether this is the kind of thing we'll have to contend with in the future. We transport more than eight hundred thousand youngsters a day in this state."

As the search gathered momentum and widened, the press began to gather, sensing a story of cosmic proportions. Bewildered parents waiting in what would become a bedlam answered the same questions over and over again. They flinched as the hot television lights went on and off every time Dymally or some other official stepped forward, always to say there was nothing new to report. Theo Wilson, the peripatetic newswoman who is the de facto kidnapping expert from the New York *Daily News,* arrived ostentatiously from Los Angeles in a taxi. The bill was $200. Soon there would be hundreds spreading as well as reporting rumors and interviewing one another and fighting over the sixty telephones the Pacific Telephone Company had scrounged from phone booths at stores and filling stations. As always happens in celebrated criminal cases, the press became as big a show as the search, and many of the townspeople not even related to the children came to watch.

Some brought casseroles and buckets of chicken, and remained to drink coffee and share the agony of the parents, much as they would do after a funeral.

Encouraged in part by questions from the reporters, the dis-

77

traught parents began to fantasize unspeakable fates for their children. They recalled to each other that the deranged Zodiac killer, who had terrorized the Bay Area years earlier but had never been caught, had once threatened to capture a schoolbus. Perhaps the kidnappers were terrorists. Maybe someone had a grudge against the town.

Back in the slough Angus had been joined by Lieutenant Hickman and a detective named Seymour. He was having a hard time finding anything he could get a handle on. The technician photographed two sets of tire tracks in the moist sand about seventy feet south of the bus, and four more a short distance away. It looked as if the vehicle, whatever it was, had failed to make it up the bank the first time and had backed for a second run at it. Cooley had told Angus there were no footprints, so he began to work on the bus. He lifted eight sets of latent fingerprints from the inside of the folding pneumatic door and the hand support bar near it. Finally he took soil samples from where he had photographed the tire impressions. He finished up about 12:30 A.M.

Cooley, Whitney, and Hickman had gone to the police station to bring Bates up to date. "The kids are gone and that's our only fact," the sheriff told the reporters. "There's no blood, no evidence of foul play. I absolutely can't figure it out. I'm at a loss for words."

Cooley left Whitney at the police station to finish up the list of the missing and drove back to the bus. As soon as Angus was done he called for the big tow truck from Melvin's Garage on West Sixth Street, the only rig in town big enough to haul a bus. It would be stored at Melvin's for the time being. Then Cooley returned to the police station and told Whitney to drive back to headquarters in Madera and bring back another deputy and all the emergency rescue and medical equipment in case it would be needed later at the Chowchilla command post. He and Seymour went out and started searching every empty barn and shack they could find.

Then, for the first time in months, it started to rain. It hardly ever rains in the summer on the flatlands of California, but that night a mighty storm broke over the valley. It was almost as if nature had joined in a conspiracy to hide the children. High winds whipped sheets of water over the fields and orchards, making them quagmires, and thunder and lightning exploded overhead. For three hours during the night much of Chowchilla was without electricity.

Back at the police station the parents began to distrust the authorities. Maybe they had found blood, or even bodies, on the bus but were keeping it from them. Denver Williams was permitted to go check it out. He came back and said he found only a few towels. It was scant reassurance.

"We're becoming more and more resigned to the very worst," said Jim Dumas, the owner of a furniture store and Chowchilla's mayor. "It's just tearing this town up."

Later Dumas would tell reporters how he had been kidnapped himself five weeks earlier while he was attending a conference in Fresno. A young black with a gun had jumped him and Chowchilla city councilman Alvin Acker in the parking lot of their motel, forced them to drive a few blocks in Dumas's pickup truck, taken the money from their wallets, and then ordered them to drive away.

"It's all been crazy lately," Dumas said, adding, "I lost eighty-two bucks."

Just before 7:00 A.M. Friday, Angus got a call from the dispatcher who told him Sergeant Sam Haun wanted him to go back to the slough where the bus had been found. Angus called Haun, who told him another sergeant, Charlie Young, might have found some new clues.

Young was waiting for Angus when he got there about 7:45. The first thing he noticed was that the tire tracks had almost been obliterated by the six hours of heavy rain just past.

Young showed the technician what he thought looked like narcotics paraphernalia not far from where the bus had been parked. Angus retrieved and catalogued three cotton balls and a two-inch-square bandage with spots of blood on them, some aluminum foil

79

tied with a red rubber band, and a plastic drinking glass with a minute amount of liquid in the bottom.

Young shivered. Junkies, he thought. That's all we need.

As the country awoke to what had happened at Chowchilla, the tips started coming in from as far away as New England and Mexico. Virtually all of them were worthless. Some were aberrations from the imaginations of the unstable who are always galvanized by major tragedies. But all of them had to be checked.

During the long wet night investigators carrying half a dozen different badges had been knocking on doors along Ray's bus route, asking if the householders had noticed anything out of the ordinary, no matter how trivial. A few mentioned seeing a white van with a whip antenna and two others just like it but of different colors a day or two before the kidnapping. The all-points bulletin was routinely updated to include them, and the information was picked up by radio and television stations.

About 10:30 Friday morning the Chowchilla command post got a call from Elmot Austin, a city councilman in Los Banos, a slightly larger farming community thirty-seven miles due west of Chowchilla on a cross-valley thoroughfare, Highway 152. Austin said he had picked up a tip from a woman who did not want to be identified who said a white van had been parked in front of her house all night on the fourteenth. Austin said the woman told him a brown van had pulled up about 1:30 P.M. the next day, a man got out of it and into the white truck, and that both vehicles had taken off toward Chowchilla on Highway 152. She could not describe the drivers, but she had written down the license number of the white van.

It was a California plate, 1C91414.

It wasn't until 7:00 P.M. that Friday night that a detective in the beleaguered station could get around to calling Austin back. He repeated the story, adding that the woman told him money had been exchanged between the two men before they drove away, two and one-half hours before the kidnapping.

Three hours later the license number was turned over to the FBI, which was running down all the leads outside of Madera County.

As the engines of government rumbled into high gear, hundreds and then thousands of citizens' band radio operators joined the search. Highway 99, the neon-encrusted spine running the length of the Central Valley, and the new Interstate 5 freeway to the west of it are the principal avenues of commerce between northern and southern California and the Northwest and Mexico beyond. Fleets of trucks, most of them equipped now with CB radios, roll through the valley every day. All the drivers were on the lookout, as were the "four-wheelers," the new generation of communication buffs with two-way radios in their cars.

Across the street from the police station in Chowchilla, John Moody, a builder whose CB handle is "Blue Streak," talked to the amateurs from a base station, each transmission beginning with the salutation of their arcane new language: "Breaker, breaker . . .

"If you're here for glory, if you're here to take chances or get shot at, go home, we don't want you," he broadcast. "The kids' lives are at stake. This is a situation where we don't want heroes. Don't go in and try to take them yourselves. Radio for help. When it arrives, be ten-ten on the site."

All day Friday the command post at Chowchilla buzzed with false information.

A Merced police detective called in to say a woman schoolbus driver had disappeared shortly before the kidnapping. It turned out that she was accounted for, worked for an insurance company, and hadn't driven a bus for a long time.

About 10:00 A.M. a telephone operator called to report that at 10:30 P.M. on the night of the kidnapping an elderly woman had dialed O and had asked for the sheriff's office. She wanted to report a hit and run. The operator overheard the woman tell an officer in Madera, "A white van ran over my fence and yard. There are tire tracks in my yard." The operator also overheard Ed Mulvihill, an investigator for the Madera County district attorney's office who happened to take the call, tell the woman they were too busy to do anything about it. Nobody had heard of a white van at that point.

Mulvihill had not written down the woman's address, which was on Road 15. Twelve hours after the call a disgruntled deputy went out to look for a broken fence.

At 1:00 P.M. Sergeant Young got a radio call to go to the home of Betty Lay on Avenue 22 1/2. When he got there he was met by the woman and her son, Jeff Brazil, twelve. The boy told him that the day before the kidnapping a young man wearing a red and white T-shirt had tried to run him down with a yellow Datsun pickup as Jeff rode his bicycle on Road 7 near Avenue 22. The boy said he jumped off his bike, ran into a ditch, and hid. The man stopped, got out of the truck and looked for him, he said, and then drove away.

He didn't see the license number.

In places like Chowchilla, which bears a far greater resemblance to the midlands of America than it does to the closer cities of San Francisco and Los Angeles, people with a problem yet turn to prayer, as Ray had done in his makeshift dungeon. He didn't know that he was being joined by some of his neighbors, who went to special services on Friday.

At the First Baptist Church, the largest in the community, the Reverend Ruynolds S. Van Buskirk took his sermon from portions of Psalms 23, 37, and 91, "because they best respond to this kind of evil." In the Psalter David gives thanks for his rescue from fear and death, ruminates on the happy state of the godly and the short-lived prosperity of the wicked, and admonishes: "Surely He shall deliver thee from the snare of the fowler, and from the noisome pestilence."

"My God, why kids?" the pastor asked at the beginning of his sermon. "Only God knows why these children have to suffer, and only God knows where they are today." He concluded by asking the congregation to pray for the kidnappers as well as their victims.

82

The Reverend John Surrat recalled to a group of worshippers at the First Assembly of God Church that his own brother had been kidnapped once in Texas but had been released unharmed, he said, because of their mother's prayers. "Pray that there is no vindictiveness," he implored. "Instead, have love for the abductors, as God has love for us when we sin."

In other, more earthly precincts, there was little talk of Christian forgiveness.

"We are, you might say . . . plenty pissed," a beer-drinking rancher told San Francisco reporter Bob Cardoso at the Cotton Club, one of Chowchilla's two saloons. "Yes, that's a fair assessment of the mood of this town."

Another man at the bar wondered if the blame should be lodged against the "seasonal workers," a euphemism that has almost replaced "wetbacks" in places like Chowchilla. "Twenty-six illegals were arrested here two months ago," he told Cardoso. "Now twenty-six kids are gone. I think they're getting back at us. I believe the kids are in Mexico, long gone."

At 4:30 P.M. Sergeant Young relieved Sam Haun at the command post in Chowchilla. His log for the next four hours is a record of false hopes, false information, and frustration.

At 4:38 P.M. Moody told him one of the CB operators had discovered tire tracks and children's footprints around the Ashvien Baptist Church at Avenue 20 1/2 and Road 8. He sent a deputy, who radioed back the tracks were unlike any in the slough, and that he could find only two sets of small footprints.

Two minutes later the police department in Corcoran, a town about the same size as Chowchilla seventy-two miles to the south, called to say that three vans had been reported heading toward Los Angeles earlier in the day with several children in each. One was yellow with a telephone company emblem, one was blue and pulled a trailer carrying a motorcycle, and the third was green and white and was being driven by an MMA, western police parlance for Mexican male adult. Young passed the information to the FBI.

At 5:35 an Explorer Scout handed the sergeant a note he couldn't understand. It looked as if it had been taken by a telephone operator at the command post. It contained two names, two telephone numbers, and something about New Mexico. Again, Young sent the note down the street to the FBI.

At 5:55 P.M. a messenger told him a sixty-year-old man in Palmdale, a desert town northeast of Los Angeles, had found a child's blue tennis shoe on the highway. Dutifully Young gave the information to the FBI.

Most of the people who called simply wanted to help. Others, however, grabbed the opportunity to accuse their real or imagined enemies. One woman told Young on the phone he should check out two of her male acquaintances in Madera. Another said she had an idle conversation about 5:00 P.M. Thursday with a dark-haired, bearded man with shoulder-length hair who was driving a bus with no one on it. At 7:55 P.M. a messenger gave Young a note saying that Ron Burns, a talk-show host at radio station KDSO, had received a call from a man who said he was a spokes-man for the Christian Defense League. The man said he was holding the children and was going to kill them all "to put an end to the Jewish conspiracy." About the same time a man from Los Banos came into the substation and identified himself to Young as a "rent-a-cop." He said he knew who the suspect was, a "suspi-cious character" he had been shadowing for several years. Pa-tiently, Young read through the pleased informant's garbled "re-port" and then turned him over to an FBI agent, along with all the other "leads."

A woman named only Laura called to say she had seen a van going south on Highway 99 near Bakersfield. A man telephoned from Orange Cove, a village east of Fresno, and reported seeing two, possibly three vans at the little airstrip there. They had left tire tracks, he said. Another man came in and said that if the kidnap van had large, dark emblems on one side, he could identify the driver.

Young was getting very tired.

Chapter 13

Weariness had taken over from claustrophobia, and Ray and the children slept.

After it had become clear that the ceiling was not going to collapse, they passed around the food and drank some of the water left by the kidnappers. Within an hour their meager rations were gone, all but the water.

The truck trailer in which they were entombed was eight feet wide, twenty-five feet long, and twelve feet high with a raised platform two feet high at the front end over the tractor hitch. There was little room for twenty-seven people of any size to get comfortable, and less than eighty-five cubic feet of air space per person. In spite of the fans, the atmosphere turned foul quickly. Exhaustion fed by lack of oxygen defeated tension, and they slept.

There are varying accounts of what happened next. No two people see things in the same way. Self-image colors perception. It is also true that heroism is often a product of either fear or neurosis. There are no real heroes, only survivors. Later it would be difficult for some of the boys to admit they had been afraid.

We do know that it was twelve hours before Ray and Mike Marshall, a raw-boned youth who is the son of championship rodeo rider Bob Marshall, decided they had to escape what both of them knew could become a mass grave. Ray was convinced the kidnappers had left them there to die, and for a good deal of the morning he alternately wept and asked Jesus for deliverance. At one point, the boy recalled later, the bus driver took him to a corner and said "that he was sorry and that it was his fault and it looked like we are going to have to kick the bucket."

As the July sun beat down on the earth around the buried coffin the temperature inside began to rise alarmingly. The candle was gone, the first set of flashlight batteries had been depleted, and light from the second was growing dim. About 4:00 P.M. Ray and young Marshall stacked several of the mattresses and box springs up on the raised end of the trailer floor under the circular hole through which they had entered. Ray climbed to the top of the unsteady pile and tried with his hands and shoulders and neck to raise the steel plate. It wouldn't move.

Ray slid down and pried a piece of three-by-four lumber about sixteen inches long from the base of one of the ceiling braces and returned to the sealed opening. The steel did not quite cover the hole, and he managed to wedge the board in the crack and wrench the plate a few inches to the side, far enough for him to reach up behind it with one arm. Blindly, he felt around until his hand encountered one of the huge batteries. Mike joined him on top of the mattresses and Ray pulled the battery slowly to the side at the same time they inched the plate back. They slid the hundred-pound weight over the edge, and Ray, clutching it against his belly and the boy supporting the other end, lowered it and dropped it on a mattress below. The plate moved more easily now. They repeated the process with the other battery and then struggled with them to the other end of the trailer, against the back wall, to prevent the acid they contained from spilling on themselves or the children.

Ray raised the plate, and in the waning light of the electric torch he saw the inside of the wooden shaft and the plywood cover.

They used the block of lumber to break some slats from the bottom of one of the box springs, twisting them loose from their staples. Ray was sweating heavily and perspiration burned his eyes. He climbed back up and propped up the plate. He and Mike lifted it, eased themselves up into the cramped shaft, and let the plate down. Now they were up on top of the trailer.

Ray attempted to lift the dirt-covered lid with his broad back but failed. Then Mike jabbed one of the slats into a corner and pried upward. Dirt fell in. For the first time in over twenty-four hours they saw daylight.

Feverishly they clawed at the plywood and dirt. They were joined by ten-year-old Robert Gonzales. Ray and young Marshall enlarged the opening slightly but their torn hands could not get enough of the compacted soil to fall back and lessen the weight on the plywood. Ray attacked the opposite wall of the shaft, hammering almost senselessly against the bowed-in wood. Some dirt sifted out from the bottom of the enclosure, which sat unevenly on the roof of the trailer. He scratched with his fingers and a slat, and dirt began to fall past the propped-up plate onto the mattresses. Sand and grit filled their eyes and lungs and showered down into the face of John Estabrook, who was holding the flashlight by now, as they raked the dirt and gravel back and Ray continued to slam the wall. Soon the soil stopped coming.

Ray knew he was finished. He tumbled down the tower of springs and mattresses and felt his legs buckling under him. He tilted one of the jugs over his head and let the water wash over his face, gulping breathlessly. His chest felt like it was on fire. He flopped down on a mattress, sobbing in despair. The boys labored on.

It is not known how long Ray lay there before the primal urge to live took over again. Every part of him ached. The adrenal strength that had driven him before had ebbed away. At last he rose and climbed back up the spongy pile of padding, springs, and ticking and with the desperation of a trapped wild creature he reached up through the plate with both hands, wrapped his fingers around the edge of the plywood cover, and heaved. A piece about five inches square came away.

More dirt fell in on them, and Ray and the boys dug frantically, their hands getting in each other's way. Ray jerked at the plywood again, and a larger chunk shaped like a half-moon tore off.

87

Robert Gonzales, the smallest of the three, warily raised his head up through the opening and breathed deeply.

"Jist look, see what you see," Ray whispered. "Do you see anyone?"

"No, nobody. Just some trees and a couple old trucks."

Robert climbed out of the little hole and, with Ray urging him from where he was hunkered down under the plywood, began to scrape the dirt away with his hands. Ray and Mike pushed and lifted until the lid flopped over, spilling dirt on the ground and down the shaft.

They were free.

They tilted the steel plate up on its side. Blood spurted from two fingers of Ray's left hand as he bent back the heavy wire mesh to enlarge the opening. He dropped back to the floor of the truck.

"We're gettin' out," he told the children. "We all gotta stay together."

One at a time he helped them to the top of the mattress pile, where Mike passed them up to Robert. Jennifer Brown and Cindy Vanhoff scraped their knees and Becky and Judy Reynolds both cut their bare feet on the wire. They blinked, like children coming out of a movie theater after a Saturday matinee.

Ray was the last one out. He shivered in the early evening air, his legs unprotected and drenched in his own sweat. Where are we, he wondered? Where can we get help?

Through the trees he saw what he thought looked like a grain elevator. He started down the dirt road toward it. "Come on," he called. "We're all gonna take off and go together."

As they approached the structure Cindy Vanhoff was struck by a sign on it. It said, Safety First.

Walter Enns, a maintenance worker at the California Rock and Gravel Company quarry in Livermore, had a little over an hour left on his shift. It was almost 8:15 P.M. and he got off at 9:30. He was welding on an aggregate mill tower when he heard youthful voices behind the scrubbing machines. Damn local kids had been playing in the quarry yard after dark lately. He pushed the button sounding the mill horn to alert his partner, Gerald Teague, who was working nearby, of possible trespassers. Then he saw a gaggle of filthy children and a man in his socks and undershorts staggering toward him down the road. The man broke into a run and started up the steps of the tower.

"We're the ones from Chowchilla," Ray said. Enns was astonished.

"I heard about it on the radio while I was eating lunch," the quarry worker said.

"We was buried right out there," Ray told him. "Right behind there."

Teague arrived to find out what was wrong. As soon as he saw the group he knew who they were without an explanation. He called the sheriff's office.

Enns and Teague took the woozy band into the main shop and gave them water. The workmen found a pair of coveralls for Ray. One got him a Pepsi.

About 8:30 P.M. on Friday night, July 16, 1976, Jack Baugh settled back in his chair at Hap's Restaurant in Pleasanton, a quiet suburban community about twenty-five miles southeast of his office at the Alameda County Courthouse in Oakland. Dinner and the speeches were over, and he watched with desultory interest as a motion-picture projector was set up in the smoky banquet room.

A group of physicists from the University of California's nearby Lawrence Livermore Laboratory had come to this meeting of the state association of criminalists to unveil a discovery that would make it possible to trace any solid explosive after it had been detonated. As chief of the criminal division of the sheriff's office in the large urban county that had witnessed the genesis of violent protest at Berkeley in the sixties and the subsequent emergence of terrorist groups such as the SLA and the New World Liberation Front, Baugh had decided it would be worthwhile to attend, along with the county's crime laboratory staff, including its chief, Robert Cooper, criminalist Tony Sprague, and lab photographer Ernie Erler.

Baugh's mind wandered from the after-dinner chatter around him. He intended to pass up the inevitable late-evening fellowship at the bar so he and Marcia and the kids could get an early start on their vacation in the morning. He had already taken Friday off to have new tires put on the station wagon for the 150-mile trip to their cabin in the Sierra foothills. But he had concluded that tonight's meeting and the promise of a new method to help identify bombers were important enough to put off their departure for a day. His wife had agreed, and went to the dinner with him.

As he had a hundred times, Baugh retraced mentally the route they would take from their home in Castro Valley to the cabin: past Tracy, through Manteca and across Highway 99. He wondered whether they would be held up by any of the roadblocks that had been set up in the massive search for the twenty-six children and their schoolbus driver who had disappeared the day before just outside Chowchilla, ninety miles away in Madera County. He hoped not. He didn't relish the idea of sweating in a line of cars in the hundred-degree heat of the valley summer.

Baugh lit a cigarette and thought about what the evening papers were bruiting as the kidnapping of the century. Since the story had broken just that morning, he knew only what he had read or heard Walter Cronkite tell him from the TV set while he and Marcia were dressing to leave for the restaurant. Madera was an obscure county, but it hadn't taken Clarence Kelley long to order the FBI into the case. The White House was being kept informed. Every politician with the remotest excuse to be there had flown to Chowchilla to bask in the limelight generated by the army of reporters marshaled by all media.

For several hours it had seemed as if the bus had simply dematerialized. Finally, just before dark Thursday night, it was spotted by a search plane, parked in the foliage of a dry watercourse. Nothing was left in it. Not even the keys.

He recalled seeing a grieving mother on television asking the question that was plaguing all the parents: "Why have they taken our children?"

Like virtually everyone else in the civilized world that day, Baugh had difficulty grasping the enormity of what had happened. Why would anybody want to take, maybe even murder, twenty-six kids? As a detective with more hash marks than he liked to remember, he could easily imagine several ways such a crime could be committed. But why? There hadn't yet been a ransom demand, the papers said. It was as if someone had set out to erase a generation from a small town. It just didn't make sense. Not in Chowchilla. Not anywhere.

For a moment he wondered what his life would have been like today if it had happened in his county. Thank Christ it hadn't. He formed a picture in his memory of Gary Brown, the Chowchilla police chief he had met once at a postgraduate seminar. Poor sonofabitch. He certainly had his hands full.

Baugh's reverie was interrupted by Hap's hostess.

"Chief, there's a phone call for you."

He cursed silently, leaned over to his wife, excused himself, and followed the woman to the telephone. Clay Paxton, the lieutenant in charge at the Eden Township Substation, spoke rapidly, excitedly.

"Jack, they found the kids. They found the kids from Chowchilla." Baugh felt the hair prickle on the back of his neck.

"Where?"

"At the Cal Rock Quarry in Livermore. Jesus Christ, Jack, I can't find anybody. They're all gone—the sheriff, the undersheriff, the assistant sheriff. And where the hell are the guys from the crime lab?"

Baugh heard his own voice rising. "How many kids?" he asked.

"All twenty-six. And the driver."

"Sheeeeeeit," he breathed softly. "What kind of shape are they in?"

"It looks like they're okay. They worked their way out of some sort of cave. We have some buses on the way over there to pick them up."

Baugh thought fleetingly of his retreat in the mountains, then blocked it out. Marcia wasn't going to like this.

"Who's there?" he asked Paxton.

"Lieutenant Volpe. He was on his way home when we got the call. He got there in a few minutes." Baugh's spirits rose slightly. Ed Volpe was one of his best men, and a good friend who lived in Livermore. Ed wouldn't make any mistakes.

Quickly, Baugh told Paxton the undersheriff was out of town.

91

Keep after the sheriff, he said. If Paxton couldn't find him, track down his secretary and ask her where he was. Baugh would gather up the crime lab people at the dinner.

Just before he hung up, a vague recollection of something he had heard on the television news bubbled to the surface, something about the kidnappers perhaps having citizens' band or police radios.

"Clay, keep air traffic to a minimum," he ordered. "Use a landwire whenever you can. If they're still around here we don't want to blow it."

Restraining an impulse to run, Baugh hurried back to the banquet room, found Cooper, Sprague, and Erler and told them to meet him at his car. "Something's come up," he whispered to his wife. "You'd better come with us."

"Hey, Jack," an acquaintance protested as they threaded their way toward the door, "you'll miss the movie."

"That's okay," he answered. "I'll wait until it's on television."

Although the restaurant is only a few miles from the quarry, Baugh drove first to Santa Rita, site of the county's prison farm but also a south county headquarters for the sheriff's office. He left Cooper, Sprague, and Erler to assemble their equipment and a laboratory truck, and then drove with Marcia to the darkened quarry between Pleasanton and Livermore. He looked at his watch as they rolled through the gate. It was 9:05 P.M.

He found Volpe and Ron Lindgren, Livermore's police chief, standing near the small office. A number of dirty, exhausted children in various states of undress were being loaded onto a jail bus.

A little girl, tears carving traces through the thick dust on her cheeks, was tugging on the lieutenant's jacket.

"Is my mommy gonna spank me for not coming home last night?" she whimpered.

"No, honey," he answered, picking her up and carrying her to a waiting deputy. "No way is your momma going to spank you."

Volpe telephoned his wife at their home a mile away and asked her to come over and help with the younger kids.

Chapter 14

Ray first saw the lights of a patrol car coming down the road, then another, and fire engines summoned by the sheriff's dispatcher in case the victims needed first aid.

Some buses pulled up and they began loading the kids into them. Ray talked to a Lieutenant Volpe and another deputy named Schalk. He knew he wasn't making much sense. When they said they would take the children to someplace called Santa Rita, they told him he would stay behind. He wanted to go. He was still fearful and didn't want to let them out of his sight. Tears welled in his eyes again, and he asked to telephone Odessa. Finally the man named Baugh said they could take him to Santa Rita. First they let him use the phone in the quarry office to call home.

The next several hours were a blur for Edward Ray. It seemed to him there were hundreds of people at the prison farm, all asking him questions. They kept taking his picture. He talked for a long time to the deputies and to an FBI agent, Benedict Tisa. The only thing he was certain of was the last half of the license number on the dark van: 414.

In a commandeered portable classroom some of the children, dressed in oversized jail coveralls, passed the time between questioning by drawing and coloring. Others slept in rough jail blankets. They ate hamburgers and told the deputies and the FBI agents twenty-six versions of their odyssey. They were delighted at the attention of the press.

"Am I gonna be in the newspaper and on television?" asked Larry Park.

Finally just after 2:30 A.M., Ray and the children, accompanied by nurses and deputies, filed aboard a chartered Greyhound bus, gaily painted in commemoration of the nation's bicentennial thirteen days earlier. Two highway patrol cars escorted it as outriders. Ray sat up front. He told the driver, Walter Cairola, it looked like a pretty good bus, bigger than the one he drove. Then he lapsed into silence for the trip back to Chowchilla.

Some of the kids were talkative. Others dozed. Several, past caring, wet their pants. One little girl had a nightmare and woke up screaming "Please leave me alone! Please leave me alone!"

The first radio and television bulletins announcing that the children had been found were broadcast sometime after 9:00 P.M. Because they were based only on what the reporters working the Friday night police beat in Oakland had heard on the Alameda County sheriff's radio, they gave no indication of their condition. It was several minutes before the networks could confirm the children were safe.

In Chowchilla the parents and their friends who were not already there dashed to the police station. Reporters mobbed Lieutenant Governor Dymally in the adjacent fire station, which had been turned into a press room by the simple expedient of moving the fire trucks out onto the street.

Dymally was joined by Robert Gebhardt, assistant director of the FBI in charge of the western states. At last he stepped to the microphones. "They have been found. They are safe and well. They are being held in the San Francisco Bay Area. They will be brought back by chartered bus in a few hours. The FBI is talking to them. That's all I know."

"Where? Where were they found?"

"In Livermore. That's all I know at the moment."

The room seemed to explode. Parents cheered and clapped. Total strangers hugged each other. A table collapsed under the weight of a dozen reporters who had climbed up on it for a better view. Earl Weiner, agent in charge of the FBI office in Sacramento, joined Gebhardt and Dymally and reconfirmed the happy news.

"Oh, thank God," breathed Tom Vanhoff, Cindy's father. He started jumping up and down.

Carole Marshall, Mike's mother, clenched her fists and finally managed to speak to the reporters. "I'd like to think he took care of the others since he was the oldest," she said. "I never lost hope, but I had a lot of bad thoughts."

The parents assembled in the single courtroom to await the bus. Many of the reporters decamped immediately for Santa Rita. The rest stayed to cover the homecoming. The FBI turned its attention northward, and agents began checking out of their motels. Evelle Younger was on his way to Santa Rita.

The bus pulled up behind Chowchilla's courthouse and police station at 3:55 A.M., thirty-six hours after Ray had started his Thursday run. One by one they walked or were carried off, squinting in the night turned day by the television lights. Their parents clutched them and kissed them and cried. Bill Parker grinned and held his daughter, Barbara, aloft.

"See," he said to the reporters. "I told you she was a doll."

Ray's ordeal was not over. After he hugged Odessa, they led him to the fire department garage where they showed him and his wife to two chairs. The room was lit so brightly he couldn't see past the conference table laden with microphones in front of him. All around he heard the *whirr-click whirr-click* of motor-driven cameras, like a swarm of wasps.

Haltingly, sometimes rambling, he told the two hundred reporters and the world beyond his story as best he could recall it. When he was finished he started to rise to leave, to go home to bed.

"Do you have any feelings about what should be done with the kidnappers if they're caught?" a newsman asked.

"I do," he said. "I wouldn't let 'em live if I could get ahold of any of 'em."

Chowchilla began to feel the spotlight fading within minutes after the children were restored to their families. Some were relieved, others almost disappointed at the prospect of returning to the normal routine. Sheriff Bates would sharply criticize President Ford and Attorney General Levi after the FBI left. "They gave the case first-class treatment after the kids disappeared," he said. "We get them back and five minutes later we go from fifty FBI agents to zilch." He found it difficult to believe the investigation in Madera County was virtually over, that the solution to the puzzle lay elsewhere.

Chowchilla, its odd-sounding name now etched indelibly in the chronicles of iniquity, would return to normal. But it would never be the same. Notoriety, like a vandal, had smashed the quiet life of the town—and then abandoned it.

Part Four

Chapter 15

About 5:00 P.M. Friday, July 16, 1976, Julie Ciochetti received a telephone call from her boyfriend. Rick Schoenfeld asked her to pick him up at Fred Woods's garage apartment. She drove to Portola Valley from her parents' home in Menlo Park. Rick was nervous. He said he wanted to ride around for a while.

"What's the matter, Rick?" she asked finally.

"I can't tell you," he said. "I don't want you to get involved."

"Involved in what?" He didn't reply immediately. Julie suddenly was alarmed. He was pale and trembling, and looked as if he would be sick.

At last he told her. "You know that thing in Chowchilla with the busload of kids? I was in on it." Shocked realization came to her slowly. "I can't tell you any more about it," he continued quickly. "I can't let you get into this mess."

Dread gripped the girl. She almost screamed. "Where are they?"

"I can't tell you that. But I've gotta go back there tonight by eleven thirty. Let me borrow your car."

"No," she said, fighting hysteria. "I won't let you have the car until you promise to let them go."

The distraught young couple decided to go to Julie's house, where she would make dinner for them. Her parents were not home. They would eat and talk about what Rick had to do.

When they arrived at the house sometime between seven and eight that evening, Rick flopped on the couch in the living room and stared at the ceiling. Julie went into the kitchen and began puttering, more for something to do than to prepare a meal, since neither of them was hungry. After a while she heard Rick flick on the television set. A short time later there was a news bulletin. The children had been found. She ran into the living room. Rick was sitting rigidly, gripping the cushion, his mouth open. The bulletin was repeated with the added information that the children were safe.

"Oh, Rick, they're all right," she cried.

"I gotta make a phone call," he said.

Julie did not overhear Rick's telephone conversation. She thought he was calling his brother at home. He came back into the living room.

"I have to go down to the bottom of the hill for a minute," he said. "Then you gotta drive me to Fred's place."

Irene Bolzowski was at home in Mountain View when Fred called her at 7:00 P.M. Friday and asked her to come over. He would eat and take a shower, and meet her over the garage around nine.

After hanging up the telephone, Fred hesitated a minute and then called his parents at their home on the other side of the estate. He asked if he could drop over for dinner. They had already eaten, but invited him anyway.

As her son pushed his empty plate away about 8:00 P.M., Mrs. Woods told him that she and his father were going to visit his grandmother and asked if he would like to come along. No, he replied, Irene was coming by, and he wanted to take a shower. They left him at the house.

Irene left her apartment at 8:30 P.M. and arrived at the garage about twenty minutes later. Fred wasn't home, so she put Shelley, the adolescent collie, on a leash and took her for a walk. She could hear Fred's father's voice coming from the grandmother's house nearby.

Sometime after nine Fred drove up in his green station wagon and parked. She thought he was acting funny. As they went upstairs she chattered about some of her misadventures trying to housebreak Shelley. A few moments later the telephone rang. The instrument was down in the garage, and Fred went to answer it. She barely overheard him say Jim Schoenfeld's name.

Fred bounded back up the stairs and turned on the television set. Another bulletin about the children was being broadcast. His eyes took on a wild look, and he began pacing, almost loping, around the room. Irene was frightened.

"Honey, what's the matter?"

"I'm in big trouble," he said. "I have to go away."

"What's going on, honey?" she pleaded.

"You don't want to know."

Julie Ciochetti drove into the Los Trancos Road entrance of the Woods estate and parked. She got out of her car, but Rick told her not to come with him, to wait. As she paced in the driveway she noticed Irene's light-green Ford, but she didn't see Irene.

Rick stood in front of the garage and called softly for Fred. Julie could hear rapid footsteps on the stairs, and Woods appeared. He and Rick spoke quietly, urgently, for several minutes. Then Rick came back to where Julie was standing.

"I want you to drive me to the warehouse," he said. "Jim's there."

She was confused. "What warehouse?"

"I'll give you directions. Come on."

Upstairs Irene nervously scratched Shelley behind the ears. Something was desperately wrong, but she didn't know what it was. It couldn't have been the Chowchilla kidnapping. Fred couldn't have had anything to do with something so monstrous. Her stomach was knotted, and her chest hurt.

Fred kept some of his personal things in a cottage not far from the garage. He went there and returned with a small brown suitcase and a black duffel bag, and began hurriedly packing his clothes, toothbrush, and shaving gear. He packed a blue business suit which he also had brought from the cottage. Irene had never seen him in it.

101

At 10:00 P.M. the phone rang again. It was Fred's father. The quarry manager had just reached him at home to tell him about the children being found there. Fred agreed it was a terrible thing.

Fred told Irene she had to drive him to San Jose. When they went downstairs to where her car was parked, Rick was gone. She watched as Fred hurled his bags, jackets, and a sleeping bag into the automobile. She saw the glint of metal. It was a small pistol.

"Why are you taking that?" she asked.

"Don't worry," he said. "I won't use it." He shoved the weapon in his pocket.

Jim was waiting by his 1963 white-beige Chrysler when Julie and Rick reached the warehouse. The building lights were out, and the only illumination came from the mercury vapor lamps on the nearby Interstate 280 freeway.

Julie stood by her car while Rick and Jim talked. The main door to the warehouse was open, and in the shadowy light she could see a long dark car inside. She saw no reflections from chrome or glass other than the windshield.

Fred and Irene drove up, and Jim and Fred began to load the things from Irene's car and some more equipment from the warehouse into Jim's Chrysler. Rick went inside the warehouse and came back to Julie's car carrying what looked like a piece of tent material. He put it in the back seat along with a couple of other things she couldn't recognize in the dark.

"Where are you going?" she asked.

"I'm not going anywhere," he said. "Jim and Fred are going to make a run for it, but I've gotta talk to dad."

Rick got into the driver's side, and he and Julie drove through the warehouse gate, turned right, and stopped by the curb with the engine running and the headlights out. She saw Irene's car leave, and then the door to the warehouse was pulled down and locked. Jim's car rolled through the gate, turned, and stopped next to hers. Rick got out and had a brief, whispered conversation with his brother and Fred. He waved as the old Chrysler pulled away toward the freeway.

Julie did not know what time it was when she and Rick arrived at his parents' home in Atherton. She was sure it was after midnight, perhaps as late as 1:00 A.M. She was on the verge of nervous collapse as Rick let her into the darkened house with his key. He went to awaken his parents, and she stumbled into a bathroom and wept.

After a few minutes Julie pulled herself together, washed her face, went into Rick's room, and sat on the bed. She could hear voices coming from the kitchen, but not what was being said. She could tell from the tone of alarm that Rick was telling them about the kidnapping.

He was saying he wanted to turn himself in.

"You could get the gas chamber," his father said, aghast.

"Oh, my God," the mother murmured.

"What should I do?" Rick asked.

"I'll find out," his father assured him. "I'll talk to a lawyer tomorrow. You go to bed and try to get some sleep."

It was almost 4:00 A.M. when Jack Baugh let himself in the front door of his hillside ranch-style house. He poured himself a scotch and sank heavily into a chair in the living room. His head hurt from too much coffee and too many cigarettes. It had been a fruitless night. Even a little frightening.

Marcia was upstairs in bed. After sitting in the car in the darkness of the quarry for about forty-five minutes, she had come into the little office to find her husband.

"This place is spooky," she said. "And I don't think you need me here if those guys come back. Do you think you can get a ride home later?" Baugh started. He had honestly forgotten for a moment she was still there. He kissed her and watched as she drove away in the station wagon.

It was just after ten.

When Baugh had arrived at the quarry, Volpe told him one of the children had overheard the kidnappers say they would be back. Baugh hastily called Santa Rita and asked if they could round up enough deputies to stake the place out after the bus left. The officer on duty dashed his hopes by reporting wearily that news of the escape already was on radio and television, and that he was being deluged with calls from newspapers all over the world. So much for the old wait-for-them-to-return-to-the-scene-of-the-crime trick.

Baugh sent the children to Santa Rita, but kept their driver with him. Ray was nearly spent, on the verge of collapse and hysteria. After several unsuccessful attempts to get his account of the kidnapping, Baugh had allowed Ray to call his wife in Chowchilla, then sent him to Santa Rita for a medical examination.

As soon as Cooper arrived with his lab crew, Baugh drove back to Santa Rita to organize and direct the questioning of the children and Ray. He found utter confusion. Agents from half a dozen federal and state bureaus had arrived, along with a gaggle of other officials and politicians. Stepping over the bloodhounds and German shepherds that had been conscripted just in case they had to search the hills, Baugh spoke briefly with Tom Houchins, the Alameda County sheriff, who finally had been located and had driven to Santa Rita. Then he found Charles Bates, special agent in charge of the FBI in San Francisco, the man who had ramrodded the Patty Hearst investigation. Baugh told Bates he would not be able to scramble enough detectives in time to interview all the children that night, and asked if the FBI could help. Bates said it could.

Baugh dealt diplomatically with the state attorney general, who was on hand, and with the governor, whom he assured on the telephone that all the children were healthy. He ordered his deputies to set up a press headquarters in the old Marine Corps barracks at Santa Rita, and to keep the reporters confined there until the sheriff was ready to talk to them. Yes, that meant the guy from the New York *Times,* too.

About 2:00 A.M., all the detectives and FBI agents who had interrogated Ray and the children gathered in a small classroom in the sheriff's training building to compare notes and descriptions of the kidnappers. The results were a mess.

There had been three armed men, all wearing masks fashioned from nylon stockings. None of the victims, including Ray, could agree on what they looked like. The descriptions of individual gunmen ranged in height from five five to six five, in age from eighteen to fifty-five.

One child remembered seeing a tattoo on the forearm of one of the kidnappers.

Another said one of the men had a leg missing and used a rifle stock as a crutch. No one else could remember him.

They recalled what they thought of as funny. Like the fact that the legs of the pantyhose used to conceal his features gave one kidnapper "Pluto ears."

They said they had been abducted from their schoolbus the day before. The men put them into two vans and drove them around for a long time and then made them climb down into a hole in the ground. After a while they broke out.

One of the vans was white. The second was either blue or black or green or dark brown.

They both could have been campers or panel trucks.

Wearily Baugh had the disparate accounts and descriptions sent to the Madera County sheriff's office, and then arranged for the reporters and photographers to see the children before they were taken, with a heavy guard, back to Chowchilla.

While Houchins, Bates, and another FBI agent held what would be the first of an endless series of press conferences, Baugh talked to Cooper, who said he wasn't getting anywhere at the quarry because of the bad light. He told him to quit until daylight, and asked Volpe to set up a command post in the morning. Then he went home.

Baugh tiptoed into the bedroom and undressed, trying clumsily not to disturb his wife. Her voice came out of the darkness. "I'm awake," she said. He slipped into bed next to her and stared dully at the ceiling.

"Jack, I'm scared," Marcia said.

"Why?"

"Those could have been our kids." He had forced himself to repress the same thought several times during the last long hours. "Who are those cuckoos?" she asked.

"I don't know," he replied. "The only thing we're sure of is that there were at least three of them."

She changed the subject. "I told the kids you wouldn't be able to make it up to the cabin today."

"Yeah. Good," Baugh said absently.

It was dawn before he finally went to sleep. Somehow the scotch had helped to dispel the nervous exhaustion and bewilderment that had started to grip him after he had left Santa Rita in a borrowed patrol car. Gradually, the disciplined process that was the product of twenty years of routine and training began to take over, and he started to plan what would become the most incredible investigation of his career. One thing was certain. He would put Ed Volpe in charge of the tactical operation.

He didn't know it as he drifted into a fitful sleep, but Baugh was about to become the central figure in a manhunt that would cover six states and two countries.

It was almost 10:00 A.M. by the time Jack Baugh returned to Santa Rita, Saturday morning, July 17. Marcia had let him sleep later than he had planned. Ed Volpe was already there, along with several FBI agents and two men from the California Department of Justice: John Lilly and Norm Gard. Lieutenant Darrell Hickman and another detective, Dale Fore, were on their way up from Madera County.

Baugh knew his department was going to have to depend on extraordinary cooperation from the state and federal governments, not only because of the enormity of the case but also because Alameda County was in the middle of its first strike by county employees. What made matters worse was the fact that most of the 585 sworn officers were working twelve-hour shifts to fill in for the strikers or as part of a special task force commanded by Baugh to guard county buildings where there had been a couple of ugly incidents.

Paradoxically, the Alameda County Deputy Sheriff's Association is affiliated with the AFL-CIO Operating Engineers Local 3. It had not joined the strike.

Volpe told Baugh that little had been accomplished since the children had left for Chowchilla. Volpe had set up a temporary command post in the captain's office in the white-and-green frame building that housed the crime laboratory across the road from the entrance to Greystone, the old Marine Corps brig long ago taken over by the county as a prison farm. Cooper, Sprague, and Erler, who had not left the lab until 2:00 A.M., had returned bleary-eyed at 7:00 A.M. and were back at work in the quarry by 7:30 A.M.

"How did you get home last night?" Volpe asked.

"I stole a patrol car."

"That debriefing was a real comedy," Volpe said. "Those kids and the driver gave us twenty-seven different versions of what happened."

"Yeah," Baugh answered. "We're at square one, all right. You find out anything more about Lindgren's phone call?" When Baugh had arrived at the quarry the night before, Livermore police chief Ron Lindgren had told him the reason he was there was that his department had received a telephone tip that the kidnap victims were at the quarry.

"They checked the logs," Volpe answered. "Whoever it was called after the news was on the air."

Even though it was Saturday, Gard and Lilly assured Baugh that the state's Criminal Identification and Investigation Bureau would provide any help he needed, especially processing finger-prints. Sam Erwin, a latent print analyst in Sacramento who had earned an enviable reputation for his part in the Patricia Hearst kidnapping investigation, had been assigned full time to the Chow-chilla case.

One of the problems the investigators faced was determining jurisdiction. The presumption of a federal crime, kidnapping across a state line, had pretty well been exhausted, although there remained a possibility it had been a terrorist act. The FBI agents at Santa Rita that morning had no idea how long they would remain on the case. They talked it over and decided that sheriff's deputies and detectives, more familiar with the area, would can-vass the neighborhood around the quarry to learn whether anyone had noticed anything out of the ordinary, and that the FBI agents would start running down all the past and present employees of California Rock and Gravel Company for possible leads.

In the next few days eight agents would interview a score of quarry workers at home and on the job, virtually without results. It would be Monday before they could talk with the president of the company, Frederick Nickerson Woods III, at his Montgomery Street office in San Francisco. Detective sergeants Berni Cervi and

Bruce Tellardin would begin the first of what would become dozens of interviews with the neighbors. Although several would recall seeing strangers in cars or on foot, none would provide a solid lead.

Cooper, Sprague, and Erler were busy at the quarry. The night before, the laboratory chief had turned down a suggestion that high-intensity lamps from the county civil defense headquarters be hauled in to illuminate the scene. The area around the quarry was already crawling with curious onlookers and reporters, and Cooper didn't want to make the place easier to find. His concern was to preserve the evidence until daylight. The criminalists had ordered several inmate clothing boxes from Santa Rita to cover the tire impressions and had left half a dozen deputies guarding the perimeter.

When the three arrived at the quarry at 7:30 A.M. they met Volpe, several deputies, and six FBI agents who had been assigned to help them.

The place where the victims had been entombed was a drained lake bed that had been refilled with slag from the quarry. Except for the area immediately over the dungeon, which looked as if it had been scraped clean with a bulldozer or front loader. The depression that had been the lake was covered with cottonwoods, willows, cattails, brush, and wild grass, all crisscrossed by trails left by small animals. Cooper made a note that in the scraped area the willow roots had just started to sprout.

Methodically Cooper, Sprague, and four FBI agents measured the distances between every piece of possible evidence they could find and collected samples of all the plants for potential comparison later with the clothes of suspects—if they ever got any suspects. Erler, Deputy Killian, and another agent photographed everything in sight, including all the tire tracks they could locate. About midday a helicopter arrived and took Erler up to make aerial photos of the quarry.

Just south of the entrance to the underground chamber the criminalists found four automobile batteries buried in a shallow pit camouflaged with cardboard, a window screen, and dirt. They were connected by concealed wires to a blower fan that pumped air into the buried trailer. They also found three sections of army green tarp or tent material, another battery, several coils of wire, various pieces of lumber, duct clamps, a dust pan, a pair of pliers, and the white plastic clothes-drier vent hose that led from the end of the chamber opposite the blower. They could hear an exhaust fan, and the vent hose smelled strongly of human waste.

While they were collecting the evidence the county's district attorney, Lowell Jensen, arrived with a small entourage of assistants to look over the crime scene. A short time later they were joined by FBI special agent-in-charge Charles Bates and Robert Gebhardt, his superior from Los Angeles. Cooper and Sprague told them what had been found so far.

By early afternoon no one had physically entered the hole in the ground, although Cooper and Sprague had examined it with lights the night before. Baugh was getting anxious. "I don't want anyone to get hurt," he said, "but what if they left us a nice address or something?"

At 2:00 P.M. Cooper and Sprague let themselves down gingerly through the hole. Immediately they were assaulted by the stench of excrement. The foul air was extremely humid and, although the temperature was not unbearable, both men found themselves sweating.

They worked quickly, fearful the sagging roof would collapse. Using a strobe light Sprague took several photographs to be developed and printed immediately for the investigators. He and Cooper examined the smooth plywood interior of the truck body and found a number of recessed cleats of the type used to tie down furniture. They had been used to secure the heavy wire mesh. They stayed inside for fifteen minutes and returned to the surface, leaving everything intact.

"No doubt about it," they told the others. "It's a moving van."

While the work was under way at the quarry, the FBI sent a team of specialists led by Agent Roger Goldsberry to Chowchilla to examine the bus and the slough. He was accompanied by Maurice Brittingham and Tom Gummere of the FBI identification division, and Sam Clark, a laboratory section chief, all from Washington. In Chowchilla Agent John Baker, from the Sacramento field office, already had started fingerprinting Ray and all twenty-six children for the purpose of eliminating their prints from any the kidnappers might have left behind on pieces of evidence.

Goldsberry and his crew lifted seventeen sets of latent prints from various sections inside the bus. Then they began a microscopic and chemical examination of the outside. To the rear of the door and about two feet above the floor of the garage they found a small spot that appeared to have been freshly damaged. Chips of yellow paint had fallen away from the bus, and traces of dark green paint had adhered to the metal. Using special tape and a knife, the agents lifted the paint transfer, along with samples of the yellow bus paint.

They searched the inside for bloodstains, but found none.

When Goldsberry and the other agents walked down into Berenda Slough off Avenue 21, they muttered to themselves in exasperation. The ground was tracked over with countless footprints, obviously left by the curious who had not been kept away by the authorities. They took samples of grass, shrubs, and bushes and left.

Earlier in the day Baugh had called Rich Krimm, the department's Identikit technician, and told him to go to Chowchilla and try to make composite drawings of the kidnappers with the help of the victims, especially Ray.

Krimm arrived at the Chowchilla substation about 3:00 P.M. and found Sheriff Bates. After talking with several Madera County deputies and FBI agents who had interviewed the children, Krimm decided the best eyewitnesses among the children were Jeff and Jennifer Brown, both of whom believed they could recall the features of the man who drove the schoolbus and the one who had driven the van they were in. He completed his composites that evening, made thirty copies for Bates and his men, and called Santa Rita for permission to come home.

Over the phone Krimm received an unusual assignment. He was to be at the Rodeway Inn in Fresno by 10:00 A.M. the next morning. The FBI was going to put Ed Ray under hypnosis, during which Krimm would try to put together composite drawings.

110

Ed Ray after the long ordeal

Some of the children returning to Chowchilla

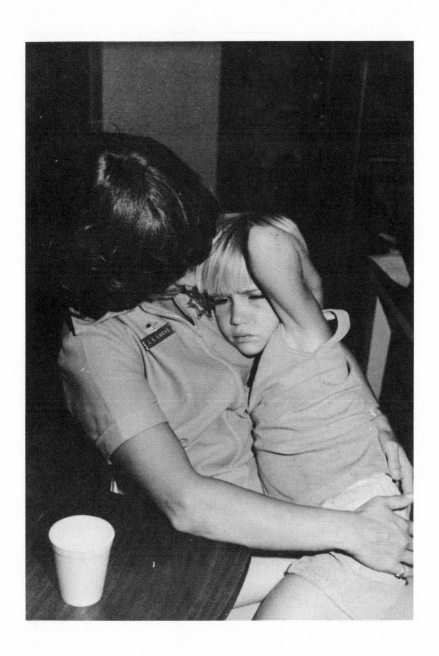

Interior of buried van where victims were held captive

Digging out the buried van

Fred Woods' garage apartment

Trailer hideout in Reno

Lifting the van from the earth by crane

Fred Woods after capture

Kidnappers in courtroom (left to right: James Schoenfeld, Fred Woods, and Richard Schoenfeld) (UPI)

The abandoned school bus in the slough

Chapter 16

For the next seven days Rick was never sure he was not going insane. For hours after he told his parents about the kidnapping no one slept at the Schoenfeld house. He listened to the radio, but heard only disjointed reports about the children arriving home in Chowchilla. He managed to snatch a couple of hours of sleep just before dawn, but he was horrified when he got up and read the San Francisco and San Jose morning newspapers. Beneath the heavy black, eight-column headlines he saw photographs of Ray and the children, tired, dirty, and frightened. He could hardly recognize them, yet he had seen them all only thirty hours earlier. The news reports said the FBI was gearing up for one of the most intensive manhunts in history. To his relief, they said they had no suspects.

Frantically he searched his memory. Had the three of them left anything behind at the quarry that could be traced to them. They had been so careful. In a way it was his fault that the hostages escaped, he thought. Fred had wanted to put more weight on the cover over the entrance to the buried trailer, but Rick had said it wasn't necessary. He knew now that he really had wanted the children to escape. What if they had died in there?

Oh, Jesus, he prayed, don't let them kill me.

Rick jumped every time the telephone rang, or he heard a car in the driveway. But as the hours dragged past on Saturday, and the radio continued to say the authorities were baffled, he began to relax a little. No one had been hurt, he thought. Maybe it will all blow over. He didn't really believe it.

Saturday Jim called and talked to his brother and his parents. He told Rick he was in Reno. He said he just wanted to make sure he had made it home safely, and that he had told their mother and father what had happened. He reminded Rick to get rid of the kids' clothes someplace where it would lead the investigators away from them if they were found.

Leonard Bethal, who lived in the trailer parked in space 19 at the Arrowhead Trailer Lodge in Reno, had been suspicious for several weeks about the man who rented the trailer in space 20. He was hardly ever there, and whenever he was he seemed to have a car with out-of-state plates.

It was raining slightly that Saturday morning when he looked out a window and saw two men unloading some things from a large older car next door. He sauntered over.

"You guys up to something illegal?" he inquired garrulously.

"No," one replied. "Why don't you beat it." Bethal retreated to his trailer and saw them pack everything they had unloaded back into the car and drive away.

Jim and Fred had about $500 between them. The car was packed with sleeping bags, clothes, rifles, pistols, a shotgun, ammunition, tools, an uninstalled CB radio, and most of the junk food they had intended to take to the children at the quarry over the weekend while they waited out the deadline in the ransom message they had never delivered. They had not even had a chance to write a final draft of it. For one thing, Jim, who was a fairly good speller, wanted to look up the correct spelling for Beelzebub, a reference they had decided to throw in to confuse the police into thinking they were dealing with zealous cultists.

After leaving the trailer park in Reno, the two drove to the airport. They decided they had to split up and leave the country. They parked at Reno International and walked past the

122

line of ticket counters to the right of the main entrance, looking for foreign destinations. United offered a 2:55 P.M. flight to Seattle, connecting to Vancouver. That would be it, then. They would go to Canada, get jobs, and wait for the statute of limitations to expire. They could still make a bundle on their story, Fred said.

Their decision left the problem of what to do with the heavily laden car. One of them would fly and the other would drive. Fred reminded Jim that he had the false passport and identification in the name of Ralph Snider. Obviously, he should be the one to take the plane.

"You don't need a passport to get into Canada," Jim protested. "Besides, nobody's looking for us yet." But in the end, as he usually had, he gave in. They decided that Fred would take most of the money, buy a ticket, fly to Vancouver, find a room in a cheap hotel, and wait for his partner. Jim would take enough to buy gasoline and would drive, crossing the border at one of the back country stations in eastern Washington or northern Idaho. If he failed to get into Canada for some reason, he could sell the car and pawn the stuff in it and go across in a bus at another port of entry. In the meantime, he could sleep in the car and eat the food they had stocked for the children.

They deliberated how they would link up in Vancouver. In some ways their planning was as impractical as some of the schemes they devised when they were plotting the kidnapping. At first they decided that each would buy a jar of red and a jar of green paint. After they arrived in Vancouver they would seek out drug stores and laundromats and would paint red X's on the sidewalks in front of them. The first of the two to come upon a red X would cover it over with green paint. When the other spotted a green X he would wait around the neighborhood.

"I think that's a little too complicated, Fred. Let's try something else," Schoenfeld said.

At last they decided to meet at Vancouver's main post office. For the first several days after arriving in the city each would go to the post office at 11:00 A.M. and 7:00 P.M. daily. After that they would visit it at the same times on Tuesdays only. If after four weeks they had not found one another, they would go their separate ways.

Ninety percent of criminal investigation is dull routine. Although every case is different, the same procedures are followed over and over. In fiction, printed or projected, police officers are portrayed either as lollipop-sucking geniuses or plodding, semihonest flatfeet who must depend either on private eyes or nonprofessional dilettantes to solve their cases. Actually the vast majority of investigators are hardworking, normal men and women who follow techniques adopted because they work.

Then there is the other 10 percent of police work, which, no matter what one reads or sees on the screen, is unvarnished luck. Some of it is good, some bad. On Saturday, Baugh and his men thought they had gotten lucky, twice.

Detective Sergeant Dale Smith received a telephone call from Jim McGettigan, a sheriff's detective in Sonora, the seat of Tuolumne County in the Gold Rush country of the Sierra foothills north of Chowchilla. McGettigan told him a prisoner in the county jail, Chuck Collier, had said that while he was in the penitentiary at San Quentin in 1974 and 1975 another inmate had told him about a plot to exact revenge from the people of Madera County by kidnapping a busload of schoolchildren and burying them in a cave.

"We've been getting a lot of calls like that since the kids got out," Smith said. "What's your boy's angle?"

"That's just it," McGettigan said. "He told me about it before the kids were found."

The detective put Collier on the phone and Smith talked with him for a long time. The ex-convict, now in jail for another offense, told Smith that while he was at San Quentin three other inmates, led by a man whose first name he could remember only, told him of their plan. The man had been sentenced in Madera County for some sort of sex charge and wanted vengeance. At first, Collier said, the three were going to kidnap or assassinate Madera policemen. Then they abandoned that plan and decided to abduct the members of the jury that convicted him. Finally they hit on the idea of hijacking a schoolbus and burying the children in a pit or cave that one of them knew about.

About 11:00 A.M. Collier called back and told Smith he remembered the would-be kidnapper's full name. A quick check of their own identification bureau revealed a minor Alameda County record for a man with the same name.

He had a Livermore address.

"We'd better get somebody up to Sonora in a hurry," Baugh said. "Call Young and tell him to crank up his flying machine."

Deputy Jim Young keeps his single-engine, six-seat airplane parked on an abandoned road behind the headquarters building at Santa Rita, primarily to transport prisoners. Although there is an airfield a few miles away, the sheriff's office finds it more convenient for him to land near the gate to the prison.

Young took off early Saturday afternoon with Detective Tellardin, Dale Fore from Madera County, and FBI agent Don Noel. The pilot gestured upward toward a line of telephone wires that flashed past overhead as the small plane gathered speed on the makeshift runway.

"Taking off's okay," he told the three investigators cheerfully. "It's a little hairier when we land." Tellardin, who had ridden Young's roller coaster before, grinned. Fore and Noel were silent.

While the four were in the air, Baugh and Volpe sent to the main courthouse in Oakland for the suspect's photographs and fingerprints. They also asked all the other law-enforcement agencies in the county to check their files. The highway patrol called back and said they had a number of cards for traffic stops. More than one of them carried notations that the suspect had a CB radio. The patrol record said he was hostile toward the authorities.

Volpe came to Baugh, excited. "Livermore PD found him in their files," he said. "We also have another report of our own. He may be a back-hoe operator who had some equipment stolen once not far from the quarry."

"Stake out his house," Baugh said. "Let's find out who his friends are."

At the courthouse in Sonora, Tellardin, Fore, and Noel talked to Charles Harry Collier for several hours that afternoon. He told

125

them that in September of 1974, after he had been sentenced to prison from Sacramento County for bad checks, he was sent to the California State Medical Facility at Vacaville, a clearinghouse where all state inmates undergo two months of evaluation before they are assigned a permanent place to serve out their terms. He met two men there. Later Collier and the other two were transferred to San Quentin, where the two introduced him to a third man, whose name he couldn't remember. Collier said he worked as a clerk, and that he had helped the suspect prepare and file his federal and state income tax returns. He recollected that the man then had a small freight business in Raymond, a town not far from Chowchilla, and that he owned six or eight Ford Econoline vans. He believed one of the trio had been sentenced from Madera County for rape. All three, he said, were heavy dope dealers in prison.

"Where was your impression they were from, before being sentenced?" he was asked.

"Livermore. The Livermore area," Collier said. "One . . . the guy . . ."

"Okay, go ahead."

"All right. They constantly were talkin' about gettin' involved in a situation such as this, like plottin' against, to destroy whatever they could destroy or take whatever they could take, for the revenge. They were bitter. I mean, I've seen a lot of bitter people but they just, you know, you could catch the vibes a mile away. They were just strongly bitter.

"They planned for hours on end how they would go about doing somethin'. They even got maps sent in to them in MAC. How that ever got accomplished, I don't know."

"What's MAC?"

"Men's Advisory Counsel."

"Okay, Chuck, keep going."

"They named, you know, well, we'll get this family, we'll get that family. They argued quite a bit, whether they were goin' to take the kids, or whether they were goin' to take the parents, or whether they were gonna take the sheriff's department on, whether they're goin' to free all the prisoners. They were goin' to

126

start a whole revolution, you know, from what they wanted to do."

"Were they revolutionary types?" Collier was asked. "Were they radicals?"

"No, they stayed pretty much to the threesome. My encounter with 'em was brief. When I sat in on a little discussion one day out in the big yard, and they were telling me what they were gonna do and how they were gonna do it, I got up and said, 'Hey, I don't want any part of this, you know.'

"I felt a little pissed myself for the way I was treated in Sacramento. But I don't think I could ever go to the extent that they had planned to do when they got out."

Although there were inconsistencies in Collier's tale, the alleged plot generally followed the outline of the kidnapping as it had happened. McGettigan confirmed that he had told essentially the same story the night before, several hours before the children were found. Collier insisted the three planned to use vans, and they were going to bury their victims in a cave.

"They argued a lot about the guns," he said. "They wanted high-powered rifles. Art says, 'No, they're too bulky, they're too noisy.' He said, 'A shotgun, nobody's gonna run from a shotgun . . .'

"Most of the main topic of anything I heard was just revenge. They wanted to get at 'em. They wanted to say, 'See here, son of a bitch, I did this.'

"It'd make me upset to hear it. In fact there was several times I'd want to tell somebody else about it, but you just don't do stuff like that in the joint, you know. It just ain't done."

Collier told the investigators he later was transferred to the minimum security Sierra Conservation Camp near Sonora, but that he believed all three plotters had been given parole dates for the spring of 1976. He said he had a photograph of himself with the three in a scrapbook he had left with Ed Ziomek, a former Tuolumne County sheriff's deputy he met while he was at the camp. He also said he had mentioned the names of the three in letters he had written to his mother in Sparks, Nevada.

The physical description he gave of the suspect was a close match with that of the man who lived in Livermore.

There was something of a debate under way late Saturday at Santa Rita over whether the man should be arrested. The files showed he had a friend named Jerry. One of the children had remembered hearing the name Jerry.

A detective was sent to the friend's home. He was literally rubbing his hands when he returned.

"His wife said she had thought he was on a trip to Oregon, driving a truck for Wards," he related. "She said he came rushing in unexpectedly Friday afternoon about three or four o'clock, grabbed some clothes, threw them in a suitcase, and took off without telling her where he was going. She thought it was a little unusual."

"That could tie in with our caper," Volpe said. "Shall we hit the house in Livermore?"

They decided to wait. Somehow it was all a little too perfect on one hand, flawed on another. For one thing, they couldn't find a record on the suspect at San Quentin, and CII had no record of a felony conviction for him. Dale Smith had spent most of the day on the phone trying to trace him through the state bureaucracy. San Quentin correctional officers went through their files looking for anyone with a name remotely like his who had been there the same time as Collier. The only similar name belonged to a man who didn't fit the description and still was in prison at Soledad.

The FBI in Reno and the Sparks police visited Collier's mother. She couldn't find any letter with the man's name, nor could she remember any mention of a kidnapping plot.

Late Saturday FBI agents Don Richards and Steve Gray located former deputy Ziomek in Daly City, where he had moved after leaving Tuolumne County. He said McGettigan had telephoned him, that he had searched the two boxes of personal possessions Collier had given him for safekeeping, but that he could find no scrapbook.

"It doesn't negate Collier's story entirely," an investigator argued.

"Yeah, but it doesn't help it much either," Baugh replied.

The Livermore home remained under tight surveillance while the investigators assembled a lineup of six photographs, one of them his booking picture. Young flew Jim Williams, a sheriff's department intelligence sergeant, to Madera with the lineup. Sheriff Bates showed the photos to the older children, who recognized no one. The sheriff unlocked the county clerk's office and, with the help of his wife, searched the court records back ten years for the name or any phonetic similarity, again without results.

As the weekend drew to a close, the frustrated investigators called off the stakeout on the now discarded suspect, who never knew that he had narrowly avoided becoming one of the most wanted men in the country, nor that the police he so often derided worked diligently until they cleared him.

Why had Collier told the story? He had asked for nothing in return, and seemed to be telling the truth. "How the hell could he make it up?" Baugh asked. "Is he psychic? Prior to the facts being known, he ran it down damn near as it went."

Baugh and Volpe still don't know the answer.

Chapter 17

What looked like the second lucky break that Saturday came in the form of a commercial license plate number, 1C91414, given to the FBI late Friday night by the sheriff's office in Madera. The Department of Motor Vehicles in Sacramento did not have the number in its computer, indicating it had been registered only recently. Because it was a weekend the DMV had to round up several people on their day off to search for the records. They finally found the registration at the bottom of an "in" basket among a batch from Santa Clara County. The papers revealed a white 1971 Dodge van had been registered July 14 to a man who gave his address as 3487 Saylor Street, San Jose.

The FBI quickly learned there was no such address, that there is no Saylor Street in San Jose nor in all of Santa Clara County.

The license number had been provided by Elmot Austin, who said he had received it from a woman in Los Banos who wanted to remain anonymous. That was no longer possible, they told Austin.

The informant turned out to be Mrs. Mary Phillips, who worked in her husband's insurance agency on East J Street, thirty-seven miles west of Chowchilla. About 6:30 P.M. Wednesday, July

14, the same date as the registration, Mrs. Phillips noticed a white Dodge van parked in front of the office, which is in the same building where she and her husband, Robert, make their home. The van struck her as being newly painted. When Robert Phillips, who had been out talking to a client, returned home about 8:30 P.M. he saw the van and mentioned it to his wife.

It was still parked in front of the agency when Mrs. Phillips opened the office at 8:30 A.M. Thursday. After several hours Phillips became curious and strolled the 25 feet over to where the vehicle was parked. The window on the passenger's side was halfway down, and Phillips saw a Pepsi-Cola can on the black console between the two bucket seats. There was a partition blocking his view into the back. He walked back to the office.

About 1:30 P.M. another van, identical except that it was light brown, pulled to the curb behind the white one. Mrs. Phillips saw two young men in the brown van talk for a few minutes. Then the passenger got out, walked up to check the white van, and returned to the driver's side of the brown one. The driver counted out what appeared to her to be a large number of bills and gave the money to the second man, who put it into his wallet before climbing into the driver's seat of the white van. It pulled away from the curb, made a series of left turns around a triangular block, and fell in behind the brown van, which had started south toward Highway 152 after making a U turn. She last saw the two turning onto the highway toward Chowchilla.

Mrs. Phillips had become suspicious when she saw the money exchanged, and jotted the license number of the van on a piece of notepaper. She stamped it with the date. When she learned of the mass abduction on the radio that night, she called Austin to tell him about the two vans and to ask his advice. He called the Chowchilla command post.

After the FBI learned that the address in San Jose was phony, Baugh asked the DMV to search their records for the current drivers' licenses issued to all males in California with the same name. The department came up with ninety-five between San Diego and the Oregon border.

One, aged sixteen, lived in San Jose.

Two FBI agents, Ervin Thibault and Dick Bernes, went to the San Jose police department and checked the juvenile records, but could find nothing on the potential suspect. After the county communications center told them there was no Saylor Street in San Jose, they looked for similar-sounding names. They found a Taylor Street, but no number 3487.

Thibault and Bernes next consulted the city directory and learned the residents of the boy's home were his father, mother and their six children. The father worked for Lockheed Aircraft in Sunnyvale. The two agents called Sacramento and asked for a list of all vehicles registered at that address. The records showed four, a 1968 Volkswagen, a 1975 Ford, a 1972 Honda automobile, and a 1971 Honda motorcycle.

Thibault and Bernes cruised by the home a couple of times to see whether there were any vans or trucks parked nearby. There were none.

Alameda County detective Rod Alvarez had joined the two agents in San Jose, and he and Thibault went to the front door of the home and rang the doorbell. Bernes remained on guard outside, in case a suspect should try to make a break from one of the other exits.

At first, the father didn't know what they were talking about, although he was very cooperative. His son, who would be seventeen in October, didn't own any trucks, nor had anyone in the family owned one except for a Chevrolet van he had sold sometime in the late sixties. The family had lived in San Jose for twelve years. He could account for his son's whereabouts all day July 15, and the day before, for that matter.

He couldn't understand why someone would borrow his son's name.

Back at Santa Rita the investigators checked again with Sacramento. The prior legal owner of the white van was listed as Defense Projects Disposal Services, a federal agency in Alameda. After several telephone calls they found the chief disposal officer for the Naval Supply Center in Alameda, LaVar Beck, at home. He agreed to meet a deputy at the base Sunday morning.

"Maybe we're getting somewhere," Volpe said.

132

"Yeah? Where?"

"I only said somewhere," Volpe answered.

Saturday afternoon Baugh and Volpe had gone back to the quarry with Sheriff Houchins and a group of reporters and photographers. After an impromptu press conference during which the criminalists gave a guarded account of what they had found, the caravan left, and Cooper, Sprague, and the others began a careful examination of a little picnic area south of the hole in the ground. Before leaving for the laboratory with the evidence they had collected up to that point, they covered the food wrappers and soft-drink cans and other litter to be catalogued the next day. They decided to leave the battery connected to the exhaust fan, to clear the air inside the trailer as much as possible.

At Santa Rita, Cooper and Sprague told Baugh, Houchins, Volpe, and Agent-in-Charge Bates they were certain from soil samples that the van had not been buried longer than the winter just past.

"There's a ton of physical evidence in the damn thing," Cooper said. "Most of it's been contaminated by the victims, but there's a possibility that something usable exists in there."

The criminalists restocked their truck for the next day and went home about 7:00 P.M.

During the day Baugh's relationship with some representatives of the media had deteriorated. The phones rang constantly with queries from all over the world, and the reporters housed in the old Marine Corps guard barracks were complaining about the lack of communication out of Santa Rita. There was a single pay phone near the gate to the prison. A deputy told Baugh they wanted phones installed in the barracks.

"Bullshit," he said. "This is all going to be over someday, and there's no sense in our ending up with the only county jail farm in the country with its own city room."

Baugh was also beginning to have trouble with Sheriff Bates in Madera, who was furious at the FBI for pulling most of its small army of agents out of the Chowchilla area. He telephoned Baugh and read him a statement he was working on, blasting FBI Direc-

133

tor Kelley and Attorney General Levi. Baugh tried to assure him the FBI was cooperating heroically in the investigation, but Bates was inconsolable.

"Get Sheriff Houchins on the horn," Baugh ordered after another call from Bates. "We have to go down there and talk to the sheriff in Madera. We need information, not his goddamn press releases."

During the day the calls from tipsters mounted into the hundreds, both at Santa Rita and the Eden Township Substation, the patrol headquarters in Castro Valley south of Oakland. Some of them were demented, all of them useless.

Baugh left Santa Rita about 10:00 P.M. Saturday, not knowing whether or not they were any closer to a solution.

Earlier that same Saturday Fred Woods's father had noticed that the horses had not been fed. He went to his son's apartment, but he was not at home. He called the Schoenfelds and asked if they had seen Fred. Rick did not talk to him. His father told Woods he didn't know where Fred was.

Saturday evening Rick was with Julie. Her parents asked the young people to join them for dinner at a local restaurant. They accepted. Somehow, Rick got through the meal without betraying his panic.

Sunday morning Irene got a telephone call from Fred's parents. They invited her to lunch.

"I'm really not very hungry, Mrs. Woods," she said.

"Oh, come along. Bring Shelley. You know how she likes to run."

At the table, Woods asked, "Irene, do you know where Fred is?" She tried to keep from crying.

"No," she said.

"We're not sure what's going on, but I called the Schoenfelds awhile ago, and they don't want to talk to us for some reason. Jim is apparently on some kind of trip, and Fred left without telling us."

"Yes, I know," Irene said.

134

"Did he say good-bye to you?" Mrs. Woods asked.

"Yes."

"Did Fred take a gun, Irene?" his father asked.

"Yes, he did."

United Air Lines flight 887 from Seattle arrived on time at the Vancouver airport shortly before 6:00 P.M. Saturday, July 17. Ralph Lester Snider deplaned and nervously stood in line for immigration control. Her Majesty's Government was not on the lookout for fugitive kidnappers that evening.

"Nationality?" the officer asked.

"American."

"Purpose of your trip?"

"Just visiting."

"How long will you be in Canada?"

"Oh, a few days." The immigration agent stamped a five-day visitor's card and handed it to Woods.

"Next," he called.

He didn't even ask my name, Woods thought as he made his way to the customs area to pick up his bag.

So far the trip had gone without a hitch. The 2:55 P.M. flight from Reno had landed in Seattle at 5:10. Woods, who had checked his luggage through to Vancouver, simply walked to another gate, showed his ticket to the man at the desk, and walked on board the evening shuttle to Vancouver.

Woods was unsure whether his American dollars would be welcome. He found the airport branch of a bank and exchanged some currency. Then he took the bus into town, put his bag in a bus station locker, and began looking for a place to stay.

Isabel Lay, the desk clerk at the St. Francis Hotel, looked up as the smiling young man approached. "May I help you?" she asked.

"How much for a room?"

"That depends. Do you want a plain ordinary room or one with a shower?"

"One with a shower, I think," he said.

"The rate is forty-two dollars a week."

135

"That sounds okay. Can I see the room?" Mrs. Lay had several vacancies, and she showed Woods three rooms before he selected no. 103. He registered as Ralph Lester Snider of Reno, Nevada, and paid a week's rent in advance. Mrs. Lay thought it was odd that an American would pay in Canadian bills after arriving on a weekend. She asked him if he had any luggage, and he told her it was at the bus depot. Later that night she saw him walk through the lobby carrying a single bag. He's a real country boy, she thought. He must be a logger or a cowboy.

Woods awoke the next morning, showered, shaved, and went out for breakfast and to look around his new haven. The St. Francis Hotel, on Seymour Street just around the corner from the old Canadian Pacific Railway Station that fronts on Vancouver harbor, was not quite on Skid Row but close to it. The big lobby, with its red and green linoleum-covered floor, was furnished with venerable overstuffed chairs, many of them occupied by equally old men reading newspapers. He saw there was no coffee shop, just a coin-operated coffee machine. The entrance to what he thought might be a restaurant turned out to be the door to a barbershop.

He spent most of the day exploring Vancouver on foot. He discovered Stanley Park, the magnificent forest that is one of the city's greatest sources of civic pride, and watched a gaggle of elderly and middle-aged men and women dressed in flannels and crisp white dresses lawn bowling, many of them chattering in British accents. It was difficult for him to fathom the object of the game, and he tried unsuccessfully to figure out the rules.

That night after dinner, about 8:45 P.M., he went to a telephone booth with a pocketful of Canadian change. He dialed the operator and gave her Irene Bolzowski's number in Mountain View and dropped nine quarters in the slot. Stephanie answered the phone. Irene wasn't home.

"Where is she?" Woods asked.

"I don't know, but she went to your folks' house for lunch today."

"Yeah? I wonder what she told them."

They chatted for a couple of minutes, then Stephanie asked him when he would be coming home.

"Maybe four, five months," he said.

"Where are you?"

"I can't tell you," he said. At that point the operator broke in on the conversation to say his three minutes were up, and that he would have to deposit more money. He hung up quickly. He must be in the United States, Stephanie thought. The operator had no foreign accent.

Just as Fred was stepping out of the telephone booth, Jim Schoenfeld was pulling his car into the Canadian border station at Kingsgate, British Columbia, north of the Idaho Panhandle. He was tired, having driven all night and most of the day, taking naps when he could and living on potato chips and soft drinks. He was nervous. In addition to all those guns Fred had thrown in the trunk in San Jose, he knew he was carrying a lot of ammunition. But he had driven to Canada before, and he was aware the customs examination usually was cursory.

Dick Crumb, officer-in-charge, Canadian Department of Immigration and Manpower, looked at the sleeping bags and clothes heaped in the back seat of the old Chrysler. He noticed a bumper was crushed and that it rubbed slightly against the tire. Jim, who knew from listening to the radio that no suspects in the kidnapping had been identified, gave the officer his correct name and address.

"What's your destination?" Crumb asked after looking at his California driver's license.

"I'm going to visit a friend of mine who works at the Alberta Game Farm near Edmonton."

"What's his name?" Crumb inquired

"Mark Muldown."

"Is he a Canadian subject?"

"No, he's an American. He's a friend of mine from home."

"How long do you plan to stay?"

"Oh, maybe a week or so," Schoenfeld answered. "Then I thought I might drive to Montreal to see the Olympics."

"With all this stuff in the car, it almost looks like you're planning to stay longer," the officer said. Schoenfeld rubbed his sweating palms together. They hadn't looked in the trunk. He hoped they would not. "Have you ever been convicted of a crime?" Crumb continued, his pencil poised over a clipboard.

Schoenfeld thought he had better tell the truth. They have ways of finding out, he said to himself. "Once, in 1974," he answered aloud.

"Where?"

"In California. It was only a misdemeanor, tampering with a motor vehicle."

"How much money do you have?" Crumb asked. By now Jim was blushing.

"Just a few dollars, but I'll be staying with this friend so I won't need much."

"I'm sorry, son," Crumb said. "I'm afraid we can't let you in." He smiled. "You have to admit your story's a little thin."

Schoenfeld made a U turn, and Crumb watched as the crestfallen young man drove back to the U.S. side of the line, stopped to hand the U.S. Immigration Service guard a chit certifying he had not entered Canada, and then drove away. He did not see him turn southwest.

Chapter 18

When Cooper, Sprague, and Erler returned to the quarry at 7:30 A.M. Sunday, the first thing they noticed was the silence. The exhaust fan had stopped sometime during the night. The big 150-pound industrial battery was dead. None of the deputies guarding the site could say when it had failed because they were too far away to hear it.

It was reasonable to conclude that if the children had been inside they would have been dead by then.

At 9:00 A.M. Sunday, Sergeant Williams and Deputy John Ratcliffe found LaVar Beck at his office at the Naval Supply Center in Alameda. They gave him the number of the government release form submitted to the DMV when the white van was registered. With it he located a file folder showing that on November 24, 1975, a man using the name Mark Hall and the Saylor Street address in San Jose had purchased three 1971 Dodge armed forces police vans, two for $1,000 each and the one now licensed as 1C91414 for $1,750. The original notice of award, statement of ownership, and release documents bearing Hall's signature had been forwarded to the federal records depository in Ogden, Utah.

Beck agreed to call Ogden Monday morning and have the papers mailed special delivery to Volpe.

Since they had been shore patrol vans, often used to carry prisoners, the vehicles had no side windows, Beck said. He added they had been painted black when they were sold.

The investigators ran the engine numbers of the other two vans through the DMV. Only one of them had been reregistered, on July 13, 1976, at Los Gatos, to the same phony identity in San Jose. It now bore license number 1C90730.

At 9:30 A.M. Rich Krimm, the Identikit technician, pulled into the parking lot at the Rodeway Inn in Fresno. In room 1805 he met FBI agents Dick Burris and Dick Douce, who had arrived earlier with Dr. William S. Kroger, a psychiatrist from Beverly Hills. While Krimm waited in another room, Dr. Kroger put Ray into a hypnotic trance at 10:45 A.M.

The bus driver was an easy subject and quickly reached a state of hypermnesia, the accentuation of subconscious recall. The doctor turned him over to Burris and Douce for questioning. They took him through the events leading up to the abduction, but he could remember nothing he had not already told the investigators. He was able to furnish one complete license number and part of another, 1C71414 and 13531. It confused the agents that Ray insisted the first number was on the dark-green van, not the white one.

Shortly before noon Dr. Kroger began to bring Ray back to consciousness. "With each hour and day that passes you will become more calm and objective in your recollection," the physician commanded. "You will be able to report additional details clearly and concisely to the authorities. You will call the sheriff as you remember these things."

Ray returned to normal. He blinked.

"How do you feel?" Dr. Kroger asked.

"Better than I have since it happened," Ray said.

Burris, Douce, and the doctor sat down with Krimm to talk over the results. They decided it would be more useful to wait a few days to put together the composite drawings, until the post-hypnotic suggestion Dr. Kroger had planted in Ray's subconscious took hold and his memory of the physical descriptions of his kidnappers was sharper.

Kroger told Krimm that Ray could remember only what he thought he saw under extreme stress, and that he had perceived the third figure on the full plate as a seven. After an ordeal as long and arduous as Ray's had been it would have been easy for him to mix up the plates and the vehicles. It was the psychiatrist's opinion that the license number he saw doubtless was 1C91414.

Krimm drove back to the Chowchilla substation, where Sheriff Bates told him he wanted a composite drawing made from the descriptions provided by a woman who said she had seen two men, one about thirty and the other fifty-five, loitering the day before the kidnapping at the pool where the children went swimming. The witness, Beverly Hansen, came to the substation and worked with Krimm for nearly an hour on the two drawings. Before leaving for Santa Rita, Krimm picked up all the fingerprints and physical evidence collected by Angus and the FBI agents and locked them in the trunk of his patrol car.

Earlier Sunday, after getting another angry telephone call from Sheriff Bates about what he thought was a grievous lack of federal help, Baugh sent Sergeant Williams to Chowchilla. He reported that the substation there still was a scene of some confusion, with reporters all over the place. "I don't know who's running the operation here," Williams said. "They're going to pull the command post back to headquarters in Madera Monday morning."

"That makes sense," Baugh said. "We're moving back to ETS tomorrow, too, when the regular work week starts." He told Williams to set up a meeting in Madera the next day between Sheriff Bates and Sheriff Houchins, who would fly down with Jim Young.

Back at the quarry the criminalists finished collecting all the potential evidence above ground early Sunday afternoon, including several pieces of willow brush six to seven feet long and from half an inch to two inches in diameter. These had been cut and shoved into the ground around the entrance to the underground

141

chamber to hide it after Ray and the children had been sealed inside. Cooper saw that all the branches had been jammed into the soil when it was wet because dried, caked mud adhered to them when they were pulled up. He made a mental note to find out the precise times of Thursday night's unseasonal rain.

At 2:00 P.M. Cooper and Sprague lowered themselves into the trailer. By that time the civil defense people had put a borrowed telephone company breather and ventilator into the hole so the two men could work safely. They started a meticulous search of the moving van, tagging and listing everything. When they found bloodstains on a bedspread they sent a radio message to Santa Rita to find out whether any of the victims had been cut. If not, the stains might be the blood of a kidnapper. Baugh relayed the request for information to Chowchilla, but Bates sent back word that some of the children and Ray had said they had spilled blood in the trailer.

Among the dozens of items the two criminalists picked out of the moving van were several pieces of wood, including some two-by-fours.

Starting Saturday, sheriff's deputies using backhoes had begun to dig the trailer out of the ground. It was a chore that would take two days.

Meanwhile, Baugh had a visit from Dick McMullen, the FBI resident agent in Hayward, a man highly regarded by the sheriff's officers who deal with him. McMullen introduced Baugh to Goldsberry, Brittingham, and Gummere and lab chief Sam Clark.

"The Director is very interested in this case," McMullen said. "These are some of our best people, when it comes to gathering and preserving evidence. Kelley told them to come out here and stay as long as it takes. He said something like, 'See you all next spring sometime.' "

"Let's go out to the quarry and talk it over with Bob," Baugh suggested.

At the quarry Baugh had a private conversation with Cooper. In the year and a half since his promotion to chief of the criminal division, Baugh had grown to know the crime laboratory chief well, and he trusted him completely. His admiration for the sixteen-member crime lab staff was strong and well-founded and shared by the dozen police departments in the county that used their services.

"Bob, those boys over there are from the Bureau," Baugh said. "They say they're ours as long as we need them. Now this is going to be a big job, but I'd like to keep it in the family if we can. Are we equipped to handle a case like this?"

"Hell, yes, we are," Cooper said. "There's nothing here we can't handle, including the latents. Besides, the lab is close by. Washington is three thousand miles away, for Christ's sake."

Baugh walked back over to McMullen. "We're going to keep the evidence here," he said. "We appreciate the offer, but we think it would be better if we do it ourselves."

McMullen and the others were skeptical. "The Director sent them out here," McMullen repeated.

"As I said, we appreciate it," Baugh told him. "By the way, we also would like the stuff you got in Chowchilla. I don't know where the prosecution will be, if there is one, but we might as well not have part of the evidence in Washington."

"What about fingerprints?" one of the agents asked.

"DOJ in Sacramento has given us Sam Erwin for our very own."

"That's not too shabby," the agent admitted.

"Okay, you're the boss," McMullen said. "Call it any way you want. But I wish you'd think it over."

"Do that," one of the others added. "We'll go back to our motel, and if we don't hear from you by tomorrow, we'll go home."

"It's a deal," Baugh said. "And I wasn't kidding. We really are grateful for the offer."

Baugh returned to where Cooper was standing. "I'll tell Volpe to have Krimm grab all the stuff in Chowchilla before he comes back tonight," he said. "We don't want anybody changing his mind."

The criminalists and technicians, both at the quarry and in the laboratory, were elated. They had been working what amounted to double shifts since the victims had been found, and although they didn't say it out loud, they resented the idea of turning the case over to the FBI.

Of course, they didn't know then they would process over 3,000 items out of 4,800 pieces of physical evidence before it was all over.

Early Sunday morning fourteen-year-old Andrew Silberman and his brother, Jimmy, nine, took their half-brother, David Smith, twenty-eight, visiting from Wisconsin, on a hike near their home in Saratoga, a semirural suburb in the eastern foothills of the Santa Cruz Mountains at the south end of the San Francisco Peninsula. On Pierce Road about a quarter mile north of Highway 9, the old road that winds from the South Bay across the mountains to Santa Cruz on the coast, the three spotted a black vinyl suitcase and some clothes wrapped in a green tarp about twenty feet down an embankment. They decided they had better take the lost suitcase to the firehouse about a half mile down Highway 9 and turn it in.

As they walked up to the station, they saw a Santa Clara County sheriff's patrol car parked outside. Inside they found a Deputy Alford. They gave him the suitcase, told him about the other clothes, and resumed their Sunday-morning outing.

Alford chatted for a while with the firemen, and then drove to where Smith and the two boys had come upon the suitcase. He picked up the green canvas and rummaged through it for some sort of identification.

He found a Madera County schoolbus driver's card bearing a picture and the name Frank Edward Ray, Jr.

Unaware of the significance of what he had discovered, Alford collected the tarp, put it in the trunk of his car with the suitcase, and drove back to the fire station. A few minutes later he glanced at a newspaper on a desk. Ray's photograph was on the front page.

"Oh, my God," the deputy said.

Volpe put down the telephone. "Hot damn!" he said. "Tellardin and Pennington, get over to Saratoga. It looks like they found the kids' clothes."

Volpe had just talked with Santa Clara County Sheriff's Sergeant Jeannie Smith. She told him of Alford's discovery, and that she had photographed the scene and had left two reserve deputies to guard it until someone could get there from Alameda County.

Sergeant Tellardin and Deputy Andy Pennington met Alford at the first station. He showed them where the suitcase and tarp had been found, and Pennington took measurements and pictures. Although no one had opened the suitcase, there was no doubt the canvas contained some of the victims' clothing. Pennington rolled comparison fingerprints of the deputy, Smith, and the two Silberman boys, who had been called back to the station. Then they bagged up the evidence, including a few beer cans Alford had found.

"All this stuff is dry," Tellardin said. "Have you had any rain over here?"

"It rained from about seven thirty to nine thirty Saturday morning," Alford said. "We had a little rain last night in the mountains, but I don't know how heavy it was."

The two Alameda County officers raced back to Santa Rita to deliver the bags to the laboratory. Hurriedly but carefully the criminalists went through the contents.

There was no ransom note.

"The Peninsula's beginning to look pretty hot," Volpe told Baugh. "San Jose, Los Gatos, and now Saratoga. These guys may not be so far away after all."

"Maybe so," Baugh said. "I wish to Christ they'd call us up and tell us why they did it."

Before closing down the command post Sunday night and making arrangements to reopen it the next morning at Eden Township substation, Volpe called the quarry office and got the name of the head of the private patrol service that guarded the property. One of the security people had said the guards kept logs of any unusual contacts they made, especially with trespassers. The investigators needed those logs.

Sunday night the news broke about the recovery of the children's clothes. Dr. Schoenfeld told Rick that the lawyer he had talked to in San Francisco over the weekend would not take the case, but that he would call another lawyer for advice early in the week.

Rick could not decide whether to run or go to the police. He called an old friend of the family, Fred Larson, an aerospace engineer who lived in Redwood City. With studied nonchalance he told him he was thinking of taking a trip to Brazil, and asked Larson for the name of an acquaintance he had mentioned once, a newsman who worked in Rio de Janeiro. Larson gave him the friend's name and a telephone number in Lexington, Massachusetts, where Rick could reach the reporter's mother for a current address.

Monday evening Larson dropped by the Schoenfeld house after work. Rick was there with Julie.

"How are the plans for your vacation going?" Larson asked. Julie shot a sharp glance at Rick, who looked at his shoes and shrugged.

"I might go later this month if I can manage it," he said. He had already told his friends he wanted to sell his horses and motorcycle to finance a trip.

Chapter 19

Monday morning Sheriff Houchins, Baugh, and Jim Young flew to Madera. Sergeant Williams, who had stayed there to act as a liaison officer, met them at the airport. At the county building the two sheriffs met cordially and planned a press conference for the reporters still in town. First they had a private briefing with agents from the state justice department and the FBI resident agent from Fresno.

About 11:15 A.M. Baugh was called to the telephone. It was Volpe.

"They uncovered the name on the outside of the moving van," the lieutenant said. "Now I think I know where 'somewhere' is."

"What was the name?"

"Palo Alto Moving and Storage," Volpe said.

"The Peninsula again. You'd better have someone call down there."

"You wound me, chief. The head man is named John Pipkin. He said he sold the trailer for cash on November 20, 1975, to a young party named Fred Woods."

"Woods?"

"Double U, double O, D, S."

"That's the name of the quarry owner, isn't it?"

"You got it, baby. It's his son. Butch Kelly, the production manager at the quarry, says that the kid is listed in his payroll records as having been an employee there from January 1972, with no termination date."

"Where does he live?"

"At his folks' estate in Portola Valley. It's called The Hawthornes. Apparently they're very big bucks."

Baugh returned to the room with the other officials and told them what Volpe had learned. They actually cheered.

Although Bates and Houchins did not reveal the new information at their press conference, the reporters in Oakland learned of it by monitoring the sheriff's radio. Several of them reached Pipkin in Palo Alto before Volpe's men got there.

Pipkin had told Sergeant Gull that Woods lived in a separate house on his parents' estate in Portola Valley, an area of ranches and large homes in the rolling hills behind Stanford University. Pipkin said he had been to the moving company several times inquiring about buying used equipment.

He described Woods as a white male, in his early twenties, about five feet eleven inches tall, 165 pounds, with light, sandy hair, long but not down to the collar.

Volpe dispatched a teletype to all Bay Area law-enforcement agencies for any files on Fred Woods, and asked for similar information from CII in Sacramento and the FBI in Washington.

About 10:00 A.M. Monday, while Baugh and the sheriff were on their way to Madera in Young's plane, Santa Rita got a call from the Vida Youth Ranch in Livermore. The caller said the ranch had sold several mattresses to a man driving a white van.

Volpe sent some deputies to the ranch, but they came back empty-handed. The mattresses used at the camp were totally different from those found in the trailer.

At 11:00 A.M. Deputy John Ratcliffe received a telephone call from the Oakland police, who said the sales manager at Miracle Auto Painting at Eleventh and Webster in Oakland might have had a conversation with one of the kidnappers. Ratcliffe took

Krimm and his Identikit and drove over to see the manager, Bill Billetter.

He told the two officers that at about 10:30 A.M. that morning an average-sized white man about thirty, with dark-brown hair and a mustache, wearing a red shirt and blue pants, had driven a green van into the shop and asked for prices for a quick paint job. The man seemed nervous and irritable, Billetter said, and was more interested in how fast the work could be done than he was in choosing a color. When he was asked his name he mumbled only "Larson." Billetter said he picked up a work order and the two men started walking toward the truck. When the sales manager asked Larson for the license number, he abruptly said, "You're getting too damn nosy" and broke into a run. The man jumped into the driver's seat, started the engine, and screeched out of the shop onto Webster Street. The startled Billetter ran after the van and saw that it had no license plate.

The next day, after Ratcliffe and Krimm had filed their report and a composite drawing of the suspect, Billetter called the sheriff's office again. He was nervous.

During the lunch hour Tuesday, he said, a man telephoned the shop and asked for him. Assistant Manager Mike Becerra told the caller Billetter was out and asked if he could help. The caller said simply, "Tell the fucker to keep his mouth shut," and hung up.

Ratcliffe called the Oakland police and asked them to take a report from Billetter and forward a copy. A short time after the Oakland officer left the shop Billetter received another telephone call, this one answered by Ed Ball, his supervisor. "I guess Billetter will have to learn the hard way," a man said in a deep, accentless voice. "We saw the cops."

Billetter was worried that someone was watching him.

Between the time the first Oakland police officer left the shop Monday morning and Ratcliffe's and Krimm's arrival, Don Martinez, an East Bay reporter for the San Francisco *Examiner,* had called and asked him about the man who had wanted to have his van painted. A story naming Billetter appeared in the newspaper's first edition Tuesday. Obviously that was where the caller got the manager's name.

149

Billetter received no more threatening calls after that, and Baugh and Volpe concluded the incident was unrelated to the kidnapping. But that didn't explain why the man wanted his truck painted so quickly, or why he had no license plate for it.

After Baugh returned from Madera late Monday, he and Volpe closeted themselves at Santa Rita and went over the previous three days.

"Has anybody talked to Fred Woods, the kid's father, I mean?" Baugh asked.

"An FBI agent, Dave Evans, talked to him today at his office," Volpe replied. "He was very cooperative. He said he'd worked Cal Rock and Gravel for thirty years. It's a family company. The quarry has been there at least that long. It's about five hundred acres and it's never been excavated deeper than ninety feet."

"What about the buried trailer?"

"I don't think Evans knew who owned it when he talked to Woods," Volpe said. "Woods did say that he never heard of any vehicles being buried there, although there are a lot of stripped-down trucks around waiting to be sold for scrap. But Butch Kelly says that all those are in plain sight, above ground."

It was nearly 10:00 P.M. and both men were weary. "We have to get those logs from that patrol outfit, Security Eye, I think it's called," Baugh said. "It just doesn't make sense that someone could bury a goddamn moving van without somebody seeing them do it."

Volpe rose to go. "Maybe we'll get something from Sacramento tomorrow," he said.

"I don't know," Baugh answered. "Not too many kids in Portola Valley have rap sheets."

Monday, Woods glanced through the want ads in the Vancouver *Sun* and the Vancouver *Province* to see if there were any jobs available. He had tried to get a paper Sunday and was surprised to learn that Canadian newspapers didn't publish that day.

He asked Mrs. Lay if the hotel had any parking space available. "Oh," she asked, "do you have a car?"

150

"No, but a friend might be joining me."

When he asked her for directions to the main post office, she told him there was a branch closer to the hotel, at Granville and Hastings, but he said he had to go to the main branch. He arrived before 11:00 A.M. and loitered in the lobby for some time. There was no sign of Jim, nor was there when he returned at 7:00 P.M. that evening. He began to feel uneasy. It had been longer than two days since they parted in Reno. He should have made it by now.

Most of Monday afternoon Woods sat in a wine-colored, shabby chair in the lobby of his hotel, watching television. Over the next few days Mrs. Lay would notice that his favorite programs were the afternoon reruns of *The FBI.*

Jim Schoenfeld had learned a lesson from his initial attempt to enter Canada. First of all he had to get rid of the guns in the trunk, and second he needed enough money to make his story about visiting Mark Muldown plausible. He chuckled to himself. Mark was in the army at Pensacola, Florida. He had once introduced Jim to a friend who worked on the provincial game farm in Alberta. He wondered if Mark would think all this was funny.

Monday afternoon Jim pulled into a service station in Spokane, Washington. While the attendant was refueling the car, he consulted the yellow pages in the telephone directory to find a shop that bought used guns. He asked the attendant for directions.

Just before 3:00 P.M. he parked in front of Sportsmen's Surplus on North Division Street outside the city limits. He went inside and approached Mike Miotke, the co-owner of the store, at the counter.

"I have some stuff I'd like to sell," Schoenfeld said.

"Where is it?"

"Out in my car." Miotke walked outside with Jim, who unlocked the trunk. He pulled aside a couple of sleeping bags, revealing several guns and a set of tools.

"I'd like to sell all of it, including the tools," Schoenfeld said.

"I'm not interested in them," the store owner said.

"I'll take forty dollars for them," Jim bargained. "They're worth at least a hundred."

151

"I don't doubt it, I just don't want them. But I think we can make a deal on some of these guns."

After some dickering, Miotke offered Jim $180 for a lever-action .30–30 rifle, a .22 rifle, a 20-gauge shotgun, a .22 revolver, and a .38 revolver. The package included 3,000 rounds of .22 ammunition, 200 .30–30 cartridges, and 200 rounds of .38 pistol ammunition. Schoenfeld also tried to sell him a modern replica of a .58-caliber muzzle-loading rifle and a .44 cap-and-ball revolver, but Miotke said there wasn't much of a market for them.

Inside, the store owner made out a bill of sale with the name and address from Jim's driver's license, and Jim signed it. Pocketing the money, he got in his car and turned north again toward the Canadian border.

At 6:00 P.M. Canadian customs agent Grant Jannaway looked warily at the driver's license proffered by James Leonard Schoenfeld of Atherton, California. The bearer was dirty, had a few days' growth of beard, and appeared on the brink of exhaustion.

"What's your itinerary?" Jannaway asked.

"Well, I'm going to visit a friend at the Alberta Game Farm at Edmonton, and then I thought I'd drive east to the Olympics, and then I want to go down to visit my girlfriend in Kentucky."

"What's your friend's name in Edmonton?" the agent asked.

"Mark."

"Last name?"

"Uh, I don't remember."

Jannaway looked at the clutter in the car. "All right, young man," he said. "Let's take a look through your automobile. Open the trunk, please."

Under the sleeping bags he found the tools, food, winter clothing, and a coin collection. He turned his attention to the interior of the car, and opened the console between the two front seats. Schoenfeld had gone inside the office to answer some questions for an immigration officer. He heard Jannaway's voice through the open door. "Well, what have we here?" He looked out and saw the agent holding a small, nickel-plated pistol. He hadn't known it was in the car.

"Oh, no," Jim muttered under his breath. "You've sunk me now, Fred."

Actually, Jannaway found two .25 automatics in the console, both Fred's. Jim's heart sank as the agent came into the office and picked up the telephone. "You can't take handguns into Canada," he said as he dialed. Jim started to speak, but was interrupted by Jannaway's voice. "Brian, I'm seizing some contraband. Could you come to the border?"

Constable Brian Fleming of the Grand Forks Detachment of the Royal Canadian Mounted Police arrived a short time later from Christina Lake. He joined Jannaway as they virtually took the car apart.

Concealed behind the spare tire they found the two muzzle-loaders, a half pound of black powder, shot, and some loading equipment. From behind the rear seat they recovered two license plates, one from Montana and one from California with a 1972 validation sticker on it. In the console they found a personal identification card for someone named Frederick Newhall Woods, a library card in the same name, a letter to Woods from the Navy Disposal Center in Alameda, and a Nevada driver's license in the name of Ralph Lester Snider.

"How about these license plates, Schoenfeld?" the constable asked.

"The Montana plate is for a tractor registered to my uncle that my dad has," he said. "The other one is for a car I have stored."

Fleming took him back into the office. "You're going to be with us for a while," he said. "Make yourself comfortable. Would you like a soda?"

"Yeah, sure," Jim said.

"What kind? We have Coke, orange, grape, and root beer in the machine."

"Orange, thanks."

Jannaway and Fleming ran the serial numbers of the guns, the license number on the car, the numbers of the two license plates found in the back seat, and Jim's name, address, and description through the RCMP, FBI, and U.S. Customs computers.

While they waited for the answers from Ottawa and Washington they searched Schoenfeld. They found only about a hundred dollars in cash, but Jim volunteered that he had more. He produced a plastic bottle with a fishline around it he had hidden in the car.

"How do you make your living?" Fleming asked.

"I buy and sell antique cars."

"What's this place?" the constable asked, holding up a photograph of the Rengstorff mansion he had found in the trunk.

"That's my house," he replied.

Fleming looked through the coin collection, which was in a Chinese puzzle box. In addition to American and Canadian proof sets he found Soviet, Brazilian, and various Caribbean currencies.

"I've been collecting foreign money since I was twelve," Jim explained. "I bought that Russian bill from a kid in the seventh grade for a quarter. I'll sell the collection if I need money."

"Now, you say these pistols belong to Fred Woods?" Fleming asked.

"Yeah."

"What's he need them for?"

Jim laughed. "He likes to scare kids with them."

"He what?"

"He gets his jollies scaring little kids."

Fleming's superintendent called with the information that neither Jim, the guns, nor the license numbers were wanted. The policeman regarded the tired young man.

"We could arrest you for trying to smuggle illegal weapons into the country," he said, "but I don't think that would do any of us much good. I'm afraid we can't let you cross under the circumstances, though."

"What about the guns?" Jim asked. "I'd really hate to lose the muzzle-loaders."

"You can have them all back," Jannaway told him, "but the law says you have to pay a seventy-five-dollar tax." Schoenfeld paid the fine, retrieved his possessions, and ruefully drove to the American side. U.S. Immigration and Naturalization officer Bill Ramsaw, who had been briefed on the telephone by Jannaway, talked to him briefly and waved him through.

By Tuesday the newspapers and broadcasters had Fred's name as the owner of the buried moving van. The reporters made the connection between Woods and his father, the owner of the quarry. That evening Irene drove to the Schoenfeld house and asked to see Rick, ostensibly to have him check her car for a mechanical malfunction.

"Oh, God, where is he?" she asked.

He lied. "I don't know."

"Fred called me Sunday and again today, but I wasn't home," Irene said. "Stephanie was there, and she said it sounded like long distance."

"Probably was."

"I had lunch with Fred's folks Sunday. I think they know."

"Yeah, Dad said Mr. Woods sounded pretty suspicious."

"Rick, what are you going to do?"

"I don't know. We just have to wait."

"I've been so scared and nervous that I keep throwing up," she said.

"Yeah. Me too."

Chapter 20

Baugh had been wrong. Frederick Newhall Woods did have a record. According to the CII, Woods, now twenty-four, had been arrested October 6, 1974, in mountainous Sierra County north of Lake Tahoe with two other young men, James Leonard Schoenfeld, now twenty-four, and his younger brother, Richard Allen Schoenfeld, now twenty-two. The brothers lived with their parents, Dr. and Mrs. John Schoenfeld, in Atherton, another Peninsula suburb. They had been caught stripping a car. The charge originally had been grand theft, but it had been reduced to petty theft and auto tampering, and the three had pleaded guilty and paid fines of $125 each.

The booking photos and fingerprints taken in 1974 at the sheriff's office in Downieville, the tiny Sierra County Seat, were on their way to Oakland from Sacramento, along with their driver's license pictures.

While the investigators were pondering this new information, the sheriff's office got an urgent call from Charles Bates at the FBI field office in San Francisco. The day before Agent Charles Hiner answered a telephone call from a San Francisco attorney who said he thought he had some information about the Chowchilla kidnapping. The lawyer said a Dr. John Schoenfeld had called him Saturday morning, July 17, and asked him if he would be willing to represent one or more possible suspects in the case. The attorney told Dr. Schoenfeld he wasn't interested, but the physician kept him on the phone, asking whether he thought the kidnappers would get the death penalty, and if he believed they should surrender.

Agents Jim Watters and Jean Hughes had gone to Dr. Schoenfeld's office in Menlo Park, not far from his home in Atherton, Monday afternoon and questioned him about the call. He seemed upset and was somewhat evasive.

Dr. Schoenfeld told the two FBI agents that on Friday he had received a call from a patient whose name he said he couldn't recall. The patient told him that a friend or friends may have been involved in the kidnapping, Dr. Schoenfeld said, and asked him if he could help find an attorney. He said the patient was mainly interested in knowing whether the kidnappers would be sent to the gas chamber and if they could surrender without being killed by the police. He couldn't remember the patient's name, he repeated, but even if he could, he would be bound not to reveal it because of the doctor-patient relationship.

The agents, who had not heard of James or Richard Schoenfeld at the time, asked the doctor how he had selected the attorney in San Francisco. He said he got the name and telephone number Saturday from his cousin's husband. He was distressed that the lawyer had gone to the FBI, but promised he would call the Bureau himself if the patient called him back.

However, he added as he showed Watters and Hughes to the door of his office, he doubted he would hear from the patient again.

"One and two makes three," Volpe said happily.

Tuesday morning all the investigators who had worked on the case, including FBI agents, state justice department agents, and a lieutenant from the highway patrol, held a briefing session at the Eden substation. They agreed that young Woods and the Schoenfeld brothers were the primary suspects, but that so far everything was circumstantial. The two fathers—Woods and Schoenfeld—had to be questioned again, and they had to start interviewing all the friends and associates of the three they could find.

The tentative first plans were laid for a search of The Hawthornes, the Woods family's estate.

The reporters, who had picked up Woods's name the day before from Pipkin in Palo Alto, were clamoring for more information. Sheriff Houchins said Cooper was ready to pull the trailer out of the ground. To provide a little theater and allay the newspeople he asked Baugh to arrange for a press conference and for representatives of the media to be at the quarry when it happened. Houchins also called Sheriff Bates in Madera and offered to send a plane to pick him up so he too could be on hand, and he accepted.

Watters, one of the FBI agents who had interviewed Dr. Schoenfeld the day before, went to Palo Alto to talk again to Pipkin, who had searched his records further. The terminal manager said the moving van was not the first surplus vehicle he had sold to Woods, who had visited the yard several times. On October 17, a month before he bought the trailer for $500, Woods paid $750 in cash for a 1956 International tractor that had hauled moving vans a total of 323,612 miles in the past twenty years. On both bills of sale Woods listed his address as P.O. Box 4337, in nearby Mountain View. Watters asked for a description of him.

"He's about five foot ten, five eleven, slender build, a good-looking kid about twenty-four, I'd say," Pipkin recalled. "He has a sort of western air, acts sort of like a country boy. But he's a hell of a businessman. He really knew the value of the stuff he was shopping for, and he drove a hard bargain. We ended up selling the truck and trailer for a lot less than we wanted."

On a couple of occasions, Pipkin added, Woods was accompanied by another man about the same age, only a little bigger. He couldn't remember anything else about him.

Watters drove to the Mountain View post office and talked to a postal worker named Pat Caldwell. He learned that Woods had taken out the box in April 1970 and that it was still active. Six years earlier Woods had given his address as 1184 Bonita, Apartment 3, Mountain View.

Caldwell told the FBI agent the box was also listed to receive mail for something called Townhouse Enterprises.

At the apartment house Watters found out that Woods had moved back to the family estate in June 1974 and that his address there was 800 Los Trancos Road, Portola Valley.

Later the same day, Watters checked with the Atherton police department for any additional records on the Schoenfeld brothers. James had been issued five traffic citations, but had never been arrested. Richard had two traffic citations and no arrests. Both had registered concealable weapons, James an old army .44 revolver and Richard an 1811 .69 flintlock pistol.

It occurred to Watters that criminals seldom register their guns.

At 11:00 A.M. Tuesday, Bruce Tellardin and Rod Alvarez arrived at the Livermore office of Security Eye Patrol, the company that furnishes night and weekend guards for the Cal Rock quarry and adjacent property owned by Lone Star Industries. They met Gerald Bell, the firm's director, and Dan Twohey, one of his employees.

Bell told the two detectives that the night before he had received a telephone call from a former security guard with the company, Harry Striplin, who lived in Union City. Striplin had read in the newspapers about the children being found in the quarry, and he said he remembered seeing somebody working with a bulldozer on a weekend, when the sand and gravel operations were shut down. He thought he had made a note of it in the patrol logbook.

Bell had gone through the logs and found the references on the page for December 7, 1975.

Twohey told the two investigators that the Sunday after that, December 14, he saw two men drive a blue-and-white dump truck into the quarry and park it near an old moving van. Bell, who happened to be visiting the quarry at the same time to check up on his men, wrote the truck's license number, 47776V, in the log.

Bell went on to say that several months later, he couldn't remember when, he stopped a young man who was sorting through a pile of scrap metal at the quarry. The man produced a driver's license identifying him as Fred Newhall Woods of The Hawthornes, Portola Valley, and said he was the son of Cal Rock's owner. Bell checked with Butch Kelly, who confirmed Woods's story. "He said he pretty much had the run of the place, and that he had his own key," Bell recalled. Woods told Bell he was looking for some scrap for a friend in San Francisco.

Tellardin called Harry Striplin's home and learned that he worked now for an aluminum company in Oakland. He telephoned the former Security Eye guard at work. He agreed to meet Tellardin and Alvarez at the Eden substation on his way home that evening. They took the logbook after promising Bell they would return a Xerox copy of it.

Tellardin learned from the DMV computer that the dump truck was registered to a John Andrew Hunt in Marysville. He asked the Yuba County sheriff's office to find him. A deputy called back and told him Hunt had sold the truck through an auctioneer in Yuba City a year earlier. Tellardin asked the FBI to find out who bought the truck at the auction, although he already had a pretty good idea who it was.

Sergeant Berni Cervi, who the day before had driven a geology engineer to the quarry to take soil samples to estimate when the trailer had been buried, returned Tuesday morning to help supervise the vehicle's removal. Deputy Bob Ferguson had removed the dirt from around the moving van with a backhoe, taking care to preserve the walls of the original cut made when it had been interred. The criminalists would photograph the blade marks left by the kidnappers for later use as evidence. Another deputy, George Garibaldi, had hauled a bulldozer over to the site from Santa Rita on a flatbed truck and had used it to dig a ramp down to the front of the trailer. On Tuesday morning Deputy Tony Trean arrived and set up a television camera to record the removal on video tape.

After Ferguson uncovered the entire trailer, Garibaldi jumped down into the hole. "The wheels and tires are in great shape," he

160

called up. "They even look like they may be new." Garibaldi climbed back out of the excavation and told Cervi that whoever had buried the trailer had taken exact measurements. The rear wheels were in two short trenches dug to accommodate them, while the front was resting on higher dirt.

"When they backed it into the hole, it just dropped into place like a piece of a puzzle," he said. "They didn't even have to level it up."

Cervi climbed into the van through the hole in the roof and removed the front vent pipe, a piece of aluminum four inches in diameter with a flange on the inside. Garibaldi hooked his bulldozer to the trailer hitch and Ferguson attached the line of a crane brought over from Santa Rita to the roof. At 10:30 A.M., with the sheriff, press, and a number of visiting VIPs watching, Ferguson and Garibaldi started their big machines. The van groaned, but the rear wheels refused to come free of the two trenches. They shut down their engines. "According to the association, we're operating engineers," Garibaldi said. "We ought to be able to do better than this."

They waited while Ferguson drove to Santa Rita and returned with a truck tractor. He backed the truck down the ramp, hitched it to the trailer, and attached the bulldozer to the front of the tractor.

"I guarantee the son of a bitch will come out this time," Ferguson said. It did, as the cameras rolled. The van was driven under highway patrol guard to Santa Rita, where it was stored in a property warehouse near the laboratory.

When the trailer was out, the investigators found several soft drink cans in the hole, along with the cardboard box that had contained the ventilator covers. They were marked for evidence and sent to the laboratory to be dusted for fingerprints.

Harry Striplin arrived at the substation about 5:15 P.M. Tuesday. Tellardin took him into an office with the Security Eye logbook. Striplin glanced through it. He found several entries with his initials next to them.

11–30–75 1350 hours.: (3 men 1 driving a blue & white dump truck, other two driving a Palo Alto storage truck in Cal-Rock main gate. Had their own key.)

Striplin told Tellardin that on November 30, 1975, while he was on his way to check one of the gates at the quarry shortly before 2:00 P.M., he saw a white moving van with black lettering on it pull up to the main gate, followed by a blue-and-white dump truck. He drove to a place where he could watch as a man got out and unlocked the gate, returned to the cab, and drove the van inside. After the dump truck pulled in behind, another man got out of it and locked the gate. A third man climbed down from the cab of the moving van, and the three appeared to check over the trailer to make sure nothing had fallen off it. Striplin watched unseen as both trucks were driven to a storage shed north of the office, beyond some conveyor belts. The van was parked next to a second moving van, this one painted orange and black. At a distance two of the men appeared to be blond, and the third had darker hair. All three were wearing work clothes.

Assuming they were quarry employees, Striplin continued his patrol.

12–7–75 1535 hours.: ST(Men working with Cat west of Cal-Rock).

Striplin told Tellardin that entry was made after he heard a noise coming from west of the office, and he circled around to investigate. Through the brush he saw two men working, one driving a bulldozer and the other guiding him with hand signals. They had a hole started a few feet deep. Again assuming nothing was wrong, Striplin continued his rounds.

12–7–75 1700 hours.: (Cal-Rock, men still working).

Striplin recalled thinking it was odd that the company would have men on the job on a weekend. He usually was alone on Sunday.

162

12–7–75 1800 hours.: (LSI & Cal-Rock security tour completed. Men still working at Cal-Rock on Palo Alto Van truck. LSI quiet and secure. All gates locked. All seems secure.).

Just before dark, Striplin said, he started another round and heard the bulldozer engine. He wondered how long the men would remain there, and if they would turn on the lights to continue working. He peered through the brush and saw the hole was now four or five feet deep, about twenty-five feet long, and the width of the bulldozer blade.

12–7–75 2300 hours.: (LSI & Cal-Rock secure and quiet.).

Striplin remembered driving his patrol car near where the tractor had been working. He turned off the engine, rolled the window down, and listened. He heard only the crickets chirping. The men had left. At midnight Striplin was relieved by another guard and went home.

"I guess they never saw me," he said.

"Did you ever see them again?" Tellardin asked.

"No," Striplin answered. "But about three weeks later, on a Saturday or Sunday, I thought I heard some kids talking. Someone had been stealing fire extinguishers, and Mr. Kelly had left a pickup truck out in the yard over the weekend to make it look like someone was there all the time.

"I climbed a hill to see if I could spot the kids. I noticed the place where the bulldozer had been working was flat again. The hole was gone."

"Did you ever see either moving van again?"

"No."

"How about the dump truck?"

"Never saw it again, either," Striplin said.

"Is this the van?" Tellardin asked, producing three Polaroid color photos taken while the trailer was being hauled out of the ground that day.

"That's it."

"Now then," Tellardin continued, "do you recognize any of these men?" He showed the former security guard a lineup of eight photographs, including the pictures from the driver's licenses of Woods and the Schoenfeld brothers.

"I've seen that guy working at the quarry several times," Striplin said, indicating Woods's picture, "although I can't remember any dates. And I feel like I've seen this guy before, too, but I can't remember where." He was pointing to the photo of Richard Schoenfeld.

Just after Striplin left the substation, Tellardin got a call from Bell at Security Eye. He had searched his files for the field interrogation card he filled out the day he had stopped Woods at the quarry. It was dated May 2, 1976.

Baugh called the district attorney's office at the main courthouse in Oakland Tuesday afternoon and asked Jensen if he would mind coming to the command post. The D.A. promised that he and his chief deputy, Dick Haugner, would drive by after their office closed at 5:00 P.M.

"Things are getting out of hand, Ed," Baugh told Volpe after hanging up the telephone. "We're going in too many directions at once, and we're going to end up with no one person knowing all the facts."

"We do seem to be making what you might call your rapid progress," Volpe said.

"I'm still supposed to be running the strike task force," Baugh continued, "and as I sit here I can't even remember when it's supposed to end."

"It'll be over Thursday. We ought to have all the help we need to search the Woods place."

"That's a blessing. Look," Baugh said, "we'll need one person who knows everything that's going on to be the affiant on the search warrants. I have a feeling we may enforce quite a few of them before it's over. You're elected. You've been in charge since the investigation started, and you're the only guy who knows everything that's happened."

"Okay," Volpe said. "Who replaces me here?"

"I'll take over the day-to-day shit. You get ready to have a long

164

and meaningful relationship with Jack Meehan in the D.A.'s office."

Jensen and Haugner listened as Baugh and Volpe brought them up to date. The district attorney agreed that the Schoenfeld brothers were solid suspects, especially after the doctor's call to the lawyer, but he and Haugner didn't believe enough evidence had been uncovered to justify a search of the Schoenfeld home.

Getting a search warrant is not the automatic procedure depicted in police movies, at least not in California. Judges must be convinced not only that there is reasonable cause to believe the person named in a warrant request has committed a crime, but also that there is an immediate danger that evidence will be destroyed or hidden. Otherwise a warrant has to be served during business hours. In a case as complicated as this one it is not uncommon for an investigator's affidavit, meticulously composed by the district attorney's office in the proper legal jargon, to run thousands of words long.

The case against Woods was another matter, Jensen said. He was convinced that any municipal court judge in San Mateo County, where Portola Valley and Atherton are located, would grant a warrant to enter the Woods estate. He said he would send Meehan, an expert on the laws covering the seizure of evidence, out to the substation in the morning to go over the entire case with Volpe.

Baugh was called out of the office. "Barbara Walters is on the phone," he was told.

"Tell her I'm too busy to talk to her," Baugh said. "No, tell her it's too early to comment on the progress of the investigation . . . or something like that."

A deputy came back a few minutes later. "She's very insistent," he said.

Baugh blew up. "Tell her I'm out arresting some clown for impersonating a human being. Tell her anything, but tell her to get off my goddamn phone."

Chapter 21

On Tuesday, July 20, Fred went to another telephone booth in Vancouver and tried to call Irene. Stephanie was home alone again.

"I have a long-distance call," the operator intoned.

Knowing it was Fred, Stephanie said immediately, "Irene's not here." She heard Fred's voice.

"Forget it, operator, can I get my two dollars back?"

"I can only return the last twenty cents," the operator said. "I'll give you an address for a refund."

"No, that's all right," Fred said. "I'll talk to anybody. Stephanie, is that you?"

"Yes."

"How's Irene?"

"She's scared and nervous. She's just sick, Fred. What have you done?"

"I did something, that's all. What about my folks? What do they know?"

"I don't know." There was a pause. "Fred?"

"Yeah."

"Why don't you come back and give yourself up?"

Stephanie heard him hang up the telephone.

Early that same morning Jim drove into Coeur d'Alene, Idaho. After his second attempt to enter Canada had failed, he had returned to Spokane and turned east. He looked up pawnshops in the telephone book, and parked in front of Forest Brothers Salvage on North Ninth Street, waiting for the store to open. He shivered. Even though it was July, it was cold before sunrise in the Bitterroot Mountains.

When Jack Forest unlocked the store, Jim went inside. The transaction was swiftly concluded, and Forest gave Jim cash receipts for a box of tools, a CB radio and antenna, a pair of four-foot bolt cutters, two .25 pistols, a drill, and a pair of fur earmuffs. Jim asked where he could buy a newspaper.

About 11:00 A.M. Elmer Williams answered his front door on Coeur d'Alene Street. "I'm interested in a truck I saw advertised in the paper," Schoenfeld said.

"That's it out front there," Williams told him. "It's a fifty Chevy van. It belongs to my son, Jeff. He's the one selling it."

"Mind if I take a look at it?"

"Go right ahead. Help yourself. The price is two hundred and fifty dollars."

Williams watched as the disreputable-looking young hobo walked around the panel truck and looked inside. He came back to the door. "I'm interested in it," he said, "but I'll have to come back later."

"Fine. Can I give Jeff your name?"

"Ralph Snider."

Jim Schoenfeld parked in front of Rodell Motors on North Fourth Street in Coeur d'Alene in midafternoon. He went inside and found the owner, Chester Rodell. "Do you buy used cars?" he asked.

"Sometimes, if they're in good shape."

"Could I show you mine? It's real reliable."

"Sure." Rodell walked outside with Jim and looked over the 1963 Chrysler. "What do you think it's worth?" the dealer asked.

"I need two hundred and fifty dollars."

"Well, you're out of luck, young fella. You have some heavy rust marks on the frame, and it's pretty well beat up. I probably couldn't wholesale it for more than twenty-five or fifty bucks."

Schoenfeld look disappointed. "Well," he said finally, "if that's the best you can do."

"Okay, let's go to the office. Where's the title?"

"I don't have it with me."

Rodell stopped. "Well, I'm afraid I can't buy it then."

A short time later "Ralph Snider" returned to the Williams residence. "The best I can do is two hundred and thirty-five dollars," he said.

"All right," Williams said. "Jeff isn't here, but I think that'll be fine."

"I'll come back for the van," Schoenfeld said. He drove away in the Chrysler. Within an hour he returned on foot. "I walked over from where I'm staying with some friends on Fourth Street," he told Williams. "Where do I register the truck?"

"Over at the courthouse," Williams said. "But it'll be closed now."

The next morning Jim presented himself at Emogine Schively's counter at the Kootenai County Assessor's Office and changed the registration for the 1950 truck from Jeff Williams to James Leonard Schoenfeld, Atherton, California. She gave him a temporary permit, and told him he should return the old license plates to the former owner. Jim went back to the Williams house and gave the plates to the father. Then he drove ten blocks to the corner of Fourth and Boise streets for one last look at his old Chrysler. The night before he had transferred his remaining possessions to the panel truck. He had decided since he couldn't sell it, he had better abandon the Chrysler before the police started looking for him.

He glanced at the big car in his rearview mirror as he pulled away. He was about out of money, and he hadn't slept in a bed in five days.

Volpe and Meehan got down to work the first thing Wednesday morning. The narration of the facts supporting the search warrant would be lengthy, and Jensen didn't want any mistakes. They would be asking an unknown judge in another county to allow a small army of deputies from a foreign jurisdiction to raid the estate of a very prominent citizen.

Baugh had the Woods estate staked out, and he ordered black-and-white, color, and infrared aerial photographs taken of the property as well as the quarry. He learned that the heavily wooded estate had two entrances, one at 4411 Alpine Road, where Woods's parents lived in the main house, and another at 800 Los Trancos Road, where Fred lived most of the time. Also staying in houses on the Los Trancos Road side of the ranch were Fred's uncle, Edwin Woods, and his wife, and his paternal grandmother, Frances Newhall Woods, an elderly invalid attended by nurses full time. For insurance Baugh ordered a stakeout at the Schoenfeld home as well.

The press, already aware of the identity of Fred Woods, learned of the stakeouts by monitoring the sheriff's radio. About midday Baugh got a call from one of his detectives in San Mateo County.

"We have reporters damn near in the back seat," he reported. "They're all over both locations. They're more of them than there are of us. One of the news stations even has a chopper hovering over the Woods estate. And I just saw a reporter go up and ring the Schoenfeld's doorbell."

Baugh cursed. "Keep the stakeout going, but don't answer any questions," he said. "And use the phone whenever you can instead of the radio. If a reporter spooks one of the suspects, don't let him get away. Bring him in for questioning."

As Baugh dictated a strongly worded press release pleading with the media "not to try and do our field investigation for us and hold off until we have some positive information to release," a reporter was chatting at the door with Richard Schoenfeld. The young man said he didn't know what all the excitement was about.

Baugh had his secretary, Theresa Schwarz, who had left his Oakland office to work with him at the Eden substation, order a large classroom blackboard. She started a running log of assignments and made a list of the names of every friend or associate of Woods's or the Schoenfeld brothers' who had the remotest chance of being involved in the kidnapping.

169

Baugh tried to divide his detectives into teams according to specialties or particular talents. Larry Santos and Ken Tiers, for instance, the experts on banks and bad-check cases, were assigned to get all the information on the three that they could from financial institutions and credit-card companies. They would ask the postal inspectors for mail traps on all three suspects, and would begin the process of getting lists of telephone numbers they had called from home. "And," Baugh told them, "call all the major oil companies and find out if any of them have credit cards. It might be interesting to find out where they've been buying their gas lately."

Other teams were equipped with photo lineups including pictures of the three and were sent to show them to potential witnesses such as workers at the quarry, the clerks at the state motor vehicles offices in Los Gatos and San Jose, and the garages on the Peninsula where the vans had been certified for compliance with California's air pollution control laws before they were registered.

Deputies Jake Negley and Ron Kolodzieczak (called simply Kolo by his fellow officers, who can't get their tongues around his name) were detailed to interview the senior Fred Woods at his office in San Francisco, and Deputy Andy Pennington was sent to question Dr. Schoenfeld.

Negley and Kolo, accompanied by two San Francisco police inspectors, were ushered into Woods's office at 11:45 A.M. After they introduced themselves, he asked them if they would mind waiting while he called his attorney to have him sit in on the interview. The lawyer, Herbert W. Yanowitz, arrived just after noon. Following a private conference with Woods, Yanowitz came out of his office. "I would like to inquire as to what questions you intend to ask my client," he said.

"Among other things, I want to ask him if he has a son named Fred Woods and if the son has access to the Cal-Rock quarry in Livermore," Kolo answered.

"I have already advised Mr. Woods not to answer any questions at this time," Yanowitz said. The four officers left the office.

At about 3:30 P.M. Pennington and FBI agent Jim Watters met

Dr. Schoenfeld in his office. He was asked again if he could remember the name of the patient who had called him seeking a lawyer. He said no.

"When did you get the call?" Pennington asked.

"I really can't remember," Dr. Schoenfeld said. "It was either Friday or Saturday."

"The patient hasn't called back?"

"No."

"Do you know anyone named Woods?" Watters asked.

"The only Woods I know well is a neighbor, Bea Woods. I also know a Fred Woods, who owns a quarry somewhere in the East Bay." He paused. The two investigators waited quietly. "My two sons, Jim and Ricky, were arrested once with his son, Fred. They were supposedly taking parts from an abandoned car someplace in the mountains."

"What happened?"

"They were acquitted by a jury," the podiatrist said quickly, unaware that his two interrogators had seen the record. "I think at the time they went to trial the whole car had a value of about fifteen dollars. There really was nothing to it."

Dr. Schoenfeld said that aside from that scrape none of his children, including an older son, John, a butcher, had ever been in trouble. Woods and Jim spent most of their time buying automobiles at places like auctions and flea markets and fixing them up for resale.

"Do you know where Jim and Rick were on Thursday, the fifteenth?" Pennington asked.

"No," he replied. "Wednesday evening I went over to my other son John's house in Menlo Park to help him pour a concrete patio in his backyard, and both Jim and Ricky were there helping. I don't know exactly where they were Thursday night, but I think Friday night they were at home with some friends."

"Who were they?"

"I can't remember. I think there was a girl there with her boyfriend from Palm Springs," Dr. Schoenfeld said. "I'm not sure, but I think her name is Glick. I think Jim met her at her sister's wedding a few months ago.

"I do recall that Jim loaned his motorcycle to someone that night," he added.

"Who was that?"

"I don't remember the name, but they returned it on Sunday, I think."

"Where are your sons now?" Watters asked.

"Jim left Saturday on a trip, to Los Angeles, I think. He said he would be back later this week, tomorrow or the next day. Ricky is at home, as far as I know."

There was another brief silence.

"I know that neither of them could be involved in anything like this," Dr. Schoenfeld said slowly. "But if they were arrested and wrongfully convicted, I don't think they could handle the hardened element in the prison system. They haven't led the type of life that would prepare them for imprisonment."

"If you receive any further information about the case, or your sons' possible involvement in it, will you call our office?" Pennington asked.

"I'd have to think about it," Dr. Schoenfeld said. "Maybe." As the two left he turned to Watters. "They shouldn't be sent to a maximum security prison," he said almost beseechingly.

"Good-bye, doctor, and thank you," the agent said.

Outside Pennington spoke to Watters. "Do you think we ought to pay a visit on Ricky?"

"Does a bear shit in the woods?"

The investigators reported the results of their first interview to their superiors by telephone. Pennington learned that a search warrant for the Woods estate probably would be ready in time to serve that night. Baugh had gone home for a quick dinner while Volpe and Meehan finished the affidavit. They were arranging to take it to a judge's home in Redwood City to be signed.

By the time Watters and Pennington reached the Schoenfeld home in Atherton, the doctor was home with his wife, Merry. They told the couple they wanted to speak to Rick.

"He's not here," Mrs. Schoenfeld said. "He wasn't home when I came in at four o'clock, and we don't know where he is."

The detective and the agent left after the parents promised to give both their sons a message that they wanted to talk with them.

172

Earlier Baugh had received a call from Sergeant Dave Bricknell, who was in San Jose with Don Cordes questioning possible witnesses and showing them photographic lineups. He said that John Pipkin at Palo Alto Transfer and Storage had come up with another interesting piece of paper. In addition to his other duties, Pipkin is a state-certified weighmaster for commercial vehicles. On July 14, he said, a young man using the San Jose identity they had learned was false drove a 1971 Dodge van on to the truck scales and asked for a weight certificate so he could register it. The man, in his early twenties, was accompanied by a woman. It definitely was not Fred Woods, whose face Pipkin knew well.

During the day Wednesday Cooper received copies of the handwritten, signed statements Woods and the Schoenfelds had given the sheriff's office when they were arrested in Sierra County. At the laboratory the criminalists compared the handwriting with signatures on the DMV registration applications for the two vans. They concluded Fred Woods was the Mark Hall who registered the white van. Jim Schoenfeld had signed the same name to register the other one.

In the afternoon, Baugh called Sam Bass at the civil defense office and asked him to ready the county's mobile communication center and move it to the courthouse in Redwood City, the San Mateo County seat. The unit, a forty-five-foot air-conditioned trailer equipped with radios, teletype and telephone switchboards, would be the field headquarters for the search at the Woods estate. Because of the size of the place, they would raid it with about forty-five detectives and deputies divided into two teams, each headed by a lieutenant.

Because the multiplying calls from reporters and the public were swamping the dispatchers at the Eden substation, Baugh ordered new lines installed, along with a special circuit direct to Sheriff Houchins's office at the courthouse in Oakland. The installer arrived from the telephone company shortly and went to work. When he was finished Baugh had three new telephones on his desk. One was red, one was white, and the third was blue.

"I know the bicentennial was only a couple of weeks ago," Baugh said, "but don't you think that's a bit much?"

The installer grinned. "I couldn't think of a better place to put them."

Late in the afternoon Sergeant Williams, who still was in Madera, called the command post. Hugh Phillips, a Chowchilla truck driver, had called the sheriff's office there to report that he had visited the Woods estate July 11.

"I went to his house and talked to Phillips," Williams said. "He said he was delivering a load of hay to a stable up in Woodside, and mentioned to the customer he was looking for a used house trailer. The customer told him to go see Fred Woods, that he had dozens of old vehicles on the place, from fire engines to hearses."

"Yeah, we know," Baugh said. "They showed up on the aerial photographs."

"Phillips said he bought an old twenty-foot trailer that once belonged to a construction company. It was full of old mattresses. He also said the pink slip had been endorsed over to Woods by someone named James Schoenfeld."

"You get the pink slip?" Baugh asked.

"Yeah. I'll bring it up with me. One more thing," the sergeant added.

"What's that?"

"Phillips said Woods has a sort of hideaway, an apartment or something, over a garage."

Elimination fingerprints of everyone who had handled any evidence—victims, investigators, criminalists, witnesses—were sent to Sam Erwin in Sacramento Wednesday, along with the latent fingerprints taken from the moving van by the crime lab.

Baugh called San Mateo County sheriff John McDonald and told him Bass would be arriving shortly with the communications trailer, and that he expected the search warrant to be ready by early evening.

"Thank God," the sheriff said. "The press is all over me. What should I tell them?"

"Nothing," Baugh said.

174

Chapter 22

Marcia Baugh was ticked off. Her husband had called earlier in the day to say he would be home for dinner for the first time since the investigation started. He had called back repeatedly, moving up the time he would get there. She sighed and went into the kitchen when he pulled into the driveway at 4:30 P.M.

"It's going to be a long night," he told her when he walked in.

"Would you like a drink?"

"Maybe a little glass of wine. I want to be on my toes. The office will call as soon as Volpe and Meehan are on the home stretch with the warrant."

Baugh was keyed up, intuitively convinced there soon would be a break in the case. Systematically, almost as a rookie would, he checked over the equipment in his unmarked car: shotgun, flashlight, tape recorder, notebook. Marcia noticed he was humming to himself as he checked his Smith and Wesson. Volpe called a few minutes before 6:00 P.M.

"We'll be ready by eight thirty," the lieutenant said. "Jack Meehan doesn't think we can get a warrant for the Schoenfeld place, even with Jim's handwriting on those phony auto registrations."

"Keep trying," Baugh said.

He hung up the telephone, strode quickly out to the car, kissed Marcia in the driveway, got in, and backed into the street.

"You can't take the cat," she wailed suddenly. "You can't take the cat." He slammed on the brakes and looked in the back seat. Tina, the family's slightly overweight half-breed Siamese, was languishing on the cushion. She obviously had climbed in while the door was open to lie in the sun. He shoved the purring animal at his wife.

"On a normal day you couldn't force that thing into this car in a box," he said. "Maybe I ought to put a leash on her and take her to the office and let her compete with the canine units, sniffing out dope."

"Nice puss," Marcia crooned as her husband's tires squealed around the corner.

Baugh stopped by the substation and picked up Bobbie Alvarez, a dispatcher who would keep the running log Theresa Schwarz had started that morning. When they arrived at the county government center in Redwood City, Bass told him all the telephones and radios in the mobile center were operational. Baugh discovered that Sheriff McDonald had set up a press conference for himself and Houchins. The Alameda County sheriff delivered himself of a brief invective on the subject of press interference, and left the briefing without answering any questions.

In the trailer Baugh talked on the radio to Volpe, who was in a speeding patrol car on the San Mateo Bridge, on his way to see Municipal Judge Wilbur R. Johnson in Atherton. Ironically, his house was only a few hundred yards from the Schoenfeld home on the same street. "I don't have a warrant for the Schoenfeld house," Volpe advised. "Jack said we still don't have enough to make it fly."

Baugh was disappointed. "Ten-four. Let's not push it. If we don't have enough we soon will." He radioed the cars in Atherton to cancel the stakeout. "It wasn't doing a hell of a lot of good anyway," he told Houchins.

The sheriff said that about twenty-five reporters would accompany them to the estate. Marilyn Baker of KPIX-TV in San Francisco had suggested she go in alone as a pool reporter, he added. Baugh laughed.

"How did that go over?" he asked.

"The others told her she could go pool herself."

McDonald had arranged for deputies and detectives from his department to handle perimeter security at the estate, and to provide a backup force in case of trouble, although Baugh didn't expect any. Some of the San Mateo officers thought it would be wiser to start the search in the morning, when the light would be better.

"We'll go ahead," Baugh said. "We've got forty-five people committed to this damn thing now. If we don't find anything right away we can keep a few people on the grounds, then bring the rest back in the morning. If it takes five days, it takes five days."

Sheriff Bates arrived from Madera, and he joined Baugh, Houchins, McDonald, and FBI Agent-in-Charge Charles Bates at the Woods home on Alpine Road. Before they went to the door Baugh took the FBI chief, who had brought a squad of agents with him, aside.

"I'm afraid it's going to take us a long time to pay back all the favors we're going to owe you people when this is all over, Charlie," he said.

"We try to do the right thing," Bates drawled.

McDonald rang the doorbell at 10:35 P.M. "We've sort of been expecting you," Woods said. Volpe and Baugh huddled on the sidelines as the three sheriffs and Bates served the warrant. "As soon as they leave, I'm headed for the Los Trancos side," Baugh said.

Woods was extremely cooperative and polite. Baugh liked him immediately.

"We'll want to go through your home, sir, but the main thrust of the search will be aimed at the place where Fred lives over on Los Trancos Road," Baugh told him.

"I'm sure Chip isn't there," Woods said. "We haven't seen him since last Friday."

"Chip?"

"That's Fred's nickname."

"We didn't really expect that he would be there," Baugh said.

Woods was particularly concerned about his elderly mother, and said he hoped there was some way to prevent disturbing or alarming her.

"We anticipated that, Mr. Woods. She won't see any uniformed or armed people. The only person who will visit her house will be one of our women detectives," Baugh said.

Accompanied by a procession of reporters, Woods, Baugh, and Volpe and the others drove to the intersection of Alpine and Los Trancos roads, turned, and entered the driveway. They were met by Ed Woods, whose home was off Los Trancos Road. Sergeant Duane Gull told him they would have to search his house. While Woods accompanied Sergeant Nicki Lee into his mother's home, Baugh sent a group of detectives to the apartment over the garage. Another team started combing through the trees and the derelict vehicles scattered among them. Baugh was rejoined by the senior Fred Woods, who had the family lawyer, Yanowitz, with him. They were standing at the base of the stairs on the outside of the garage. Sergeant Dale Chambers began to yell.

"Son of a bitch, we've got it. Yahoo."

Baugh glanced quickly at Woods and Yanowitz. "Tell him to shut the hell up," he hissed at Volpe through his teeth.

Upstairs, Chambers was holding a piece of lined, three-hole binder paper he had found in a manila envelope on top of a china hutch.

Handprinted on it in a precise scrawl was a list headed with a single word, "Plan."

Below that it began: "Stop a bus . . ."

Fred waited until 7:30 P.M. that Wednesday night before he telephoned Irene in Mountain View. He had heard his name mentioned on the evening news. They had dug up the trailer and learned that he owned it. If the police started nosing around, it wouldn't be long before they got Jim's and Rick's names. And where was Jim? The television report had not carried Fred's picture, but he decided he would move to another hotel.

Irene was home this time. She burst into tears when she heard his voice.

"Now, simmer down, honey," he said. "I'm okay. I want you to do me a favor."

"What's that?" she asked.

"I want you to go over to Jim's house and see if his car's there. Don't call, or anything, just drive by and look for the Chrysler."

"Why?" she asked. "Aren't you and Jim together?"

Fred became suddenly suspicious. What if they had tapped her phone? he thought. "Something funny is going on here," he said abruptly.

"But, honey . . ."

"I'm not paying for this call," he said, and slammed down the receiver. He walked rapidly away from the telephone box.

On Wednesday the doorbell had rung, and Rick answered it. A reporter said the sheriff's office was staking out that address, and asked if Rick knew why. Rick expressed surprise, and told the newsman he should ask the deputies.

The time for decision was past. Convinced that he might be killed by the police if he tried to flee, Rick told his father he would give himself up. Dr. Schoenfeld agreed to call an attorney, Edward Merrill, and make the arrangements. "We can trust him," he said. "He'll do whatever he can."

At 3:30 A.M. Thursday, Baugh departed the Woods estate with most of his men, leaving five detectives under the command of Duane Gull to continue searching through the night as San Mateo County deputies patrolled the boundaries of the property. He and Volpe could hardly believe what had been uncovered in the first hours.

"They left us a road map," Volpe said.

"Except to where they are now," Baugh reminded him.

They had not known what to expect when they went to The Hawthornes, but certainly not what they found.

The main house on Alpine Road occupied by the gravel company owner and his wife was relatively modest, decorated with

<Plan

~~Stop~~

Stop a bus   (must be according to plan + must be fast)
transfer the occupants   (hope for best)
Put occupants to sleep   (hope for best)
Take occupants to hide-out   (hope for best)
Lock them in   (safeguard)

What's wrong
Passers by, uncooperative, non cooperative
sight of occurrence
overload + traction problem, non-cooperation
dangerous, inflamible
CHP thizard
Suffocation, water, food, cold

<Ransome
Take clothes and leave in suitcases   (hope + safeguard)
Police find clothes & instructions   (safe guard)
Police follows instructions with certain precautions   (do best)
<Occupants return unharmed   (Hope for som)
<Investigation
Police backtrack
     Police know → Moving Van Used
          → Wire fencing used
          → welder used
          → Dodge Vans used & color & license no.
          → approx size, voice, age of captors
          → tire prints
          → Cadillac & description of buyer
          → Light from Car Palace
          → Steel Plate with dirt
          → Note
          → Examination of suitcases
          → Guns used
          →
          →
          →

sights wrong person finds
foot prints
dangerous, police policies unknown, sight, offense, deals, sight, CHP,

Don't leave cool
burn
-
-
dispose of Vans
keep cool
dispose of tires
keep cool wipe
wipe
treat
caution
wipe, caution
dispose of & shells

"Plan" referred to on page 198

You're bus has been kidnapped
Put 2½ Million dollars in each of the suitcases, total 5 Million
Use old bills
Have ready at the Oakland Police station
Further instructions pending until ~~~~~~ 10:05 ~~AM~~ PM Sunday
We are ~~~~~~ Beelsabub

10:05 PM Sunday
   Take suitcases to Oakland airport Int'l
Have CHP plane pickup and transfer same
at ≈ 1000' Above ground level to Santa Cruz direct then
follow Hwy-17 back to Oak Int'l.
Speed should be ≈ 120 MPH est Ground speed
~~Drop suitcases~~ Rest of message in 5 min
~~~~~~ (call Fred at other phone)
   Fred calls and delivers final message : Watch for lights, red, green,
blue, Red, Green, Blue, White, then drop ~~and run~~, return to Oak Int'l
End message.

Ransom message referred to on page 199

Schedule

5 weeks   30 days   Dead line 30 Days

Left to do

Need first →   Pass ports   2 weeks
To get Passports   Drivers licenses   6 weeks
                   Vans   prep   4 Days
                   Livermore Prep 1 Day
                   Disguises 1 Day
                   Research ~~days~~   5 more realistic
                   Practice 2 Days
                   Contingency ~~5 Days~~   15
                   Prep Escape 2 Days

"Schedule" referred to on page 199.

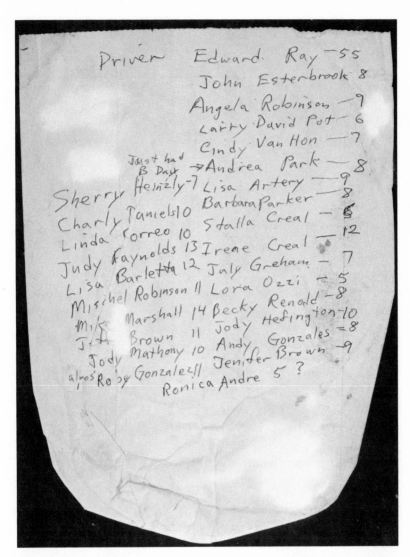

List of names and ages of victims written by kidnappers on back of Jack-in-the-Box bag

Left on R.D. 15
Step 1 girl
Left 20½

Step 2
right 14
right 21
Left 15
Step 2
Left 21½
Right or right
Step
Left to end turned around Left on 22 th

right turn 16 ¼
Step.
R turn 22 Bus ½ Dell
Made U turn
Step 2
right turn 16
Step
Step
Made U turn
Left 18
Step

DectA Ave
L. B.

615

List referred to on page 212

± 3   13 TO
       19   LEFT

N.G.   STOPS
        AT.
        SMO.

_____

SURANY

CREW

WHITE VAN

30 MPH TOP
     35

22 + 11   NO STOP
     BOTT NO H.

                    √S

22 + 12 STOP HS

13 + 22 ✓

RIGHT in 22½

RIGHT ROBERTS LEFT 22
                    NO H
   RIGHT ON 14
      THEN LEFT
                    r
ABOUT   Hr H.
  30

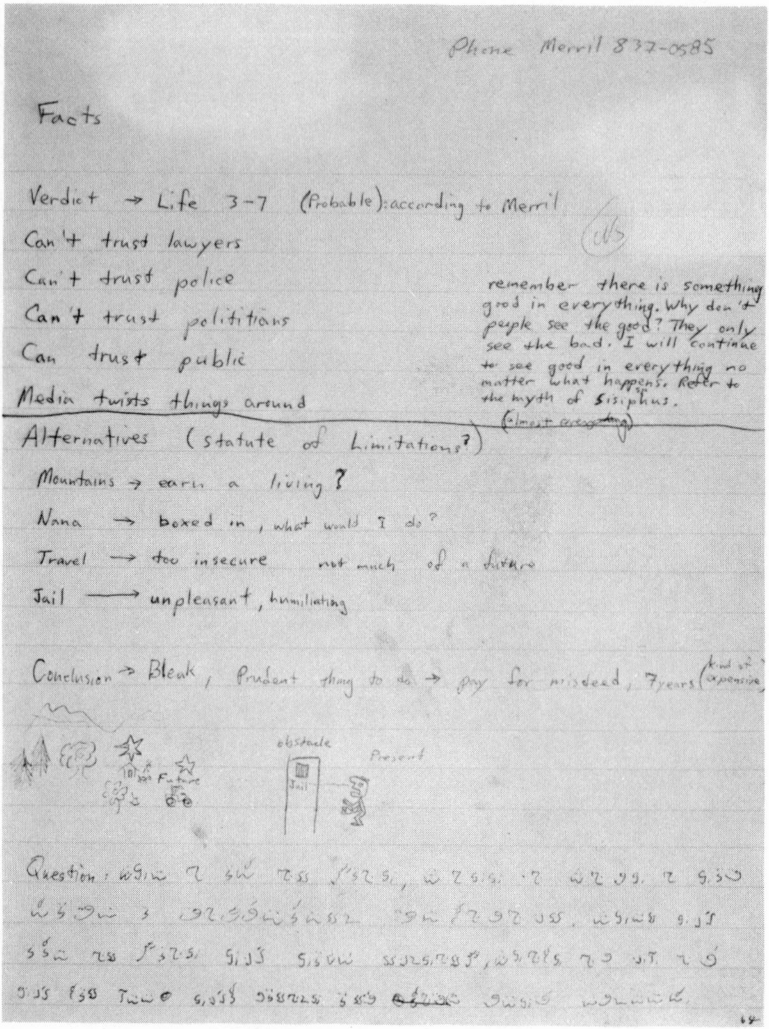

Phone Merril 837-0585

Facts

Verdict → Life 3-7 (Probable): according to Merril

Can't trust lawyers

Can't trust police

Can't trust politicians

Can trust public

Media twists things around

remember there is something good in everything. Why don't people see the good? They only see the bad. I will continue to see good in everything no matter what happens. Refer to the myth of Sisiphus. (almost everything)

Alternatives (statute of Limitations?)

Mountains → earn a living?

Nana → boxed in, what would I do?

Travel → too insecure not much of a future

Jail → unpleasant, humiliating

Conclusion → Bleak, Prudent thing to do → pay for misdeed, 7 years (kind of expensive)

Future
obstacle
Jail
Present

Question:

Papers found in van after James Schoenfeld's arrest. Written before he was caught, they reflect his thoughts on surrender.

I can live with myself because I know that I would not
have hurt anybody permanently, or bodily.
"Turn yourself in, its the only respectable thing to do!"
  Can turning oneself in be respectable when to commit a crime in
itself shows disrespect for the law, and inturn by deffinition under
these circumstances one cannot be respectable.
  Figuring

Basket weaving Job   400 mo.

Apt/mo   175

Food/mo   100

Tax/mo   100 → get most of buck   fugetives any more,
                    375   but not till end   they become prisoners.
misc/mo   25   of year. Fugitives
                    400   don't get refunds
                          or else they will
                          get caught and
                          then they aren't

  Trouble is, you don't want to put down roots or build an estate because
at any time it could all be taken away. The big Q could take you away
at any time, up to 7 years from the ███ time a warrant was put out.

See it from laws view point

A Crime was committed → criminals should be punished by imprisonment.

The Crime was big → punishment should be big

No if, ands, or buts

The Crime should not be copied therefore those responsible should be made
examples to those with similar ideas.

  Correct Attitude but I hope they take into effect that we will
never do a dishonest thing again and that the initial verdict
of life would sufice as a deterant. Perspective criminals will
expect to get life (they may not rate the 3-7 probation)

24

nautical antiques and relics of California's Gold Rush. Fred still had a bedroom in the house, although he seldom used it. His bedroom in his parents' home still reflected the preoccupations of a teenager and was decorated with things like pennants, decals, and a "liberated" street stop sign. The front door, with its horseshoe knocker, was guarded by a display of wheels—a wagon wheel, a huge gear wheel from a piece of mining equipment, a stone grinding wheel—and the garage and land nearby were littered with scores of elderly vehicles of every kind. There was an antique Rolls-Royce, an ancient fire engine, a broken down Checker cab, bicycles, an old house trailer, another moving van.

It was as if the family were obsessed with wheels.

In a garage near the main house Baugh saw a long black Packard. His secret vice is restoring examples of that extinct line of automobiles. He walked over and quickly identified it as a 1948 sedan, of the senior series with the nine main bearing engine and the cormorant hood ornament.

"Uh, have one of the lab photographers bang a few candids of that," he ordered. "Have the prints isolated for me later."

"You think it figures in the case?" a detective asked.

"No, I think I may try to buy it."

The garage on the other side of the estate was littered with junk, most of it mechanical or related to cars. The upstairs apartment, similarly messy, had bare pine walls.

"If these people are rich, they sure don't live like it," Volpe said.

The envelope Chambers had found contained twenty articles, including a black harlequin mask of the type made famous by the Lone Ranger and a list of the kidnap victims and their ages printed on the side of a Jack-in-the-Box hamburger bag.

"We've got a new suspect, chief," the sergeant said solemnly.

"Yeah, who?"

"Rodney Allen Rippy."

"That's real cute, Dale."

The first piece of paper Chambers took from the envelope, lined with three ring binder holes, was divided into columns headed "Plan" and "What's wrong." It was a blueprint for the kidnapping, accompanied by a list of potential mishaps. In between, in

188

parentheses, were written comments or solutions to the problems.

It was obvious the kidnappers had hoped not to harm the children, and that they would have delivered a ransom demand with the clothes and other personal articles they had taken from the victims—if they had not escaped. Chambers pulled a second piece of paper out of the envelope.

It was a handwritten draft of a ransom note.

The other papers in the envelope included a list of males born between 1944 and 1955, all of whom had died between infancy and the age of twenty-four.

"Well, we know some of the aliases they may be using," Volpe said. "We'd better start checking for driver's licenses, social security cards, and passports."

Charles Bates said he would assign FBI agents to interview county clerks in and around the Bay Area to learn whether duplicate birth certificates had been ordered for any of the names on the list.

The investigators were perplexed by three sheets of paper in the envelope bearing what appeared to be Arabic or Russian Cyrillic writing. They decided to call the foreign languages department at the University of California in Berkeley in the morning for a translation.

On another piece of binder paper was a schedule of things to do in the last month before the kidnapping.

Chambers pulled out a receipt for $900, made out to a Norm Phillips of Oakland, for the purchase of a surplus x-ray machine from the naval supply center in Alameda.

"Now what the hell do you suppose they wanted that for?" he asked.

"Or where it is," Sergeant Gull said, looking around the room.

Gull inventoried the other papers in the envelope: a Bay Area rapid transit district schedule, travel brochures for Mexico and New Zealand, apparently meaningless scraps of paper with notes and numbers on them, a license plate tag, and a plastic syringe.

"Do you think our boy's a junkie?" Baugh asked.

"The neighbors we've talked to say he doesn't even drink beer," Bates said.

Baugh sought out Dick McMullen of the FBI and asked him if the Federal Aviation Agency could plot the drop site for the ransom from the sketchy directions in the note. McMullen took the information and said it would be some time the next day before he could find out.

After the manila envelope had been found, Baugh, anxious to avoid revealing the existence of the evidence over the air, looked for a telephone. He didn't want to use one at the house where he might be overheard by reporters.

He drove to a nearby local pub and had a brief argument with Lloyd Boles, a staff writer for the Oakland *Tribune* he knew well and liked, over the single pay telephone. Baugh won.

As Boles stood a short distance away, trying to look as if he were not straining to hear, Baugh covered his mouth with a cupped hand and spoke to Sergeant Larry Santos and Bobbie Alvarez at the command trailer.

"We'll need a force of sixty or seventy people for tomorrow," he said. "I want them assembled at ETS at seven A.M. for a briefing before we come back here."

"How's it going?" Santos asked.

"Eureka," Baugh said. "We've struck gold."

Chapter 23

After leaving Coeur d'Alene, Jim turned west again in the truck. It was two years older than he was, but at least he could lie down in it and sleep, and he had an acquaintance in Atherton who had just paid $900 for something similar. Maybe I can sell it for a profit, he thought. If I live.

At the little town of Post Falls near the Washington State border, he stopped at the Pay Rite drugstore on the main street. He went inside and browsed in the stationery section, finally selecting a seven-by-ten-inch pencil tablet. He paid fifty-five cents for it at the counter and left.

That night, bedded down in the truck, he resumed his encoded journal:

> I heard on the T.V. that the kids were found. Only one thing to do, i.e. run.
>
> I save swear words for bad situations but all I could think of was oh shit!
>
> I was not surprised but I was bewildered, what will I do next? Answer, collect valuables and go. My trustworthy friend (my Chrysler) and I would have to do it alone.
>
> And boy! If that car didn't carry over a thousand pounds of cargo

with me and Fred. Bald front tires, 99000 on the clock and it went twenty four hours a day at sixty-seventy; without a miss. Darn that's been a good car!!!!!! While driving. I just left my best friend, I feel very depressed.

If I get pulled over by a Smokey I will do nothing to prevent my capture. I am not afraid to go to jail, my major concern is Mom & Dad. That they might feel that they failed with us. They only failed in not being strong enough to force us to get out on our own and settle down.

Thought for the day; I think therefore I am, and I think the world is still beautiful; especially where people haven't ruined it. I still believe most people are good at heart.

As I go to prison I will find a way to make the world a better place.

If I should meet my maker at an untimely time, like the near future, then I hope I should be exemplified so others shouldn't make the same mistake. (Though I hope not to be a martyre [sic]) ask yourself if you could really get along by yourself?

Somebody tell me it's all a dream.

At 7:00 A.M. Thursday, a weary Baugh met Lieutenants Keith Boyer and Lou Santucci at the Eden substation, which is a short drive from his house. He told them what had been found the night before and dispatched them to lead the enlarged search party.

"Have Killian take some daylight color pictures of that Packard, by the way," Baugh said.

"Any particular reason?"

"I'm hoping Mr. Woods will put it up for adoption."

Then he drove home for another hour of sleep.

Before he had left the estate Baugh had a candid conversation with Mr. and Mrs. Woods and Attorney Yanowitz.

"I have to tell you we have sufficient information to arrest your son at this point," Baugh said. "If you know where he is, you should try to talk him into surrendering. We don't want anyone to get hurt."

"We honestly don't know where he is," Woods said. "If we did we would tell you."

"I believe that," Baugh said. "Do you have any ideas where he might hide?"

"No. We do have some other property, though."

Voluntarily, Woods listed a cabin on 380 acres near Columbia in Tuolumne County, another on a 7-acre parcel near Bolinas in Marin County north of San Francisco, an abandoned gold mine in Sierra County near the hamlet of Allegheny (that's where Fred and the Schoenfelds had been visiting when they were arrested), two 40-acre parcels in Nevada (no one in the family knew exactly where, he said), two unimproved lots on Chappaquiddick Island and another near West Tisbury, both in Massachusetts, ancestral home of the Newhalls, his mother's family.

Volpe is going to be busy dictating search warrants, Baugh thought.

The highway patrol agreed to loan the sheriff's office a helicopter and pilot, and early Thursday a detective flew to Sacramento carrying latent prints lifted from the quarry and some of the documents found the night before in Portola Valley. The aircraft set down on the lawn in front of the CII building. Forty-five minutes later Sam Erwin called Baugh.

"You have a make," the analyst said. "James Schoenfeld's prints are all over the plan." Minutes later he called back and said he had found Rick's fingerprints along with his brother's on several pieces of evidence. Then Cooper called from the laboratory.

"James Schoenfeld wrote just about everything in that envelope," he said, "including the plan and the ransom note."

"Ed," Baugh said to Volpe, "get back in the box. We need a warrant for the Schoenfeld home, and this time I don't think we'll have any trouble."

Charles Bates called from the FBI office in San Francisco. A woman who worked in a San Jose real estate office had tipped them that the previous December she had rented space in a warehouse at 1011 Knox Avenue, San Jose, to Fred Woods. He said he wanted it to store and rebuild old vehicles for sale.

"While you're at it, Ed, do us one for San Jose. And it wouldn't hurt to take a look at that cabin in Tuolumne County."

"Maybe you'd like me to do your laundry."

"Thanks, Ed."

Volpe drove down to the courthouse and moved in with Mee-han at the D.A.'s office. By now he could practically recite the affidavits by heart.

By 9:00 A.M. Thursday nearly seventy officers were at work at The Hawthornes. During the day the teams under the command of Boyer and Santucci seized hundreds of pieces of potential evidence. From the glove compartment of a yellow pickup truck garaged at the main house they recovered an oil company road map of California, folded and refolded to the section for the Merced-Chowchilla area. Several guns of old and recent vintage were found, along with full and empty ammunition boxes. They collected more mattresses and pieces of tarp, which would be sent to the crime laboratory for comparison with the pieces of canvas found in the quarry and with the victims' clothing. In the glove compartment of a battered Plymouth parked near Fred's apartment, Deputy Ed Frye found a wallet containing miscellaneous papers bearing James Schoenfeld's name, along with a driver's license in a false identity.

In the same glove compartment Frye found two sheets of paper listing road and avenue numbers and bus stops.

"They shadowed the bus," Frye said. "They must have followed it for days before they decided where to hit it."

Ironically, the Plymouth was a retired San Francisco police cruiser that Woods and Schoenfeld bought at an auction. The papers they used to set down the route of Ray's schoolbus were expired police "hot sheets," columns listing stolen cars, that had been left in the car when it was sold.

Over the garage they found a couple of General Electric citizens' band transceivers. There was a lot of radio equipment scattered around the place.

"You guys are going to be busy for weeks," Baugh told Cooper at the laboratory.

After learning from Bates about the San Jose warehouse, Baugh sent Sergeant Dale Smith and Deputy Kolodzieczak to the address to stake out Unit No. 5, the space rented to Woods, until a search warrant arrived. The plan was for Volpe, as soon as the warrants were typed, to fly from Oakland to the San Jose Municipal Airport, drop off a warrant there, and then fly on to the small airfield at Columbia in Tuolumne County, not far from the Woodses' mountain cabin. Baugh had sent a search crew headed by Sergeant Al Poerink in patrol cars to Columbia to wait for the plane.

Smith and Kolo found the warehouse and parked across the street. It was a modern, two-story building housing a number of commercial and industrial tenants. Units No. 1 and No. 2 bore a sign for a company called Lifetime Plastics.

"Let's go talk to the neighbors while we're waiting," Smith suggested.

Moises Robledo, who operated Lifetime Plastics, told the two detectives he had seen three men in their twenties working in Unit No. 5 often. He remembered seeing a couple of black navy panel trucks a couple of months earlier, and said he believed they worked on cars inside the garage. He couldn't be sure because the three always pulled down the big overhead door when they went to work. Their schedule was irregular. He wasn't positive, he said, but he thought they might have expanded their operation into Unit No. 6. Once when the door was open he had seen that a partition had recently been built between the two spaces.

About 6:30 P.M. John Pedersen, an investigator with the Santa Clara County District Attorney's Office, arrived with the warrant for Unit No. 5, Smith, Kolo, and Pedersen banged heavily on the door. "We're from the Alameda County Sheriff's Department," Smith yelled. "We have a search warrant. Open up."

They waited for several minutes. Then, each with one hand on his gun, they manipulated the lock and rolled up the door.

Immediately in front of them was a dark-green van. Parked to the left of it was a white van, license 1C91414. Next to it was a third van painted a brown gold. Smith gazed around.

"Jesus," he said. "It's all here."

Thursday, Fred moved to the Almer Hotel on West Cordova Street, just around the corner from the St. Francis and directly

195

across from the train station. The newspapers had his name, but still no picture. That night on the news he heard about the raid at his parents' estate, and that the authorities were searching for him and the Schoenfeld brothers "for questioning." It had been five days since he left Jim in Reno and he still hadn't arrived. It looked as if he would have to make it on his own, and he knew it would be years before he could go home safely. He had better start shepherding his resources and trying to find a job, he thought.

At the Almer he booked room 120. It was smaller than his previous accommodation, but it had a two-burner hot plate and a small refrigerator. There were no chairs, just a bed. The rent was $30 a week. He paid in advance and asked the manager, Omer Lumden, if he had any odd jobs available. Lumden said no, but referred him to a hotel nearby where he thought the management might need casual help.

"He seemed like a big dunce of a kid," Lumden said later. "He dressed like a cowboy and grinned all the time."

"This search is going to take monumental manpower, I'm afraid," Smith told Baugh on the phone from San Jose. "The place is just packed with stuff. All three vans are in there. And it looks as if the suspects rented the garage next door, too."

"We'll have to get a search warrant for Unit Number Six," Baugh said.

"Pedersen is already on it," the sergeant said. "As soon as we saw what we had, he went back to the D.A.'s office here. He'll swear out a warrant based on Volpe's affidavit, the information we got from Robledo, and what we saw when we opened the door.

"By the way," Smith continued, "there might be a loft, or some kind of concealed living quarters upstairs over Unit Number Five. Only the entrance seems to be a stairway leading up from Unit Number Six."

"You think those yo-yos might be holed up there?"

"Could be. We got it secured as best we can, but it's sort of hard for the two of us to yell, 'Come on out, you bastards, we have you

196

surrounded.' Pedersen called the San Jose cops, and they ought to be here in a couple minutes."

"We'll send some more men from here," Baugh said, "and we'll have the lab send the criminalists down. Keep me posted."

"You'll be the first to know."

Within half an hour Sergeants Iver Edwall, Don Cordes, and Dave Bricknell arrived at the warehouse from Alameda County, along with a sergeant and two uniformed officers from San Jose. They took up positions at points where they could cover all the exits from both garages and settled down to wait for the second warrant. Just before 10:00 P.M. they were joined by Cooper, Sprague, and James Stam from the laboratory.

"Even if they aren't in there, they could have booby-trapped it," Kolo said. "Judging from some of the stuff we found in Portola Valley, these lads are fair mechanical hands."

"Let's get a dog." Smith radioed for the sheriff's canine unit. About 11:00 P.M. Deputy Jim Pelham arrived with a German shepherd. The animal lay down and napped as they continued to wait.

At 11:45 P.M. Pedersen returned with the additional warrant. The officers drew their guns, and Cordes hammered on the door of Unit No. 6.

"This is the Alameda County Sheriff's Department," he announced loudly. "We have a search warrant. Open the door." There was no response. He repeated the demand twice.

"Okay, let's hit it," Smith said.

In addition to the main roll-up door similar to the one on Unit No. 5, Unit No. 6 had two regular-sized hinged doors. When the officers tried to force one they found it barricaded with furniture. They kicked open the second door and jumped aside. "Come out with your hands up," Cordes ordered. After a few more minutes Smith motioned to Pelham. The shepherd darted noiselessly through the door, and they could hear him sniffing around inside. He came back out to Pelham wagging his tail.

Cordes and Smith, accompanied by two San Jose policemen, ducked through the door one at a time. Moving quickly they swept the interior with flashlights, but saw no one. The four went back

197

outside and waited while Pelham went in with his dog and searched the ground floor for explosives. He came back out. "It's negative," the deputy said.

Smith and the others reentered the garage and found the lights.

"Now, what the hell is that?" Cordes asked. He was looking at a 1965 Cadillac Fleetwood. It was sprayed completely with dull black primer—even the chrome and the rear windows and the hubcaps. Only the windshield and rear window were unpainted. The hood was up and the battery was missing.

"That," Smith replied, "is a very strange Cadillac. That's what that is."

Sprague groaned softly as he looked around the room. The volume of potential evidence they would have to examine was staggering.

Immediately to the left of the main door were stacks of old furniture. The floor was littered with paint cans and unused two-by-fours similar to those found in the buried moving van and at the Woods estate. He saw several piles of clothing, and a bag that appeared to contain children's clothes. There were mattresses, tarps, more junk furniture, more paint cans, jars of peanut butter and jelly, and loaves of bread. From under the Cadillac an officer pulled a Remington pump shotgun.

They climbed the rough-hewn staircase into a makeshift mezzanine that had been constructed over both garages. The one above Unit No. 5 contained dozens of boxes, a stereo console, a television set, a couch, and a chair. Behind the couch, Smith saw several boxes labeled lighting fixtures. In the middle of the floor stood a green wheelchair.

A catwalk parallel to the stairs connected the two mezzanines. On it were two rolled carpet remnants. Above Unit No. 6 they found empty cardboard boxes with lettering indicating they had contained "water displacing compound" and "lacquer, camouflage black" and "Hunter 12" ventilating fans, "60 cycle, 115 volts." Smith saw two stacks of Edison dictating machines and four large pieces of black electronic equipment. He looked at the serial number plates. They were navy radar scanners.

"What *are* these guys?" he asked of no one in particular.

On the far side of the mezzanine they found forty single-bed mattresses and several headboards. "They must have figured on snatching a whole school," one of the officers said.

Smith returned to the ground floor. The windows in both garages had been reinforced with chain-link fence backed with canvas and mattress covers to block the view from outside. Back in Unit No. 5 the searchers found acetylene and oxygen tanks equipped with gauges, hoses and a torch, and several floodlights.

"We'll take pictures of the interiors of the two places and secure for the night," Cooper said. "We're going to need a lot of people to go through all this."

One of the things they photographed was a certificate of achievement awarded to Darla Daniels for her participation in the summer school 4-H youth program in Madera County.

At 1:00 A.M. Rod Alvarez arrived with four deputies to guard the warehouse overnight while the criminalists went home for a few hours of sleep.

Sergeant Poerink and his men had been waiting for Volpe when Young's plane set down at the airfield near Columbia, a restored Gold Rush village in the Sierra foothills. They were with Sergeant McGettigan, the Tuolumne County detective who had helped question Charles Collier five days earlier.

"Did he ever change his story?" Volpe inquired.

"Nope. Still insists it's God's truth."

"Weird," Volpe said.

Earlier that day McGettigan had surveyed the Woods property in another plane. He said the place had two access roads leading to one fairly large white house, two smaller houses secluded in some trees, and an old house trailer. It all looked pretty rundown. He had seen no signs of life, nor smoke coming from any chimneys.

They drove to the Woods place after stopping in Sonora to have a judge sign Volpe's search warrant. The land and all the buildings on it were deserted. It did not appear as if anyone had been there for several weeks.

"You can't win them all," Poerink said to Volpe as he prepared to fly back to Oakland.

"Well, two out of three ain't bad," Volpe said.

Chapter 24

Earlier Thursday, about the same time Smith and Kolo were setting up their surveillance of the warehouse in San Jose, Sergeant Cervi was working with one of the search teams at the Woods estate. A small slightly built young man with a blond mustache came to 800 Los Trancos Road and asked for Mr. or Mrs. Woods. He said he wanted to know where he could find Fred Woods. Cervi decided he had better talk to him.

The youth identified himself as Craig Hunt, eighteen, the son of a retired business executive and his wife who had recently moved from Los Altos to Carmel. Craig had stayed behind, living in a small hotel in Palo Alto, partly because he had a part-time job working as a mechanic for Fred Woods, helping to restore old vehicles for resale.

"How did you first meet him?" Cervi asked.

"I met Fred through Jim Schoenfeld," Hunt said. "I was gonna buy a diesel tractor off of Jim, which I ended up doing, and he told me his buddy had another one, and he brought me out to Fred's house and showed me his buddy's tractor, and through that I met Fred. Then I was looking for work and Jim Schoenfeld told me that Fred had, uh, you know, work available for me and I could, uh, you know, work for him, and I've been working for him about a year and a half now . . . I worked, you know, maybe three or four days a week, just to keep some money in my pockets."

Hunt told the detective he had planned to use the truck tractor to go into the business of hauling hay in the summer from the farm areas of the Central Valley to the Peninsula, where many of the residents stable riding horses. He was unable to keep up the payments on the $2,000 he had borrowed to buy it from Schoenfeld, however, and it had been repossessed.

"When was the last time you saw Fred?" Cervi asked.

"I really can't swear. I think it was . . . I was out here Thursday and I saw him Thursday evening."

"Last Thursday?"

"Uh-huh."

"The day before the kids were found?"

"I don't know what day they were found on, but it was a Thursday."

"Okay, where did you see him? Here at the house?"

"Down here at work. He usually comes out in the morning and, uh, you know, we talked for a little while."

"What time were you here on Thursday?"

"Probably my usual time, about ten in the morning."

"And how late did you stay?" Cervi asked.

"Just to about three. And he was in and out a couple of times during the day."

"So you last saw him about what time, then?"

"I guess about three, three thirty, somewhere around there, when I left. And I came back Saturday to see if I could get paid, and, uh, he was gone. Then he came back . . . you know, I went . . . I mean I came back Friday too and he wasn't here, and the same . . . up to now I haven't seen him."

"Okay, now wait a minute," Cervi said to the stammering youth. "Let me back up a little bit. You came out here to work Thursday morning about ten?"

"Uh-huh, yeah."

"And he was here?"

"Uh-huh."

"And he was here on and off during the day?"

"Uh-huh."

"And you left about three?"

"Yeah, about three."

"And he was still here then?"

"Yeah, uh-huh."

"Okay," Cervi said. He looked hard at Hunt. I wonder if this kid is telling the truth, he thought.

"I think . . . I think he was up at the house," the boy volunteered. "Now, if they'd of taken Jim's car, you know, he might of been gone earlier, a little bit earlier than that, no later than about one, 'cause he was here when I went up to the store to get something to eat."

"So he could have left anytime then between one and three o'clock on Thursday," Cervi said.

"Uh-huh, unless he was up at the house at that time."

"And you say they could have taken Jim's car," Cervi added. "What kind of car does Jim have?"

"It's about a sixty-three Chrysler. It's beige and four-door."

Hunt told Cervi he had never seen the vans on the Woods place, although Fred had told him never to go into the barn. As far as he knew, reworking and selling surplus vehicles was Woods's sole livelihood. Cervi asked if he was any good at it.

"Some, but he was really lazy, and, you know, he really didn't like to do it. He had me, and I did most of it."

"Was he a drinker?"

"No, uh-uh."

"How about narcotics?"

"Nope . . . Fred's as straight as a board. Both of them seemed to be like that. I've never even seen Jim drink beer."

Hunt said he would be staying at the hotel in Palo Alto a few more weeks, and that his mother had promised to wire him money to live on until he could find another job. He told Cervi he had no idea where Woods and the Schoenfelds might have gone to hide. He could not conceive of them kidnapping anyone. He was sure that all of the cars and trucks that Woods drove regularly were still at The Hawthornes.

202

"Okay, thanks very much, Craig. I appreciate talking to you."

"Okay, I hope this works out."

Cervi watched the youth walk away. "What do you think?" asked a deputy who had listened to the interview.

"He told two different stories. He said Woods was here at three P.M. and then he said he hadn't seen him after one P.M."

"How long does it take to drive to Chowchilla?"

"From here, two and a half, maybe three hours if you obey the speed limit. The busnap went down about four."

"What if the kid's story holds up. Is it good enough for an alibi?"

"It's possible Woods could have made it in time. But I have a feeling it won't hold up anyway."

Thursday afternoon Jensen called Baugh from the D.A.'s office. "I just heard from Ed Merrill," he said. "He said that when we come up with the name, he'll surrender a suspect."

"Suspect singular?"

"Yes."

"Anyone we know?"

"I'm not sure, but I'm betting it's one of the Schoenfeld boys."

Later Baugh heard again from Sam Erwin in Sacramento. He definitely had identified fingerprints of all three principal suspects on pieces of evidence taken from the Woods estate. When he closed the command post and went home at 10:00 P.M., Baugh was certain he knew who had planned the kidnapping and basically how they did it.

Friday morning Jensen called Baugh again. He told him that Merrill had said he would surrender Rick Schoenfeld to the D.A. and the sheriff at 2:30 P.M. Although no arrest warrants had been issued, the Schoenfeld family knew from news reports that both brothers were prime suspects, and that the authorities were closing in. The newspaper stories said they would soon have a warrant to search the Schoenfeld home.

Baugh called Sheriff Bates in Madera and asked him to send Ray, Mike Marshall, and one other child who had been in the

203

white van to the warehouse in San Jose to identify the vehicles. Dick Haugner would draw up warrants charging Woods and the Schoenfelds with twenty-seven counts of kidnapping and sixteen counts of armed robbery and send them to Chowchilla to be signed by the judge there.

Dick McMullen called from the FBI office in Hayward to tell Baugh the FAA had charted the course for the ransom drop from the instructions in the note. It appeared to be an isolated spot in the Santa Cruz mountains.

Baugh sent Sergeants Edwall, Williams, Al Lerche, and Deputy Ratcliffe to the Santa Cruz County Sheriff's Office, where they arranged to fly over the site. Edwall, an experienced pilot who had given up recreational flying after a near accident, climbed warily into the cockpit of a small plane with a Santa Cruz County deputy at the Watsonville airport. As they took off, an engine mount broke loose and the pilot had to make an emergency landing. Pale now, Edwall went back up after the plane was repaired. Near where the FAA had plotted the drop zone he caught sight of a white cross among the trees about two hundred yards from a mountain road west of the Highway 17 summit. He marked it on a map, and they returned to the airport.

"Don't you *ever* send me up in another one of those goddamn things," Edwall told Baugh later.

"Did you find the spot?" the chief asked, grinning.

"Yeah. It doesn't look like that's it, though. We didn't find any lights. He had to hike in from the road. Climb is a better word for it because it's goat country all the way. It definitely is not a likely place to pick up a couple of suitcases loaded with five million bucks. We almost had heart attacks."

"What about the white cross?"

"It was reinforced plastic staked to the ground. It's been there a long time. We think it's a forest service aerial survey marker."

Smith and Kolo returned to the San Jose warehouse a little after 9:00 A.M. Friday with Sergeant Cervi, Deputies Clyde McCreary and Tom Ziegler, and Sprague, Stam, and Richard Schorr from the crime laboratory. While the criminalists began processing the evidence for latent fingerprints, Smith turned his attention to a large, thirty-two-cubic-foot dumpster behind Lifetime Plastics. Moises Robledo told the detective he exclusively rented the big trash container, and that he had given no one permission to use it to dispose of refuse. Nonetheless, Smith wanted to search it, especially after Robledo told him it had not been emptied for two or three weeks. Robledo shrugged and signed a search consent form. Somewhat bemused, he watched as Kolo and McCreary started sifting through the garbage.

On the floor near the stack of two-by-fours in Unit No. 6 Sprague found a newspaper addressed to John B. Schoenfeld in Atherton and a copy of the San Jose *Mercury-News* with a front-page story on the kidnapping.

Right after lunch Ray arrived, having been flown to San Jose from Madera, to look over the vans. He was accompanied by Lee Roy Tatom and a Madera County sheriff's deputy, but the two children Baugh had asked to be sent were not aboard the plane. Apparently no effort had been made to locate them.

At the warehouse Smith handed Ray a pair of plastic gloves and told him not to touch anything in the garages.

"That looks like the white van that stopped us," Ray said. "And the green one looks like the one I was taken in, but it had a rug on the floor. This one don't."

"We found the carpeting out of this van in the other garage," Smith said. Ray looked at the right-hand door of the green van and saw traces of yellow paint.

"That could be where she hit the bus, I guess," he said. Ray walked around the van several times. "This is the closest thing I've ever seen to the vehicles used in the kidnapping," he said. "There's a way to make sure. Sometime during the night, while he was driving around, I fumbled around and tried to unlatch the back doors. I got my fingers up between the two doors, and I could feel a hole, about a one-inch hole. The sheriff down home has had me look at the rear doors of all kinds of panel trucks, but we didn't find any like it."

Smith led him around behind the van. Inside the edge of the

205

right rear door they found the hole. "This is it," Ray said. "This is it for sure."

At 5:00 P.M. the searchers stopped work for dinner. They took Ray along. At the restaurant he asked the investigators in passing if they had found his keys.

"What did they look like?" Smith asked.

"It was just a ring with six keys," Ray replied.

"We haven't found anything like that yet."

"Wait a minute," McCreary said, reaching into his pocket. "I found this key ring in the garbage, but it only has two keys on it." He handed it to Ray. The bus driver examined it.

"Those are mine," he said. "The master lock key is for my tool box, and the International Harvester key is to the bus."

Smith laughed. "Well, what do you know," he said. "Mr. Robledo's going to be pissed when he finds out those guys were throwing their trash in his dumpster."

Late Friday afternoon Attorney Merrill met Jensen and Sheriff Houchins at the courthouse. He had Rick Schoenfeld with him. The young man was escorted quickly to the jail on the tenth floor, where he was met by Hal Walker, chief of the sheriff's headquarters division. Walker read the legal admonishment with Merrill present.

"Do you understand each of these rights I have explained to you?" Walker asked.

"Yes."

"Having these rights in mind, do you wish to make a statement now?" Schoenfeld, obviously agitated and nervous, looked at Merrill, who shook his head slightly.

"No, I do not want to make a statement at this time," he said.

At the command post at the Eden substation, Baugh drew a line through the name Richard Allen Schoenfeld on the blackboard list of suspects. He picked up the public address microphone and announced: "Ladies and gentlemen, the score is now Lions one, Christians zero."

"All riiiight," a deputy said, as a ripple of applause went through the building.

At 8:00 P.M. Friday, Volpe and a force of detectives led by Sergeants Santos and Tim Splan arrived at the Schoenfeld home with a search warrant. The distraught parents accepted service and showed the officers into Jim's bedroom. They tagged, photographed, and seized a wealth of evidence.

On top of a filing cabinet they found a notice of transfer for the sale of a trailer to Hugh Phillips in Chowchilla. From a dresser they took a note headed "Go to Livermore." Under the bookshelves the officers found eighteen U.S. Department of the Interior topographical maps of sections of California, from Sacramento in the north to Fresno in the south, and from the Pacific to the foothills of the Sierra. On them virtually all of the rural schools were circled.

The searchers picked out the map for the Chowchilla Quadrangle. Five schools were marked. Two of them, Alamo on Avenue 23 1/2 and Ashview on Avenue 20, were crossed off with the notation "gone." In the margin near where Dairyland School was circled someone had written "possibilities." On Avenue 21 the bridge over Berenda Slough was circled with the words "way into canal—good cover." On Avenue 21 1/2 they found the notation "last chance."

The site of the school, the spot where the bus was stopped, and the dry slough where it was hidden all were encompassed by a larger circle made with a ball-point pen.

"They must have cased damn near every country school in central California before they decided on Dairyland," Volpe told Baugh on the telephone. "This stuff is incredible."

From under the bookshelves the detectives recovered a dozen other maps, most of them for the area of the Sacramento and San Joaquin rivers delta upstream from San Francisco Bay. From a nightstand drawer they took a 7.65mm automatic and some ammunition. On a desk they found a passport issued May 19, 1976, to James Schoenfeld.

"Well, it's a safe bet he's not using his real name," Volpe said.

On top of the dresser Splan found a spiral-bound shorthand notebook. The pages were covered with what appeared to be

Cyrillic characters or code. "What do you make of that?" he asked.

"It looks like some of the papers we picked up at Portola Valley," Volpe said.

"This might be helpful," another detective said. Earlier he had tagged a Russian-to-English alphabet chart.

They moved into Rick's bedroom. On a lower closet shelf rested a brown wooden box containing his personal papers. Among them was the navy's notice of award releasing the three vans along with two hand-drawn maps of the disposal center in Alameda.

On Friday Justice Court Judge Howard Green in Chowchilla signed arrest warrants for Woods and the Schoenfelds. Rick's was served on him at the courthouse jail in Oakland. The other two were broadcast in an all-points bulletin throughout the United States. At 10:00 P.M. Sheriff Bates formally asked federal assistance in capturing the fugitives, on the assumption they had fled California. In Sacramento, U.S. Attorney Dwayne Keyes went before Esther Mix, U.S. Magistrate for the Eastern District of California, and obtained warrants accusing Woods and James Schoenfeld of unlawful flight to avoid prosecution. As had the judge in Chowchilla, she set bail at $1 million each. The FBI alerted all of its field offices.

The teletype warned the two were armed and dangerous.

That day Baugh dictated a commendation to all personnel:

"It may be premature to express thanks before our job is complete, but I feel we have to boast about the acknowledged excellence of our department . . . We did build an excellent case. We identified three suspects, recovered the primary kidnap vehicles, preserved an excellent crime scene, secured excellent physical evidence (our own people even pulled the trailer out of the hole), and we did it in seven days. On the eighth day of the investigation we chased one suspect into our jail.

"I just want to say thanks for a super job, and let you know your efforts are appreciated by all concerned.

208

"I want you all to know that the press, in general, gave me a pain in the ass too."

It should be noted that, on the part of the reporters, the feeling was mutual.

Late Friday night, Sheriff Houchins found Baugh and Volpe at the substation.

"I'm ordering you two home for the weekend," he said. "Walker can take over the command post tomorrow and Sunday. You brief him."

"Cooper and Sprague and those folks could use a little time off, too," added Baugh.

"We'll rotate the lab staff over the weekend so everybody can get at least a day," the sheriff said.

"What about the search warrant for the Woods mine in Sierra County?" Volpe asked.

"I've already arranged with Dean Hess to go up there with him. I'll enforce the warrant myself. I could use a day in the country."

Baugh talked with Walker, and told him about the continuing searches under way at San Jose and Portola Valley. The headquarters division chief promised he would spend Saturday reading and trying to arrange logically the scores of investigative reports that already had been dictated.

"You're a sweetheart, Hal," Baugh said.

"I know."

As they walked out to the parking lot, Baugh and Volpe silently shook hands. "You got any scotch at your house?" the lieutenant asked.

"If we don't, I know a place that delivers."

Part
Five

Chapter 25

On Saturday Jim and Fred both learned from the newspapers that Rick had surrendered, and that they were wanted for kidnapping, armed robbery, and unlawful flight. The bail was set at $1 million. Woods was impressed by the figure. Schoenfeld turned for home. He was sapped. There was no question of going to Canada now. He would give himself up.

"Question: While I am in jail will I wish I had made a different decision?" he wrote in his journal. "When you are in jail you have nothing which is ok if you can keep your sanity and self respect."

Later he would write a grudging tribute to those who had found him out:

"I am very proud of the F.B.I. They do what they have to and they seem to be staying within the law and not disregard people's rights, like I imagine the KGB and Gestapo do."

Sunday Woods decided to go for another walk in Stanley Park to sort out his future. He had enough money to carry him for a few weeks, but he would have to get a job, maybe up country where he wasn't so famous. His picture was in all the newspapers, but it wasn't very good and nobody recognized him.

Near the park entrance he saw a girl, about nineteen, walking by herself. Unexpectedly, he felt lonely.

"Do you mind if I walk along with you?" he asked. The young woman appraised him for a moment.

"Well . . . no, I guess not," she said.

"What's your name?" he asked, after they had walked awhile.

"Valeria Janzen," she answered. "What's yours?"

"Ralph."

"Ralph what?"

"Just Ralph."

They walked and talked for three hours. He told her he had been in Vancouver for about a week and a half, and that he planned to stay until the middle of September if he could find a job and get a car. Eventually, he said, he hoped to return to Canada permanently.

Fred told Valeria he was an only child whose father had run away from his mother when he was six. He said his mother was thinking about moving from Reno to California. He had left Reno himself because the girl with whom he had been living had decided not to marry him. It was all very tragic. About 4:00 P.M. they found themselves standing in front of the Almer Hotel. Fred invited the girl up to his room.

On the second floor, as Woods unlocked the door, Valeria noticed the ladies' bathroom next door and excused herself for a minute. Once inside his room they sat on the bed, since there was no other furniture. He put his arm around her and began to fumble with her clothes. She tried to push him away, but he was insistent. She continued to resist, and abruptly he stopped and apologized. They talked until about 7:30 P.M., and then went out for a snack. They would see one another a few more times.

On that same Sunday Jim Schoenfeld arrived back in the Bay Area. He knew that his parents' home probably was being watched and that their telephone might be tapped. He had very little money, but he didn't want to involve any of his friends in his dilemma. He was convinced the police might shoot him if they came upon him on the street. He had to think. He drove across the Santa Cruz mountains to Half Moon Bay on the coast south of San Francisco, turned south and camped near San Gregorio beach.

Several strangers talked to him there. Nobody recognized him from his picture in the newspapers.

In Vancouver, Woods sat in his room most of the day Monday and wrote letters. Expressing himself orally was difficult, in writing it was agony.

He needed a way to get mail to his parents and friends without risking interception by the FBI. He didn't know how those things worked, but he was sure the FBI was reading the letters received at The Hawthornes.

His first message was for Steven Battaini, a classmate at Woodside High School with whom he had maintained a somewhat indifferent friendship. His spelling, syntax, and punctuation were primitive.

> Steve, old man, did I spell your name right? Guess who this is, It's your old friend! I talked to you about a month ago You know we wrecked a VW, and blamed it on Gemco Parking Lot! Now you know who this is. Don't tell anybody about this letter I mean anybody! I don't want to get you involed [*sic*] in anything. But I need an inside man badly. If your mad for what we did and don't want to stay my friend I'll understand! But, I could really use some inside info! I'm trusting you as a friend not to tell anybody where this letter came from or my address. Please dont fink out on me and turn me in. Also burn the envelope right now before your foreget [*sic*]. If anybody sees that you & I could get screwed. Don't put my name on anything you send me.
>
> | Just put | Mr. R.L. Snider |
> | (what your zip | General Delivery |
> | code) | V6B 3P7 |
> | | Vancouver |
> | | British Columbia, Canada |
>
> I can get mail in that name! Your the only person in the US that knows where I am Please keep it that way! What I mainly need is to get a letter to my folks All you need to do is put this letter that says Ma & Pa on it. Not this thing I'm writing on! Put there deal

in an envolpe [*sic*] address it & stamp and mail to them from Menlo Park or whatever. Also dont have your fingerprints on my paper or the envolpe [*sic*] wipe off everything before yout mail it. To protect you. What ever you do dont call or write to my folks That will get you and your house staked out fast. Well thats about it old man, write as soon as you can tell me a little whats going on Like how long the team is for, etc. Also write me soon I want to see if you got this letter. Also see if this letter has been preopened. Well I'm waiting to hear from you, <u>Steve Burn</u> this note now Write down the name & address Put on it "An Old Friend." or something and burn this—Good luck to you! F.

In the second letter, addressed to "Ma & Pa," Woods pleaded haltingly with his parents not to hate him for what he had done, and said that he still loved them. He said that "everybody has to try it once," and that everything had worked out until the children escaped, and that he would not make the same mistakes again. The letter was directed primarily at his mother, and gave specific instructions for the sale of some of his possessions, including the x-ray machine. He asked them to keep a 1957 Chevrolet that he wanted to use when he returned some day.

He said that he would not be taken alive, that if the police came, all they would find was a dead body.

Woods sealed the letter to his parents, folded it inside the note to Battaini, put both of them in an envelope, addressed it, and walked to the post office. Jim was not there again. When he returned to the hotel he went up to his room and immediately began writing three more letters. The first was for Battaini:

Steve. This is an important letter. Can you please get this inside part to my girlfriend I don't want her to know where I am. I trust her but I don't want her to know, so she can say that, and not be a lie. But I sure am trusting you old friend! I'll pay you some day for all of your time and gas used, but I really need the help! My girl friend name is Irene Bolzowski. She about 5'3" and fat. Long dirty blond hair. She works in Wells Fargo Bank on El Camino in South Palo Alto, do you know where that is. I'm sure that her house is staked out, so could you go to the bank and give this note to her. The bank is on the corner of California Ave. & El Camino. The entrance is on Calif. Ave. She does real estate loans so you walk into the bank go way to the rear on your left. The window should say statements our [*sic*] something! Who evers at the window just ask for Irene Bolzowski. If you can't get it right that's OK, they'll know who it is. When she comes just hand it to her & leave. She doent know who you are and I want to keep it that way. What ever happens I don't want to get you into trouble. Also can you come back to see her, also get a letter from her in 3 days after you go the first time no more than 3 no less. Give her time to get some stuff together for me. Well I got to get this letter to you, so I hope alls going well with you and hope you didn't lose my address. If you did, if I haven't hear from you in a week, I'll write you again with the address. I'm writing this just after I wrote the last one.

Good luck to you old man.

P.S. Write me back. I want to see if you got this. Burn this now.

The second letter was for Irene:

Dear Honey, I love & miss you so much! I hope you still love me. The person that give you this is our contac [*sic*] from now on, he'll come back in three days so get a letter ready for me. What's going on down there? Have you hear from my parents and are you staked out? Can you please take this inside letter to Dave's house, even tonight if he isn't there let his mom read it and take. Dave owes me some money from something he sold. A "lincoln letter" it should have sold for $600 so I get $300. Tell his mom to give the money to you. If she doesn't have it, tell her to get in touch with Dave and get it soon! Also his brother Bob owes me $125 which his mom can get fast. If you know where I am don't tell them at all! I don't trust him! If she, Dave's mom, can't get the money in three days, tell the contac to phone you at the bank every 3 days or so. Give him the phone #. If you can't get the money can you sent 1/2 of it in blank travel checks in 50's That way I could put my name on it. For the records could you just put a fake name and address or your name so if they get lost in the mail. Sent 1/2 If I get that then I'll write for the rest! Can you get me 70 Chevy wagon from my parents? I want you to have that car. I hope the Ford still runs. I want to see what happens to Rick before I come back! This could be the death penalty. Then I am not coming back. I love you, and I need money bad so get in touch with Dave. Bye bye sweetheart.

Woods's reference to a "lincoln letter" in his message to Irene concerned a historic document passed down to him through the family which he had asked David Boston to sell for him through an autograph dealer.

The third note was for Boston:

Dave, if you want to make real by money, ever on a movie, write it about our deal! I think it would make a damn good movie of the week if not a feature. Its big, real big, and a hot item, everybody wants to know about it. You'll have something no body else could have, inside info. But keep that quiet, or you will not get anything. I will tell you everything that happen up to it and to where it ended and I'll tell you how it should have gone up to the end. My ending is not exciting enough, so you might have to kill some people or something! If you do make it into a film All I want is a % of it, you make it up I don't care how much but be fare.! I'm glad you were not in on it now, it was a good plan. That night I wanted to put more weight on the cover but Rick said, "Oh no, they can't lift that." Wait till I see him again! They'll hang him for sure anyhow! Oh well, from now on all the money you get from Sobathys or if you get any money from Pill give the money to Irene I trust her to keep it for me until someday, give her the money from the Lincoln Letter now, and if you can get my $125 that Bob owes me too. He's got my V.T.R. Tell him if he wants to keep and use it its OK with me, I don't need it right now. I do need cash! He has a gun of mine to If you want to keep it its OK with me, its a black powder It looks really good. If you need to write to me, give the letter to Irene, she doesn't know where I'm either but by a chain she can get it to me. I hope your not staked out. Give Irene the cash fast! If you want to know about the story let me know.

/s/ Fred.

Chapter 26

On the beach at San Gregorio, Jim had just about run out of food. He had read the name of Rick's attorney in the newspapers, and decided to call him Tuesday evening. Instead he reached Ed Merrill's answering service. He asked to be connected with the lawyer at home, but the service operator refused.

"If you'll leave a number, I'll have him call you in the morning," she said officiously. "Who should I say called?"

"Never mind," Jim said, hanging up.

He drove to the Portola Valley home of Irene Lile, Eileen Kelty's cousin, and rang the doorbell about 8:00 P.M. Mrs. Lile, who opened the door, gazed at her visitor. From the living room Shannon Lile saw who was at the door.

"Come in," he called.

"I suppose you know I'm in trouble," Jim said.

"Yes, we do."

"I've come back to turn myself in. I've been hiding in the hills for the last couple of days and haven't had a chance to clean up. I was wondering if you might let me take a shower."

"Sure. Would you like us to wash your clothes?"

219

"Thanks. That would be great." He went into a bathroom and handed his pants and shirt out to Shannon Lile.

"What about the stuff in the pockets?" Lile asked.

Jim chuckled. "Empty them out. There isn't anything bad in them, like a gun." Lile found only a wristwatch and a ring of keys.

While Jim was bathing the Liles had an urgent conversation in the kitchen. Should they call the police? He had said he was going to turn himself in. In the end they decided to invite him to stay the night.

The three of them stayed up after dinner and talked until midnight, avoiding the subject of the kidnapping.

"I'll call your dad if you want," Lile offered.

"No, they might trace the call, and you could get in trouble for having me here. I'll call the lawyer again in the morning from a phone booth, if you'll lend me the change."

Wednesday afternoon, Steve Battaini telephoned his boss and friend Bob Glynn, the manager of the Builders Emporium in Redwood City, where Battaini worked as a carpenter. He was agitated, and said he needed some advice. Glynn told him to come over to the store. When he got there, Battaini showed the manager the first letter from Woods. It had just been delivered. He wanted to call the FBI, but he didn't want to get his name in the newspapers.

Glynn telephoned the FBI field office in San Francisco. An agent told him to take Battaini and the letter to Resident Agent Ron Wolfe in San Mateo. At Wolfe's office Battaini turned over Woods's letter and described the contents of the enclosure addressed to his parents, which he had opened and read before he realized it was not for him.

In the Seattle office of the FBI, an agent picked up the telephone and dialed the area code for Vancouver.

"Well, the Mounties always get their man," Volpe observed after FBI Special Agent-in-Charge Charles Bates called Baugh in Oakland and brought him up to date on Woods's probable whereabouts. "Say, do they still use horses and dogs?"

"Oh, I understand they have cars and everything now," Baugh laughed. "I have a feeling we're going to get to meet young Fred any day now."

Earlier that Wednesday, about 8:00 A.M., Jim said good-bye to the Liles. Two hours later Lile called Dr. Schoenfeld and told him his son had spent the night at their house. The father gave Merrill's telephone number to Lile, in case Jim came back again.

When Jim finally reached Merrill, the attorney told him to come with his father to his office at 8:00 A.M. the next morning, Thursday, July 29. They would all go to the courthouse in Oakland, where Jim would surrender. Merrill assured Schoenfeld he was doing the right thing and warned him against saying anything to the police if he were caught in the meantime.

Jim called his father, and they arranged to meet at 7:00 A.M. the next day behind the Union 76 service station at the Woodside Plaza shopping center in Redwood City.

As he stepped from the telephone booth, a passerby recognized him. The bystander watched him get into the old green truck and drive away. Minutes later the person called the FBI with an anonymous tip.

At 8:45 P.M. FBI agent Jim Watters went to the Schoenfeld house in Atherton. Mrs. Schoenfeld said her husband was not at home, but invited him in. "I really have nothing new to tell you since I saw you last," she told him.

"Mrs. Schoenfeld, have you heard from Jim?" the agent asked.

"No." He thought she appeared to be nervous.

"We know he's on the Peninsula," Watters said. "Every police officer and agent in the area is looking for him now. We know what he's driving, and we have a license number. If you know where he is, please tell us before someone gets hurt."

She steadfastly claimed she had not heard from her son.

Lee Wallis, a fifty-year-old gardener, was on his way to work in Mountain View from his home in San Ramon about 6:00 A.M. Thursday. He had his car radio on, and heard that one of the Chowchilla kidnappers had been seen on the Peninsula.

221

As he turned north on U.S. 101 Wallis heard a description of the car Schoenfeld was driving, an old green van with Idaho plates —*just like the one ahead of him in the slow lane.*

Wallis didn't know what to do. If he pulled off the freeway and tried to find a telephone, he would lose the panel truck. At the same time he didn't know if Schoenfeld had a gun, or whether he would use it.

He pulled around the van and glanced at the driver. Even with a felt hat pulled over his eyes, Wallis could see that it was the same young man whose picture had been in the newspapers.

Wallis took the St. Lawrence Expressway off-ramp and slowed to a crawl. As the green truck went by, he pulled back on to the freeway behind it. Schoenfeld was going very slow, about thirty miles per hour. The gardener did not want to be conspicuous. He passed him again and kept the van in his rearview mirror.

Wallis kept up his game of cat and mouse until he saw that Jim had not taken the Moffett Boulevard turnoff. He knew there was a service station with a telephone at the next exit, Stierlin Avenue in Mountain View. He stabbed the accelerator and sped off the freeway. At the bottom of the ramp two police cars were parked, the officers talking with one another. Wallis screeched to a halt.

"The kidnapper, the guy in the green truck, he's going north on the freeway."

Officer Gary Lockman and Sergeant Larry Shannon of the Mountain View Police Department spotted the van less than a minute after they pulled on to the highway. They dropped back and radioed their position. The dispatcher called for help from the highway patrol and the police departments in Menlo Park, Atherton, and Palo Alto.

Schoenfeld took the Marsh Road exit from the freeway and turned west. At Bay Road Lockman turned on his red light and siren. The van pulled to the side of the road. Jim stepped out with his hands up as half a dozen patrol cars and a carload of FBI agents pulled up.

Dr. Schoenfeld sat nervously behind the steering wheel of the car he had borrowed the night before from a friend. He knew the

222

authorities had his license number, and he wanted to avoid recognition as he waited behind the service station.

Shortly after 7:00 A.M. a car with three men in it drove into the station. He recognized Jim Watters of the FBI.

"It's over, doctor," the agent said. "He's all right."

The father breathed a long sigh. "Where is he?" he asked.

"They're taking him to the county jail in Redwood City."

"What happens now?"

"You'd better ask your attorney about that," Watters said.

"We were going to his office. Jim was going to surrender."

"We know. He told us."

"I realize I should have called you," Dr. Schoenfeld said. "But I thought it would be safer for him to turn himself in to the district attorney."

"He could have been killed this way," Watters said. "He was lucky."

At 7:50 A.M. Larry Lawler, assistant special agent in charge of the San Francisco FBI office, arrived at the San Mateo County Jail. In a brief conversation, Jim told him about the plan for him to meet Woods at the Vancouver post office.

Lawler went immediately to a telephone.

By 10:00 A.M. Staff Sergeant Gerry Young of the Royal Canadian Mounted Police, Lower Mainland Division, dressed in a business suit, was strolling casually through the lobby of Vancouver's main post office, humming to himself. He took his time, examining the Canadian Forces recruiting posters and other advertisements. Corporals Harry Danyluk and Gerry Hanna were hidden behind the counter near the general delivery window. In an unmarked car in a parking lot across the street Constables Darrell Wakelam and Robert Teather watched the main entrance.

The excellent and well-earned reputation of the Mounties was going to suffer slightly that day, but only slightly. It was a mistake anyone could have made.

About 11:00 A.M. Thomas Engelhardt, twenty-six, and Norbert Werner, twenty-seven, two university students from Enlargen, about ten miles north of Nuremberg in West Germany, walked up to the general delivery window. The two were on a hiking vacation through North America, and Engelhardt was expecting some letters from his girlfriend. As they departed and walked down the front steps a man wearing street clothes approached them and asked for directions. As Werner was pulling out his city map, three other men jumped Engelhardt from behind, and the first stranger drew a revolver and ordered Werner to face the wall with his legs and arms apart.

The terrified tourists could not believe a strong-arm robbery such as this could take place in broad daylight.

Engelhardt, who was pinned to the sidewalk as the men rifled through his money belt and papers, managed to stammer that he had no more cash, that they could take the belt.

"Christ! It's not him."

All of a sudden their attackers became friendly. The four men helped Engelhardt to his feet and dusted him off, apologizing profusely. The first man took out a photograph of Woods and showed it to him.

"You look just like him," he said.

"I don't think so," the German said. "Not even remotely."

With more sincere regrets and protestations of eternal international friendship ringing in their ears, the two tourists retreated to a nearby bar to settle their nerves.

"Dammit," Young said. "I hope our man wasn't standing around watching this little circus. All right, everybody back in place."

In fact it would be nearly an hour until Woods arrived at the post office. Just before noon he walked up to the general delivery window and asked the clerk if she had any mail for Ralph Snider. She said no. As he walked toward the front door, the clerk nodded to Young. The sergeant followed him outside.

This time he was sure. Young waited until Woods was on the sidewalk. The FBI had described him as armed and dangerous, and the officer wanted to have a clear shot without endangering any bystanders if the suspect pulled a gun.

224

"Hold it, Fred," he said in a conversational tone. Woods turned around and grinned.

"You've got me," he said.

Danyluk and Hanna dashed down the steps as Teather and Wakelam ran across the street. "What's your name?" Danyluk asked.

"Fred Woods. You know my name," he answered as Hanna handcuffed his wrists behind his back. They hustled him into the back seat of a police car. Hanna and Danyluk sat on either side of him. Young got into the front seat and took out a card.

"I arrest you in the name of the Crown," he said. "It is my duty to tell you that anything you say may be taken down in writing and used in evidence against you. Do you understand that?"

"Yeah."

"Do you know what you've been arrested for?"

"Suspect in a kidnapping."

"Where have you been staying?"

"The Almer Hotel."

"Have you been using the name Ralph Snider?"

"Yeah."

"What were you doing at the post office?"

"I thought I might have a letter from Jim Schoenfeld. I know he got picked up, but I thought a letter might be here."

On the way to the hotel, Woods asked Young if there were any charges against him in Canada. The sergeant told him he had been arrested for the immigration authorities as a possible illegal alien.

"Will I be extradited?" Fred asked. "That should take some time."

"Not extradited, Fred, deported," the officer answered. "That shouldn't take more than a couple of hours."

When the four men walked into the lobby of the Almer, the manager gawked in disbelief.

"I'm sorry," Woods told Lumden, "I'm not Ralph Snider, I'm Fred Woods. I'll introduce myself as Frederick Woods." He laughed. "I don't want to leave, but it looks like I'm going to have to."

Upstairs the officers found a chair, brought it into the room, sat

225

Woods on it, and began searching. They found his clothes, money, and papers, including his false passport in the name of Ralph Snider. They drove him to the immigration office on Alberni Street, and as they walked toward the elevator Young asked Woods if he had engineered the kidnapping.

"Some of the things I did were obvious," he replied.

As they waited in a small interview room for the deportation hearing (It took only a few minutes. Woods's tourist card had expired, and he was in fact in Canada illegally), Hanna asked Woods if he drove the truck used in the kidnapping.

"No," he said. "Well, I might have at one time. So I drove it . . ."

"Fred, you say you definitely did not buy the three vans . . ."

"Put in Dodge vans," Woods interjected.

". . . used in the kidnapping?"

"One of the Schoenfelds did, but I don't want to say which one."

"What was your intention?" the corporal asked. "In other words, motive. Money?"

"Yeah—but I want to say this. No one was hurt or done any harm."

At 9:00 A.M. that morning, after he had passed the information Schoenfeld had given him earlier along to the RCMP, Lawler returned to the interview room where Jim was being held. He was accompanied by John McDonald, the San Mateo county sheriff. The FBI agent asked if the three kidnappers had any accomplices.

"There were just the three of us," Jim said.

"You mean there were just three of you there when you buried the moving van?"

"Yeah. I mean, how many does it take? Don't bang your heads against a wall. There are only three of us involved."

Lawler and McDonald left, and a few minutes later Detectives Duane Gull and Frank Perry walked into the room. "You're getting a lot of company this morning," Gull said. "I'm Sergeant Gull. I'm from Alameda County."

"Hi," Schoenfeld greeted him.

"I'm Sergeant Perry."

"Hi."

"Well, we gotta do the Dick Tracy bit, just like everybody else," Gull said. "No, not Dick Tracy . . ."

"No," Perry added, "the little heavyset guy who's got the cigar and trench coat on all the time."

"Columbo," Schoenfeld said. He chuckled. "Where's your dirty coat?"

"I've got one," Gull replied. "I keep it in the trunk of my car."

"This one's getting pretty bad right now," Perry said.

"Anyway, we've got to admonish you of your rights again," Gull said. "Third or fourth time this morning, probably."

"Oh, okay."

Perry read from his card, concluding, "Okay, having these rights in mind do you wish to talk to me?"

"Uh, I'm not supposed to," Schoenfeld said.

"You're not supposed to?"

"I phoned Mr. Merrill yesterday and, well, I was supposed to see him at eight o'clock this morning . . . and then we'd go to Alameda to turn myself in. And he said not to say anything until I talk to him first. Well, I didn't want a lawyer, but I talked to my dad and he said, you know, that the courts are so crazy and lawyers are even crazy and you can't trust either one, but . . ."

"Mr. Merrill is a good attorney," Gull said.

"Yeah, that's what my dad said. I just wanted to sign a statement and, ya know, not even have a jury and all that because, ya know, it just wastes time and expense."

Jim loosened up and, unsolicited, told the two detectives about the plan he and Fred had to meet in Canada. "Was that where you were going to stay?" Gull asked.

"Oh, well—depends on the job situation," Schoenfeld said.

". . . kinda start over up there?" Gull finished his question.

"We were amazed at how big everything just sort of blew up— couldn't believe it. We were gonna, you know, just drop the whole thing and then just, you know, drop everything Friday and then, uh, everything just got so blown up and we were scared and

227

nervous, and all that Fred and I could think of was to get out until things sort of blow over and cool down."

"What did you think when the kids got out early?" Gull asked.

"Well, I sort of figured on it."

"Did you?"

"Yeah. I just sort of figured that they might, because we didn't plan on doing anything at that time." Later in the conversation Jim said he had been worried about the batteries powering the fans, and that he would have taken the ones from the vans and Cadillac back to the quarry if the children had not escaped.

"Do you know how things are going with Boston?" Gull asked.

"Oh, Dave?"

"Yeah."

"Yeah, Dave didn't know anything."

"Nothing at all?"

"Fred was kidding around that he had mentioned something like this to Dave a couple of years ago."

"In the script form?" Gull asked.

"Yeah, and . . ."

"That's what I was working on," Gull interrupted. "See, I thought Dave wrote the script."

"Dave writes scripts and works with movies, so they were going to make a movie, and that's how the whole thing got started."

"But was that where the idea for this came from?"

"Well, we were trying to think of who thought up the idea," Schoenfeld said. "I know I didn't. I mean, Fred was saying, 'Well, Rick must have thought it up.' No, I thought Fred thought it up, because he . . . Fred told Dave and they were gonna make a movie, ya know."

"Is that what the original plan for this plot was, to make a movie? Or was it just to make some money?"

"It was just a crazy idea, just a wild idea, and I never thought we'd do anything."

"When did you first start discussing, Jim, do you recall? How long ago was it that the idea was kicked around?"

"Oh, I think Fred mentioned it a year ago, and I told him he was nuts," Schoenfeld answered. "And then we got into the cars and our house down in Mountain View, and all that. So I just dismissed it. And then Fred came up . . . well, let's do some preliminary stuff, well, that wouldn't hurt . . . bury this van, and stuff like that."

Later one of the detectives observed, "Yeah, a lot of planning went into this."

"Well, it—it was like making a movie, you know. It's like making a movie and you go through all the planning. Well, I wasn't doing anything at home, and I wasn't going anywhere, so I thought I might learn something by this experience."

At 10:40 A.M., while the Mounted Police were setting the trap for Woods in Vancouver, Perry and Gull put their prisoner in a car and started toward the Alameda County Courthouse jail in Oakland.

"I made a bulletproof vest," Jim volunteered along the way. "Can you try it out?"

Gull laughed. "No, I ain't gonna try it."

"I mean put it against something and see if it works," Schoenfeld said.

The two detectives shook their heads silently.

Part
Six

Chapter 27

The investigation continued for several months after Woods and the Schoenfeld brothers were captured, much of it aimed at eliminating their friends as secondary suspects. Several witnesses along the way had reported seeing other men with the accused kidnappers, but they never saw more than three at a time. It was not until after Jim was arrested that the investigators knew for certain that the three had used theatrical makeup, in addition to the hair dye mentioned in the tablet found at the warehouse. Among other things, Jim confirmed, they had false mustaches.

Before it was over, Baugh's detectives and criminalists interviewed 685 people, wrote 439 reports, processed countless tons of evidence, and served 13 search warrants from Reno to the Woods beach cabin in Marin County and including the banks where the suspects maintained accounts. It would be impossible to calculate the cost of the investigation to the taxpayers, especially the thousands of man-hours expended by other agencies such as the FBI and the State Department of Justice.

The staff of the crime laboratory, where the evidence underwent microscopic examination, lifted hundreds of fingerprints from the items found at the quarry, the Woods estate, the warehouse, and

the Schoenfeld home. Most of the associates of the accused kidnappers willingly allowed the detectives to roll comparison prints.
By the time all three were in jail Sam Erwin in Sacramento had
identified all but a few of the latents sent to him from Alameda
County.

Criminalists Patricia Zajac and Bob Hinkley, after nearly two
weeks of analysis, determined that seven pieces of canvas tarp—
three recovered at the quarry, one found near Saratoga that had
contained the children's possessions, two found at the warehouse,
and one taken from the Woods estate—all had matching threads.
They were able to report that the fabric originally had been a
forty-three-by-twenty-seven-foot surplus army tent.

Hinkley had a more difficult time with the lumber. He noticed
immediately that some of the two-by-fours taken from the quarry,
Portola Valley, and the warehouse had similar chalk lines on
them. These he knew to be lumberyard grading marks, but he was
unable at first to match the grain of the boards in the laboratory.
On the chance that he could, he asked the detectives to go back
to the Woods estate and pick up every two-by-four they could find.
Fred's father was cooperative, and consented to the search without demanding a new warrant. Ultimately, Hinkley was able to
prove that some of the boards found at all three locations had
come from the same tree. It was beyond the realm of coincidence
that they had not been purchased at the same time.

Some of the leads that had to be followed up during the search for
Woods and Schoenfeld brought them to dead ends. One was even
a little embarrassing.

About 10:00 P.M. Sunday, July 25, the weekend Baugh and
Volpe had been ordered by the sheriff to take off, Sergeant Dean
Hess and a phalanx of five other detectives rushed to Cloverdale,
a lumber town in Sonoma County about a hundred miles north
of Oakland, to find out if Fred Woods was hiding there with a
woman. A maid at the LaGrand Motel had told the Cloverdale
police that two people who had checked in to room 15 were
"acting furtive," averting their faces when they passed employees
and other guests. She said two towels she picked up when she

cleaned the room had hair dye on them, and that the man looked just like the picture in the newspapers of Woods.

Hess and his raiders made it to Cloverdale in near record time and were met at the police station by the local chief and a lieutenant from the Sonoma County Sheriff's Office. The motel manager and his wife also were there, and they tentatively identified a photograph of Woods as that of the man registered under the name of Johnson. The Santa Rosa address he had given was phony, according to Cloverdale police sergeant Jim Martin.

Accompanied by several local officers the six Alameda County detectives burst into room 15 just after midnight. The abashed "husband," a man five feet tall who bore no resemblance whatsoever to the fugitive, grudgingly gave Hess his true name and address. The "wife" said she had no permanent residence. In the stilted language peculiar to police reports, Hess concluded: ". . . With the information as given above, the above ACSD detectives along with Sergeant Martin and other members of the Cloverdale Police Department made contact with the subject. . . . It was found after making contact that the subject . . . had registered under a non-existent address, which will not be covered by this report. He was in the company of the female as listed above. This fact also will not be covered in depth by this report."

Throughout the investigation, the detectives continued to deal with the usual number of "confessions," soothsayers, and lunatics attracted by the notoriety the case was receiving. The following is a transcript of a conversation Sergeant Rod Alvarez had with an anonymous caller to the Eden Township substation the evening of July 29, after Jim Schoenfeld's arrest had been reported on the evening television news:

RECORDING: At the tone, one hour forty-two minutes Coordinated Universal Time.
DISPATCHER: Sheriff's Department.
CALLER: Yeah, I'm calling about John Schoenfeld.
DISPATCHER: Uh-huh.
CALLER: Yeah, you have him in here?

DISPATCHER: Who, James Schoenfeld?

CALLER: James Schoenfeld.

DISPATCHER: Who may I say is calling?

CALLER: A friend.

DISPATCHER: Hold on a second.

CALLER: . . . the one that masterminded the Chowchilla kidnapping.

ALVAREZ: Okay. You are, huh?

CALLER: There's no way you're gonna get me.

ALVAREZ: Okay, lay this on me, okay.

CALLER: [*Unintelligible*] . . . you don't e— you can't even identify me, and there's no way, 'cause I'm too smart for you guys.

ALVAREZ: Okay.

CALLER: However, if people such as James Schoenfeld w— Schoenfeld—are gonna get caught, I'm gonna arrange for their release and make sure that they are released.

ALVAREZ: Okay. You are? Well . . .

CALLER: Yes, I am [*unintelligible*].

ALVAREZ: If you're the mastermind behind all this, what are you doing calling from a phone booth?

CALLER: What?

ALVAREZ: What are you doing calling from a phone booth?

CALLER: What?

ALVAREZ: What are you doing calling from a phone booth?

CALLER: I'm not calling from a phone booth.

ALVAREZ: Okay. Well, I can hear noise in the background.

CALLER: Well, of course there's noise in the background.

ALVAREZ: Okay, you've asked . . . now, what are we supposed to do?

CALLER: I'm calling from an installation.

ALVAREZ: Okay. Who are we supposed to let go?

CALLER: James Schoenfeld.

ALVAREZ: Okay, and why are we supposed to let James Schoenfeld go?

CALLER: Well, I'm the person who masterminded the kidnapping.

ALVAREZ: Yeah, but that doesn't answer why we're supposed to let him go. If he . . . okay . . .

CALLER: [*Unintelligible*] . . .

ALVAREZ: You're saying you mas—

CALLER: . . . that's the thing. He was working for me, and as soon as he was working for me . . . you know, he did not do this on his own.

ALVAREZ: Okay. Well, ya—

CALLER: He was brainwashed, you know; he was drugged.

ALVAREZ: You conspired to do it then, so we legally have him in custody.

CALLER: Yeah, but he was drugged, you see.

ALVAREZ: He was . . .

CALLER: He was doing this under the influence of a drug, not his own mind.

ALVAREZ: Okay. What was . . .

CALLER: So, he's not really guilty.

ALVAREZ: What was he drugged with?

CALLER: Well, it's not for me to say.

ALVAREZ: Well, do you know?

CALLER: I know, yes.

ALVAREZ: Okay. Does he know . . .

CALLER: [*Unintelligible*] . . . you know.

ALVAREZ: Does he know that he was . . .

CALLER: Like I told you, I'm the one who masterminded this kidnapping . . .

ALVAREZ: . . . dr—

CALLER: . . . you're not dealing with a dummy; you're dealing with one of the smartest people in this, uh, planet.

ALVAREZ: Intelligent would be a better word.

CALLER: Yeah, right. Uh, you might say intelligent. You're dealing with one of the most intelligent persons on the face of this planet.

ALVAREZ: Okay. Then, why did you call me? You could of gone on . . .

CALLER: Why did I call?

ALVAREZ: . . . forever without me even knowing.

CALLER: Well, I'm calling to tell you that you're either to release him or else.

237

ALVAREZ: Or else what?

CALLER: Well, we'll blow up the Alameda County Sheriff's Department.

ALVAREZ: Yeah, okay. Well, it's . . .

CALLER: And we'll also blow up the sheriff's county car.

ALVAREZ: . . . it's pretty . . . it's pretty widely spread.

CALLER: Pardon me?

ALVAREZ: It's pretty widely spread. Are you gonna do all this at one time, or . . .

CALLER: What's widely spread?

ALVAREZ: The sheriff's department. It's not like . . . we don't all congregate in one building.

CALLER: Uh, well the thing is that, uh, you know, like what I'm referring to by the sheriff's department is the sheriff's office.

ALVAREZ: Okay, whe— Do you know where they're at?

CALLER: [*Unintelligible*] . . . different parts of the building, and then I am also referring to the sheriff's personal house and the sheriff's personal car.

ALVAREZ: Okay. What if I was to tell you the sheriff doesn't have a personal car, would that make any difference?

CALLER: Well, I'm assuming that he has a personal car.

ALVAREZ: Huh?

CALLER: I am assuming that he has a personal car.

ALVAREZ: Okay. Well, you shouldn't assume that . . .

CALLER: [*Unintelligible*] . . . drives a car . . .

ALVAREZ: . . . because then your threat becomes idle.

CALLER: . . . the car he drives . . . he drives . . . h—he drives, you know, a sheriff's car.

ALVAREZ: Right. Do you know what color it is?

CALLER: And . . . huh?

ALVAREZ: Do you know what color it is?

CALLER: Well, then again . . .

ALVAREZ: You don't know what color it is.

CALLER: . . . I'm calling from thousands of miles away here, you know [*unintelligible*] . . .

ALVAREZ: You're not calling from thousands of miles away, you don't have that many dimes in your pocket.

CALLER: . . . there are people, you know [*unintelligible*] . . . know better than me, because since I'm a thousand miles away, or over a thousand miles away, it would be kind of hard for me to see his car.

ALVAREZ: Okay.

CALLER: I mean, you know, I know that he has his house . . .

ALVAREZ: It's . . .

CALLER: . . . I know that he has an office [*unintelligible*] . . .

ALVAREZ: It's gonna be even more difficult for you to blow it up if you don't know what it looks like.

CALLER: Well, th— I'm trying to tell you this. I mean, you know, I'm like an executive; I don't do dirty work myself while I got all these people under me.

ALVAREZ: Okay.

CALLER: I have many people at my disposal.

ALVAREZ: Okay.

CALLER: I have people [*unintelligible*] . . . disposal . . .

ALVAREZ: Are you in the garbage business?

CALLER: . . . they're the ones . . . they're the ones who know about this.

ALVAREZ: Are you in the garbage business? You're speaking about people at your disposal.

CALLER: Well . . .

ALVAREZ: I'm tryin' to narrow this down. I'm a . . .

CALLER: Yeah, right. I know you're trying to narrow it down, but I'm saying . . .

ALVAREZ: I'm a new detective and you know, I'm talking to you so I can . . .

CALLER: Yeah.

ALVAREZ: You know . . . you know one thing you haven't even said that most people usually say about this time in the conversation?

CALLER: Yeah, what?

ALVAREZ: You're supposed to frantically say "And don't try to trace this call."

CALLER: Oh, I forgot. And don't try to trace this call.

ALVAREZ: Yeah, you're . . . you're lookin' . . .

CALLER: How do you like that?

ALVAREZ: Yeah, that's good.

CALLER: Is that good . . . ?

ALVAREZ: That's real good.

CALLER: . . . or, uh, do you want me to do it a little more, uh, dramatically?

ALVAREZ: Okay.

CALLER: And don't try to try to trace this call!

ALVAREZ: Okay, that's very . . .

CALLER: Well, anyway . . .

ALVAREZ: That's pretty good.

CALLER: You can trace the call, but you're not gonna be able to trace me.

ALVAREZ: Right.

CALLER: I'm saying . . . ya know, that's the reason . . . ya know, I didn't forget to say it; I mean, ya know, don't think I'm slipping up; it's just that, uh . . .

ALVAREZ: That's okay. Hey, do me a favor the next time you call, okay? Call two seven one.

CALLER: Oh, that phone is tapped, right?

ALVAREZ: No, that phone's not tapped; only beer is tapped.

CALLER: But it's important, uh, about James Schoenfeld because he doesn't deserve to be incarcerated.

ALVAREZ: Right, okay.

CALLER: Okay, you want me to call that immediately, or what?

ALVAREZ: No, there's nobody there.

CALLER: Oh. Well . . . okay . . . because, uh, you know something that the . . . you know . . . you say that you're . . . you're a new detective, right?

ALVAREZ: Yeah, I'm brand new.

CALLER: You're brand new, but . . .

ALVAREZ: Yeah.

CALLER: . . . you know [unintelligible] . . .

ALVAREZ: I'm embarrassed . . .

CALLER: . . . before it gets [unintelligible].

ALVAREZ: I'm even embarrassed to bring this to my lieutenant's attention.

240

CALLER: But I'm saying . . . I know that . . . damn well that you couldn't walk into the sheriff's department as a detective; you'd have to start someplace.

ALVAREZ: Yeah, well . . .

CALLER: I mean, I know that you know the ropes; I mean, otherwise I'm sure that, uh, your sheriff's making a big mistake by, uh, making you a detective.

ALVAREZ: Yeah, well, a lot of people say that.

CALLER: Well, I don't know whether you're qualified or not, but generally a detective is suspicious; he's skeptical; he's also unfriendly . . .

ALVAREZ: Yeah.

CALLER: . . . and then he's . . . you know, also has a rough personality.

ALVAREZ: Okay, but anyway . . .

CALLER: But, you know, you don't, uh, you know, even seem like you're a police or law-enforcement official. As far as I'm concerned, you, uh . . . in all, uh, practicality you sound like a friendly manager of one of those stakeout scenes in, uh, California.

ALVAREZ: Menlo Park or something.

CALLER: Yeah, something like that. You know . . .

ALVAREZ: Yeah.

CALLER: . . . to be quite honest, uh . . .

ALVAREZ: Okay, just one last question; then I'm gonna let you go.

CALLER: And I think that you are in the wrong business . . .

ALVAREZ: Okay. One last . . .

CALLER: . . . uh, you don't belong in this sheriff's office or any other sheriff's office . . .

ALVAREZ: Okay. One last question; then I'll let you go.

CALLER: . . . if you can't enforce the law.

ALVAREZ: Why . . . why did you do it?

CALLER: Uh, the devil made me do it.

ALVAREZ: The devil made you do it. That's pretty good.

CALLER: Why did I do what?

ALVAREZ: You know . . .

CALLER: Oh, yeah, the devil.

ALVAREZ: . . . the whole thing . . . dope Schoenfeld.

CALLER: Uh-huh. Well you might as well ask why I masterminded the kidnapping to begin with if that's what you want to know . . .

ALVAREZ: Yeah.

CALLER: . . . if you want to know the big things.

ALVAREZ: Who did you use?

CALLER: Ah, I used, uh, Frederick Woods, Ricky Schoenfeld, and James Schoenfeld.

ALVAREZ: Okay, is that all?

CALLER: Well, I'm not saying. Ya know, I'm saying . . . in other words . . .

ALVAREZ: Riddle me this, mastermind.

CALLER: [*Unintelligible*] . . . you got . . . you got the facts that I used these three people, uh . . .

ALVAREZ: Riddle me this, mastermind. Where were the five boxes of cereal supposed to be picked up at?

CALLER: The five boxes of cereal?

ALVAREZ: And what brand was it?

CALLER: Why do you want to know?

ALVAREZ: When you know the answers to those two questions, call me up on that number between eight thirty and five. Okay?

CALLER: And you'll be there?

ALVAREZ: Yeah, I'll be there. I'm goin' home right now.

CALLER: Why do you want to know the brand of cereal; is it important?

ALVAREZ: Because if you don't know, then you don't know anything about this whole thing.

CALLER: I do know.

ALVAREZ: Okay?

CALLER: I know a lot about this whole thing.

ALVAREZ: All right.

CALLER: But I don't know . . .

ALVAREZ: Take it easy.

CALLER: But, uh, wh— if you don't, uh, you know, have him released, uh, you know, you're all gonna be blown up.

ALVAREZ: Okay, what are we gonna be blown up with?

CALLER: Explosives.

ALVAREZ: Well, what type? There's more than one kind.

CALLER: Nitrogen.

ALVAREZ: Nitrogen.

CALLER: Glycerin.

ALVAREZ: Glycerin. Okay. I'm goin' on vacation anyway.

CALLER: I mean, nitro . . . that's nitroglycerin [*unintelligible*] . . .

ALVAREZ: Can you . . . just for me . . . for my own information, can you give me a date . . . an approximate date, 'cause I'm going on vacation?

CALLER: When are you going?

ALVAREZ: Well, I don't want to tell you, man, if you're really gonna do this.

CALLER: Well, I'm saying it will be done tonight if he's not released.

ALVAREZ: Okay. Well, tonight I'm safe, because I'm walking out the door as soon as I put this phone down.

CALLER: Yeah, but your business . . . place of business isn't safe.

ALVAREZ: Well . . .

CALLER: Your home might be safe; however, your sheriff's home isn't safe.

ALVAREZ: Okay.

CALLER: 'Cause [*unintelligible*] . . . sheriff's home the car he drives.

ALVAREZ: Do you even know . . . well, since you don't know the kind of car he has, do you even know his name?

[*Pause*]

ALVAREZ: Do you know the sheriff's name?

[*Pause*]

ALVAREZ: Okay, I'll see ya.

One of the more nettlesome loose ends was the story eighteen-year-old Craig Hunt had told Sergeant Cervi about seeing Fred Woods at home on the afternoon of the kidnapping.

On July 29, Sergeants Iver Edwall and Art Guzman interviewed Hunt again, this time at the Palo Alto Police Department. Origi-

243

nally he had told Cervi he had arrived at the estate to work for Woods about 10:00 A.M., and that he last saw Fred between 3:00 and 3:30 P.M., an hour before the kidnapping. Then he had said he wasn't sure Woods was there after 1:00 P.M. In his conversation a week later with Edwall and Guzman, the youth said he came to work at 9:30 A.M. and that Fred was feeding the horses. He said he went to lunch between 11:30 A.M. and noon, returned about forty-five minutes later and then had a brief conversation with Woods about 1:00 P.M. He didn't see his boss after that, he said.

The next detective to question Hunt was Rod Alvarez, again in Palo Alto. Only this time Craig was in custody at the Santa Clara County Jail. A Palo Alto policewoman, J. L. Mertens, had arrested him at his hotel on an outstanding traffic warrant. At the time of his arrest, Hunt admitted that a derelict red Mercury without license plates parked in front of the hotel was his. He told Alvarez that he had traded Woods a 1966 Plymouth for the Mercury after Woods told him he needed a Plymouth engine.

"On what date did the transaction take place between you and Fred Woods?" the detective asked.

"I traded with Fred either one or two days before the kidnapping," Hunt replied.

"Okay, now, the kidnapping took place on Thursday, the fifteenth."

"I made the trade on July thirteenth or July fourteenth, then," Hunt said.

"Are you sure the transaction took place before the kidnapping?"

"I'm certain of it."

Hunt then related to Alvarez how he took the red Mercury to the Department of Motor Vehicles on Friday, July 16, but was told he could not register it without a bill of sale from the previous owner. He said he went to the estate Friday afternoon, but that Fred was not home, and that his father told him he was away on a trip.

"Did he say where Fred was?"

"No."

244

"Craig, when was the last time you saw or heard from Fred?" Alvarez asked.

"The day we traded cars, one or two days before the kidnap."

Three days later, after Hunt had made bail on his traffic offense, Alvarez went to Palo Alto, drove him to the Eden substation, took his fingerprints and a four-page formal statement.

"Let's go back to Thursday, July fifteenth, the day of the kidnapping," Alvarez said. "You saw Fred in the morning. Did you see him after that conversation?"

"A little bit later in the day, it couldn't be any later than two P.M. that day."

"Why can't it be later than two P.M.?"

"I went to Menlo Park about two fifteen or two thirty P.M."

"How do you know you were in Menlo Park about two fifteen or two thirty?"

"I stopped in a little store that used to be called Super Junior's in Portola Valley and I saw a clock that indicated either two fifteen or two thirty."

"How much time elapsed between the time you last saw Fred Woods and your arrival at the store?" Alvarez asked.

"All I can say is somewhere around an hour had passed."

Alvarez reported both interviews to Volpe. "The kid has told four different stories now, including one that he wasn't even in Portola Valley on the fifteenth," the lieutenant told Baugh. "Do you think we should try for five?"

"Leave him alone," Baugh said.

The problem of how to handle David Boston was thornier.

When Detectives Al Poerink and Lou Lozano first talked to Boston a few days after Woods was identified as a suspect in the Chowchilla kidnapping, he said that he had been to the warehouse only once and denied that he had ever written a movie treatment or script involving abduction or extortion. Later, in a two-hour interview with Sergeants Duane Gull and Gary Seher, he would recant and admit writing *Chain Reaction,* and that he had visited the warehouse several times, as late as July. But he would continue to insist that he had never seen the vans or the dull black Cadillac.

245

"What do you do for a living, Dave?" they asked him.

"I'm a screenwriter. I also buy and sell things."

"Ever make porno movies?" Gull asked.

"Absolutely not!" he replied. "The only things I deal in to make money are legal."

"Would you call yourself a hustler?"

Boston thought for a moment. "Yes," he said, "a legal hustler."

"What do you think about the Chowchilla case?" Seher asked.

"I was thinking about that when I was in Southern California and I first heard about it on TV," the writer said easily. "I think somebody set up this operation and conned Fred and the Schoenfelds into pulling it off. I don't think they're smart enough to plan out and set up an operation like this."

During the interview, the detectives handed Boston a piece of paper. Baugh had asked them to get a set of his fingerprints discreetly. When they returned to the command post they turned the paper over to the criminalists.

"It's no good," Cooper told Baugh on the phone later. "That was Xerox paper. It's not porous enough to get a set of latents without smudging them."

On July 30, the day after Jim and Fred were arrested, Steve Battaini, who had already given the FBI the first letter he had received from Fred in Vancouver, returned to the resident agent's office in San Mateo. He gave Agent Wolfe the second package from Woods containing letters to him, Irene Bolzowski, and David Boston. It had arrived in the mail that day. The FBI turned it over to Baugh. He and Volpe were struck by the sentence in the letter to Boston that began, "I'm glad you're not in it now . . ."

"Now?" Baugh asked. "What the hell did he mean by now?"

"The suspects all insist they pulled it off alone," Volpe reminded him.

"Yeah, but Boston's the one who told us he didn't think they were smart enough to do it by themselves. I sure would like to read that script."

"He already refused to give Gull and Seher a copy of it," Volpe said. The D.A. says we don't have enough to arrest him, or even

246

to get a search warrant for his place, even with the letter from Woods."

On August 1, they tried to reach Boston in San Jose to set up a third interview, but learned that he had gone back to his apartment in Los Angeles for an extended stay.

A few days after that, Baugh and Volpe were talking to a reporter from Los Angeles who had flown to Oakland to cover the events following the arrests. They asked the newsman if he knew Clint Eastwood. The reporter said no, but that he knew someone who did. They told him Boston had written a movie script, and that they would love to see a copy of it.

Through an intermediary the reporter and a colleague were introduced to Eastwood, who normally makes his home on the Monterey Peninsula. The actor, a sensitive, intelligent family man whose real personality is the opposite of the violent characters he portrays in films, said he would be happy to do anything he could to help in the investigation of a crime that filled him with revulsion.

The reporters interviewed Boston about his script, and told him they would try to help him sell it to Eastwood. They arranged for Boston and Eastwood to meet in a restaurant in Los Angeles. Delighted at the interest expressed by his hero, the writer gave Eastwood a copy of the script.

Baugh and Volpe read the manuscript with great interest. Although it dealt in passing with a terrorist raid on a schoolbus, the fictional events it depicted bore no resemblance to the actual kidnapping. They returned the script to the reporters in Los Angeles.

Boston voluntarily surrendered another copy of the script to the authorities, and it was sent to Sacramento where Sam Erwin lifted samples of his fingerprints. They did not match any of those found on the evidence.

Eastwood, working as a volunteer undercover agent in a real-life drama, had provided part of the evidence that cleared Boston as a suspect in the kidnapping.

Boston had been the last one on the list.

Chapter 28

On the day that Jim and Fred were arrested, Rick was in Chowchilla for arraignment on forty-three felony counts. His attorneys, Ed Merrill and his law partner, William Gagen, had been unsuccessful in their attempts to have the hearing moved to Oakland. They were afraid the eighty-year-old county jail in Madera would not stand up to a mob.

Rick was driven to the little valley courtroom in a caravan of patrol cars manned by heavily armed detectives and deputies and accompanied by highway patrol airplanes. The mood of the town was angry, but not explosive. There were a few overt calls for summary justice. "Hang 'em," one citizen responded quickly when he was asked by a reporter what he thought should be done with the kidnappers.

Another man, Virgil Ryales, a postal clerk and volunteer fireman, said, "I offered to buy a rope and I have volunteers to build the thirteen steps—after a fair trial, of course."

Others were less vengeful.

"We're civilized. There ain't gonna be no lynchin' here," a farmer said. "That's just city talk."

Former Chowchilla mayor Bill Roscoe added, "People are

upset, of course. But we expect no violence here, because we're pretty much of a peaceful people. I would say the general mood of our citizens is one of quiet.

"But of course it's anybody's guess when it comes to some nut and what he might do."

In the end Judge Green was persuaded by arguments that Rick would be safer in Oakland than in Madera County. On advice of counsel the twenty-two-year-old defendant entered a pro forma plea of innocent. The judge continued bail at $1 million, and he was driven to Santa Rita to stay overnight before being taken back to the maximum security of the courthouse, where he was reunited with his brother.

Rick was considerably calmer at his arraignment than when he had surrendered nearly a week earlier. On that day, Gagen truly was afraid he might try to take his own life.

"He's nervous, distraught, trembling, often with tears in his eyes," the attorney said. "Rick fears for his brother's life—that is, he feels that if his brother feels as bad as he does he might commit suicide. Rick also indicated self-destructive tendencies."

At Merrill's request the young prisoner spent his first night in jail in solitary confinement. The attorneys were worried that the other inmates, most of them con-wise recidivists who adhered to the informal prison code abhorring crimes against children, might try to hurt or even kill him. After talking to Rick the next day, however, they asked jail lieutenant Frank Munn to transfer their client to the hospital tank, where he was given a cell near that occupied by former Black Panther leader Eldridge Cleaver.

"The boy needs someone to talk to," Gagen said. "He has no conception of the judicial system. I would say of all the clients I've had he's the youngest, most bewildered, and frightened-looking boy I have ever seen. His reaction to the charges and his being in jail is that of 'My God, what's happened to me? It's just not worth living.'" Gagen added that Rick had been "absolutely candid, absolutely open, absolutely truthful" in their conversations.

Cleaver, who had returned to the United States from Paris the previous year to end seven years of exile that began when he jumped bail in 1968, was trying to get his bond reduced as he waited for his trial on charges stemming from a shoot-out between the Panthers and the Oakland police. The fiery author of *Soul on Ice* and self-styled "Minister of Information" of the Panthers during their revolutionary phase had mellowed over the years. Almost as if he were gentling a scared colt, he talked to Rick. He told him what he could expect from the courts and his jailers. He described the advantages and disadvantages he saw in the legal system, and told him about being born again in Christ. He advised Rick to seek comfort in the Bible.

Cleaver became acquainted with all three kidnappers before he finally was released on $100,000 bail posted by his friends two weeks after Jim and Fred were arrested. Jim was moved in with his brother as soon as Rick was returned from Santa Rita July 30. Woods, who had been turned over to the FBI by the Mounted Police at the Peace Arch at Blaine, had spent the night in a county jail in Washington and then was flown to Sacramento. The next day he appeared before a U.S. magistrate, the federal warrant was dismissed, and he was handed over to Alameda County authorities. All three were together in the hospital tank, isolated, as was Cleaver, from the general jail population.

On August 4, the three young men appeared in Judge Green's court in Chowchilla. Jim and Fred both pleaded innocent to the charges, and sat silently while their attorneys—Merrill for Rick, Gagen for Jim, and Herbert Yanowitz for Fred—argued for bail reduction and for a look at all the evidence accumulated to that point. Yanowitz particularly wanted to see any statements made by the Schoenfeld brothers.

It was the first chance the town had to look at all the kidnappers. The courtroom was packed.

Judge Green scheduled the preliminary hearing for August 26, but Charles Hoffman, then acting Madera County district attorney, said he probably would take the case to the county's grand jury before then and seek indictments, a legal device that would move the case from the jurisdiction of the lower courts directly to the Superior Court.

They were returned to Alameda County with bail still set at $1 million each.

250

Although the evidence against them was staggering, the case was delayed repeatedly as the lawyers maneuvered for the best position for their clients. Richard Haughner, Alameda County's chief assistant district attorney, joined Hoffman in the grand jury presentation, and they were indicted August 26, on twenty-seven counts of kidnapping and eighteen counts of armed robbery. Five of the kidnapping counts alleged bodily harm to the victims, a charge punishable in California by life imprisonment without possibility of parole. Again, all three pleaded innocent as their lawyers worked to sort out the evidence.

From the time the first search warrant was returned in San Mateo County after Baugh and his men raided the Woods estate, court-imposed gag orders restricted the flow of information about the case to the public. The defense attorneys fought to maintain that secrecy against the wishes of the prosecutors and eventually in the face of lawsuits brought by newspapers. The day after the indictments were handed down, Fred, Jim, and Rick appeared in the Madera courtroom of Superior Court judge Jack L. Hammerberg. For fifteen minutes he carefully explained their rights and then asked each defendant if he understood.

"Yes, I do," Fred and Rick chorused.

"I hope so," Jim said.

The judge granted another defense motion to seal the evidence as reporters in the courtroom groaned aloud. Aside from the question of constitutionality, the gag orders thickened the aura of mystery that surrounded the case.

The defense attorneys intensified their fight to move the case from the emotional atmosphere of Madera County. On November 5, Judge Hammerberg agreed to a change of venue, and a week later, on the advice of the state's Administrative Office of Courts, selected Oakland as the place of trial.

The big questions were whether there would be a trial and what form it would take. A former Riverside County Superior Court judge, Leo Deegan, was brought out of retirement in November by the State Judicial Council to handle the case. But even before he arrived in Oakland, Merrill and Gagen asked to be relieved of the responsibility of defending Jim. They wanted to keep their first

251

client, Rick, but said they were afraid that their representation of both might lead to the brothers' making "incriminating statements" about each other. Their request was granted on the grounds of conflict of interest, and Jim became a client of Madera County public defender Lester Gendron because his personal resources were insufficient to enable him to hire an attorney. Because he was over twenty-one, his parents could not be required to pay for his legal costs. They continued to retain Merrill for Rick, however.

Haughner was joined in the prosecution by David Minier when the latter became Madera County's permanent district attorney. They successfully opposed motions by Yanowitz and Gendron to move the trial again, this time just across the bay to San Francisco. Merrill was satisfied with Oakland and did not join in the motion.

Although the legal proceedings had been moved away, Madera County remained liable for the costs for what was shaping up as one of the biggest criminal cases of the times. Worried that the expenses could bankrupt the small, agricultural county, Assemblyman Ken Maddy introduced a bill to obligate the state government to help all counties pay for trials in which the penalty could be life in prison. The bill made it through both houses of the legislature, but not the governor's office. In his veto message, Governor Brown said that he would not accept a law covering all counties, but that he would sign one that covered Madera County alone. Maddy called Brown a "smart aleck" and vowed he would introduce another bill in the next session.

Although it never was expressed publicly, one of the strategies of the attorneys was to delay a trial as long as possible while they tried to bargain for the best possible terms for their clients. Rick was ready to plead guilty to armed robbery and kidnapping without inflicting harm, which would have made him eligible for parole in about two years. But since the others still hoped to make a better deal, Merrill waited.

The case ground through the courts for months as motions were made, granted or denied, and then appealed. The lawyers explored

252

every technicality. In the meantime, the three languished in the courthouse jail in Oakland.

Perhaps no three prisoners in the country were as unprepared for custody as Fred, Jim, and Rick. With the exception of their brief experience in Downieville, they had never seen the inside of a jail. They had never encountered habitual criminals, homosexuality, or, for the most part, blacks.

The tanks on the tenth and eleventh floors of the courthouse generally house prisoners awaiting trial, although many of them are sent to Santa Rita because of overcrowded conditions. At first, all three remained together in the six-cell hospital section on the tenth floor. They could roam freely within the small cell block, but were separated from the seventeen-man dormitory tanks where most courthouse prisoners lived.

In addition to Cleaver they befriended Bill Harris, who, with his wife, Emily, was awaiting trial for the kidnapping of Patricia Hearst. The two survivors of the SLA were already serving terms from eleven years to life for their part in the Los Angeles robbery in which their victim-turned-comrade had participated. The couple would be enraged in May of 1977, when Miss Hearst was sentenced only to probation after she pleaded no contest to the same charges.

The three young kidnappers were surprised at the volume of mail they began receiving from throughout the country, some of it from cranks, some from well-meaning reformers who warned them to change their ways before it was too late, some from evangelical Christians. They kept up an active correspondence, answering the letters and writing almost daily to their families and friends. Rick was despondent when Julie told him she would be going to Lewis and Clark College in Portland in the fall of 1976, but she continued to write often and visited him on holidays. Prisoners in the jail were entitled to make one collect telephone call a week, and he talked to her occasionally in Oregon. Rick began to study the Bible and to talk about it with some of his fellow inmates, including Barry Braeseke, a confused young man accused with a companion of murdering his parents and grandfather. He began to pray every night.

253

In the fall Eileen Kelty came to California and visited Jim. He found it difficult to talk with her over the visitors' telephone as they looked at each other through a bulletproof window. After she returned to Louisville he wrote her about once a week.

When it became clear that there would be no quick disposition of their case and that they would be in no immediate danger, the three were transferred into a general dormitory tank. On December 15, a disturbance broke out in their cell block. A man on trial for robbery and assault refused to come out of his cell to go to court. The jail deputies called for reinforcements, and when they arrived they faced ten prisoners led by Harris and another inmate who formed a platoon to block the corridor. The officers used chemical agents to subdue the prisoners, and their visiting privileges were suspended for ten days. Two of those disciplined were Woods and Jim. Yanowitz appealed to the courts to block the punishment, claiming that Woods was caught up in the fringes of the demonstration and took no part in it. Fred said he was talking to his mother on the telephone in the visitors' area, and that the wall of prisoners prevented him from obeying the order to return to his cell. Even so, he was moved to another tank, while Jim and Rick remained together.

While he was with the Schoenfelds, whose easygoing personalities earned them friends among their fellow prisoners, Fred had little difficulty with the other inmates, who called the brothers "the Schoenfellers" or sometimes "the Chowchillas." On his own, his more caustic demeanor occasionally got him into trouble. Once, in an argument with another prisoner he thought was monopolizing a telephone, his nose was bloodied to the extent that he was taken to the county hospital for an examination. When he returned to his cell he found that his small cache of items purchased from the jail commissary had been stolen. He was bitter and angry, and stayed to himself after that.

Rick had a similar experience a couple of weeks earlier in which he suffered a cut over the eye in a fight with another inmate over a telephone. He spent the night at Santa Rita while tempers cooled, and found no bad blood when he returned the next day. Nonetheless, he and Jim decided to ask their friends not to come and see them to avoid the pressure to use the telephones on visiting days.

In October, three days apart, Fred and Jim turned twenty-five. It amused them that the newspapers, unaware of their birthdays, continued to say they were twenty-four.

Not too long after his incarceration, Fred received a letter from a prisoner in another jail, a woman several years older than he who was serving a year in Santa Clara County for selling narcotics. He answered her, and after a time they were writing to one another almost daily. Their correspondence continued after her release in the spring of 1977. At the same time Fred kept up his letters to Irene.

All three of them were annoyed at the inactivity of jail life. Fred began doing exercises such as sit-ups to keep in shape. In November he quit his half pack a day smoking habit, not so much for his health but to avoid the inveterate borrowing of his cell mates. Both the Schoenfeld brothers enrolled in correspondence courses through the University of California Extension. Rick took English and Jim a course entitled "Writing Magazine Articles That Sell." In February, the authorities conducted a shakedown of "C" tank to look for contraband. Jim and Rick were taken with the other inmates to another tank during the search, and when it was over only eight, including them, were taken back. Jim found that some magazines he had been saving to study for homework were missing, and had to recover them from a trash barrel.

He was forced to put up with a good deal of chaffing when he received in the mail an invitation from Sears to open a charge account and redecorate his new home. The company had apparently put his name on its mailing list because of his change of address filed in Atherton.

Fred, like the Schoenfelds, harbored no particular prejudice against blacks before he went to jail. They had all grown up in an environment of easy tolerance absent from racial tension. They had met relatively few people not of their own race, and it didn't occur to them at first that they might be viewed by those reared in the ghetto as symbols of oppression. In Oakland, as in most cities afflicted by urban blight, the majority of the jail inmates were black. The radios that were turned on from 6:00 A.M. to 11:00 P.M. were tuned most of the time by popular demand to stations specializing in soul music. It bothered them, although they didn't complain and Jim tried to solve the problem by getting some earplugs to use when he wanted to sleep during the day.

Each tank also had a color television set, tuned on weekends and in the evening to stations more or less representing a consensus of preference among the prisoners. Fred, who was indifferent to sports, grew to hate the endless parade of televised football games in the fall and winter, followed by basketball and finally baseball. In the spring of 1977, the sets in the jail, as were most of the others in the United States, were tuned for eight nights in a row to the local ABC affiliate, which ran the dramatization of Alex Haley's book *Roots,* the story of a black family from its origin in Africa through the abolition of slavery in America. Fred watched the first episode with some interest. He thought it was well done, but a little slow. He didn't like movies that took a long time to make a point. The show had a more profound effect on the black prisoners, many of whom regarded themselves as militants rather than criminals in any case. Fred suddenly was terrified by unexpected taunts and abuse. They called him a "rich pig" and accused his ancestors of keeping slaves on their estate. At first he tried to explain that his family was from New England, and that his own father had never called The Hawthornes anything other than "the ranch." As the derision grew over the next week, he retreated to his cell and trembled. In their tank, Jim and Rick saw the shows, but suffered little of the scorn Fred did.

The prisoners seldom stayed in one tank for long, and as they moved around the views from the jail windows changed. Fred saw the small sailboats on Lake Merritt when he was on the north side of the building. On the south side he gazed at the larger yachts moored along the Oakland Estuary. He became interested in sailing, and wrote for brochures on boats. He began decorating the envelopes of his outgoing letters with drawings of different kinds of vessels.

Rick and Jim read a good deal, certainly more than Fred did. Rick became enthralled with the fantasies of J.R.R. Tolkien. He read of the Hobbits and finished *The Lord of the Rings* trilogy, but failed to grasp the struggles between good and evil inherent in the stories. Instead he used the books to escape to an imaginary world.

All three of them gained a new and understandable interest in the law. Jim actually did some research, and while Yanowitz was fighting the discipline meted out to Fred for his alleged part in the near riot, Jim sent him some case law citations on prisoners' rights. He also wrote to a state assemblyman in Sacramento and asked for a copy of a new criminal sentencing bill then under consideration in the state legislature.

At his insistence, Fred's parents had been selling off the trove of salvage he had collected, and he kept careful track of any profits. In the spring he briefly considered not filing his state income tax. "What can they do to me?" he laughed. "Put me in jail?" His parents had cleaned out the warehouse themselves.

It was an irony that Mr. and Mrs. Woods, whose home and land had been ransacked by law-enforcement officers the previous July, would be visited again by police in force after their son was in jail. Some fleeing bandits had ditched their car and tried to hide on the property. The robbers were quickly arrested.

All three, but especially Fred, were impressed when the member editors of the Associated Press voted that the Chowchilla kidnapping was the biggest news story of 1976.

In March of 1977 the newspapers reported that Frances New-hall Woods, Fred's invalid grandmother, had been dropped from the Social Register, along with the remaining members of her immediate family who still had been included.

The Schoenfelds' friends remained loyal, for the most part unable to believe they had actually committed a crime of such unbelievable proportions. Many of them drove to Oakland on visiting days, even after Jim and Rick asked them not to do so. During one visit Jim was astonished when one of his oldest friends suggested that he would be better off when he got out of jail to grow a beard, change his name, and move to another country. It had never dawned on him that he could possibly be an object of public loathing for kidnapping and burying alive twenty-six children.

There is an emerging theory in psychiatry that the children of well-to-do families, reared without personal struggle, with most of the material things they want, have a latent hunger for ideals. This desire, some analysts say, can manifest itself by identification with a radical group, as in the case of the Harrises and Patricia Hearst and the SLA. Others seek identity in religion, politics, philanthropy, sometimes business or making money. It is difficult to judge whether there is a valid parallel, but Jim genuinely had convinced himself that his quixotic dreams of using part of the ransom for vaguely conceived good works justified their incredible act.

On May 4, 1977, Richard Nixon told David Frost and the American people that because he had lacked criminal motive in his handling of the Watergate cover-up, he could not be guilty of a crime. It is not known whether the three kidnappers watched that televised interview that Wednesday night, but the similarity in twisted logic is striking.

Chapter 29

On Sunday, August 22, 1976, over five thousand people, hundreds more than the population of the town, assembled at the fair grounds in Chowchilla to honor Ed Ray and the children. The throng ate four thousand pounds of barbecued beef, consumed a sea of beer, and cheered when Ray accepted awards and citations with a modest "thank you." The bus driver was awed by a message from President Ford praising his heroism, but he also was moved by a picture of the bus the children gave him after each had signed it.

That same Sunday the town dedicated a monument, a bronze plaque much like a historical marker, outside the Justice Center. Below a bas-relief profile of a schoolbus was etched this inscription: "With heartfelt thanks, the people of Chowchilla commemorate the safe return of 26 schoolchildren and their bus driver who were abducted July 15, 1976, and who escaped 30 hours later." Under Ray's name the children were listed alphabetically.

Some day that plaque will be all that remains to remind the town of that harrowing night and day. But it took a long time for normalcy to return, in part because of the massive attention from the outside, in part because the children were slow to forget, and in part because of the frustrated anticipation of some of the parents who believed that they, somehow, should get something out of it.

By the time school started again in September, the chamber of commerce had banked about $5,000 in unsolicited donations for the children and another $2,600 that had come in the mail for Ray. "None of them was hurt, so there were no expenses," chamber secretary Ned Crouch said. "It really surprises me." Ultimately the contributions to Ray were put into a supplemental retirement fund, and the chamber divided the children's share among them—$210.18 each—in the form of savings bonds. Ray thought they should have used the money to set up a special scholarship fund, but the town officials decided it would be too complicated and expensive.

Ray arrived back in Chowchilla barely in time to begin his twenty-fourth year as a bus driver. He had just wrapped up a taped appearance on *The Hollywood Squares* in Los Angeles. He won a cruise.

Darla Daniels was the only one of the twenty-six summer session kidnap victims who rode with Ray that first day of regular school, September 13. The other children on the bus, about thirty, giggled nervously as they were interviewed and photographed. The school district trustees had voted, not without debate, to forbid a television network's request to have a film crew ride the bus that day.

The first thing Ray noticed about his bus, the same one he had been driving when he was abducted, was that the scratches from the bamboo in the slough and the dents from the kidnappers' vans had not been painted out. The second was a brand new citizens' band radio on the dashboard. A company near Los Angeles had donated a base station for the district office and transceivers for all five schoolbuses. "Those wouldn't have been much help," Ray said, "because it happened so quick."

Ray found it difficult to be a national hero in his own town. The parents of some of the older children, encouraged by some juvenile exaggerations, resented the fact the roles of their sons and daughters in the escape were not as publicized as Ray's. These feelings

260

were overmagnified by some of the reporters who came through in predictable waves to write the "One Month Later" and "Chowchilla Revisited" stories for newspapers and magazines and weekend television news shows. Ray was perhaps most uncomfortable after the fall publication of his "exclusive" ghostwritten account of the kidnapping in the *Ladies' Home Journal.*

"The press created some of the problems after we came back," he said. "They tried to make it seem like there were bad feelings about me, and it wasn't true. They took pictures of my dog, Buddy, and waited for him to show his teeth so he would look mean."

On a Friday night, Saturday and Sunday in mid-October, Ray and the children went on another sort of adventure together. Accompanied by some of the parents, Mayor Jim Dumas and School Superintendent Lee Roy Tatom, they were taken on a bus to the San Jose Municipal Airport and were flown to Orange County. That evening they toured the Movieland Wax Museum. The next day they worked their way through Disneyland and Knott's Berry Farm. The climax came Sunday when they rode on floats in the annual "Silverado Days" parade in Buena Park.

The excursion was sponsored by the Buena Park Noon Lions, whose president was Dr. Charles LaRue, a clinical psychologist. "I knew how these things create emotional scars," he was quoted as saying, "so I thought we could do something to help. We had to show them there were nice people in the world too."

It is still being debated among psychiatrists and psychologists whether any aftereffects the children may suffer will come from the crime itself or the international attention it received. Shortly after the victims were returned, Mayor Dumas received a letter from Dr. Jonathan Kellerman, clinical child psychologist at the Children's Hospital of Los Angeles. As the director of psychological treatment for pediatric cancer patients, he was a specialist in the reactions of children to stress, and he wondered if the town officials had thought to seek any psychiatric counseling for the schoolchildren. Dumas called Dr. Kellerman and asked for suggestions.

"These children experienced an alternate form of child abuse—not chronic abuse, but a very strong, acute abuse," the psychologist said. He advised the mayor to call the local mental health professionals in Madera County.

It was several months after the kidnapping before a meeting was held between the parents from about half the seventeen families involved and the county mental health services staff. The parents were motivated primarily by alarming news stories they had read predicting lifelong emotional trauma for their children. The two psychiatrists, one psychologist, and one clinical social worker had not expected any children to attend the meeting, but when they came anyway "we took a look at the kids and, from a gut level, did not see anything unusual in their behavior," Dr. Raymond E. Reedy, the staff director, later reported in *Pediatric News*. The counselors concluded there could be some psychiatric casualties as the years went by, at the rate of perhaps one child in twenty. But the real problem, Dr. Reedy said, was that "some of the parents were not hurting enough." Based on his information, the medical journal reported that "For the first time, these parents, living in one of the most deprived sections of California, were being given attention, fame and popularity they had never experienced before. Questions such as whether a child might act in a movie or the strategy of civil action to recover damages complicate these people's lives now."

Some parents refused to believe the best therapy for their children would be to treat them normally, with normal expectations, and sought help from outside analysts. But, interviews with the children a year after their ordeal made it apparent that the memory of terror was fading, and that their parents, bereft of the resilience of childhood and more aware of mortality, had taken the event harder than they had. For the children it was something they could recall in as much detail as they wanted, consciously or subconsciously. For the parents, who had not been there, the experience was something that could only darkly be imagined.

Many of the other 4,600 people in Chowchilla were unhappy to see the limelight fade. Somehow, the kidnapping had become an ingredient in civic boostering. For a while there was a run on bumper stickers printed by the local weekly newspaper that said, "Now You Know Where Chowchilla Is," but sales tapered off.

Once, for a couple of weeks in the summer of 1976, the name Chowchilla screamed in a hundred languages from the front pages of newspapers from Oslo to Capetown and from Moscow to Tahiti.

"Now, when I go to meetings out of town," Superintendent Tatom told a reporter a year later, "people say the name Chowchilla means something to them, but they can't quite remember why they know the name. Soon, they'll forget the name."

Epilogue

In July of 1977 Judge Deegan convened a hearing in Alameda County Superior Court in Oakland to hear motions by the defense attorneys to quash the search warrant that was served at the Woods estate on the grounds it was based in part on evidence illegally obtained. They argued that officers on the stakeout had entered the property before the warrant was issued and recognized the dump truck that had been seen at the quarry when the moving van was buried. The presence of the truck at the estate was included in Lieutenant Volpe's affidavit supporting the request for the warrant. The prosecution quickly admitted the error, but the judge ruled that the evidence found on the Woods property was not tainted and could be used against the defendants.

They had run out of legal maneuvers.

On July 25, a year and ten days after the abduction, Woods and the Schoenfeld brothers pleaded guilty to twenty-seven counts of kidnapping for ransom without inflicting bodily injury. As a result of plea bargaining the prosecution agreed to drop the armed robbery charges, but insisted on submitting the issue of whether the victims had been hurt to the court for trial. "We're going to use the body scratches, the cuts, the nose bleeding, the claustrophobic effects of being buried underground and the emotional harm those children suffered," Madera County D.A. David Minier said. "This constitutes bodily harm in our opinion."

The defense immediately waived the right to a jury to decide the point.

"A jury would have been too sympathetic to the kids on the bus," Madera County public defender Leonard Gendron said. "It's an overwhelming prosecution case. Everything went down the drain when they found the ransom notes and other plans."

Purely by chance, Ed Ray, who was vacationing in the Bay Area after the end of the summer school session, was in court when the three changed their pleas.

"Justice has been served," he said slowly. "I'm happy. I feel better that they pleaded guilty. They should have done that a long time ago. Now I'm ready to party it up tonight."

His sentiments were echoed in Chowchilla. The townspeople were relieved that it was over. Somehow, it was like a second happy ending for them.

The trial on the issue of bodily injury began November 1 under the glaring attention of the media. Including delays, it was to last nearly seven weeks, during which time the three defense attorneys would fight doggedly to prove that the victims had not been hurt; if they failed, their youthful clients faced life in prison without the possibility of parole.

The first of the prosecution's nineteen witnesses was Ray. In a steady voice he recounted the events of that sweltering Thursday almost a year and a half earlier. He recalled riding in the back of the van.

"It got so bad I couldn't move," he testified. "They were all leaning against me. Yeah, it hurt."

He told the judge about finding the food the kidnappers had left for them in the buried truck body.

"The kids got to that right away," he said. "I got one slice of bread. I should have left it for them, I guess."

One by one the children told their stories.

"What happened after the bus got under way?" a deputy district attorney asked Jodie Heffington.

"A man . . ." the girl began. "A man. . . ." She started to sob, and then cried, out of control. Judge Deegan quickly recessed the proceedings, and the witness's father soothed her until she was able to resume her seat on the witness stand, clutching a cup of water. Later, her parents testified that their daughter had suffered from a recurring urinary problem as a result of her ordeal.

Mike Marshall said he began to hallucinate, to see things that weren't really there, after several hours as a captive. Jennifer Brown remembered how she had tried to cheer the younger children by singing.

"Lots of kids were crying and screaming," she said. "So I sang 'If you're happy and you know it, clap your hands.' But nobody did. It wasn't happy, it was sad. But there was nothing else to do.

"Then I sang songs like 'Boogie Fever' and 'Get Down Tonight.' I was hot and tired and sad and scared. Everybody was. I didn't worry, but I was scared.

"The air started to disappear and it got hard to breathe. And it smelled bad. It smelled awfully bad down where the bathroom was."

It appeared at first the case would turn on conflicting medical testimony about the condition of the children after their rescue and the effects of their confinement. Two physicians who examined them at Santa Rita said that all of the victims seemed to be in reasonably good shape.

"The best therapy was to get them home as soon as possible," said Dr. Howard Wax, a pediatrician. "They were in excellent spirits, with some of the children having minor injuries."

But Ed Volpe testified that a number of the children had been hysterical and that Ray was at the point of breakdown. Volpe was followed by a male nurse who told the court the doctors had given the children only cursory examinations.

On November 4 Judge Deegan moved the court briefly to Santa Rita, where he viewed the vans, the Cadillac and the musty moving-van trailer. As the three shackled defendants looked on nervously, he walked silently among the evidence in the dimly lit warehouse.

The state concluded its case November 31 with the testimony of a University of California pediatrics professor who said that in his opinion Ray and at least four of the children suffered from heat exhaustion.

The defense opened by showing television film taken at Santa Rita the night the victims were found. The clips showed an apparently robust Ed Ray and a gaggle of cheerful and excited children. One of the first defense witnesses was Alameda County Sheriff's Department Criminologist Dick Schorr, who testified that the blood found on a bedspread was not the same type as Ray's.

After an unsuccessful motion to ban any evidence related to heat exhaustion, the defense attorneys called as a witness Colonel Robert Herman, a doctor and a chief of the department of medicine at the Institute of Army Research in San Francisco. He said that only people doing heavy work under extremely high temperatures experience heat exhaustion, that humans recover from it quickly and that there are no aftereffects.

In their final arguments, the defense lawyers insisted that the prosecution had not proved its case, and pleaded with the judge not to commit the three young men to the living death of life in prison.

On December 15, 1977, ten days before Christmas, the trial ended. Without leaving the bench, Judge Deegan delivered his verdict. He spoke for an hour, quietly, dispassionately. As he began, Jack Baugh slipped into the courtroom and took a seat near the back.

The judge said he did not believe that the scratches, bruises, cuts and contusions complained about by Ray and some of the children constituted serious injury. Nor was he persuaded by the prosecution's hotly contested contention that the victims suffered from heat exhaustion.

But in the end, he turned his attention to the testimony of three of the girls, Jennifer Brown, Jodie Heffington and Becky Reynolds. He looked down at the defendants.

"I have resolved an opinion that the prosecution has established beyond reasonable doubt that there was bodily harm under California law," he said grimly.

"I made my finding on the testimony of these children. I don't think they have any guile about it. I think they're telling the truth.

"The kidnapping itself was a classic violation of bodily security, and this was an aggravated kidnapping."

He noted that the abductors had made "some provisions" for air, blankets, water, food and primitive toilets. "But in totality the kidnappers were indifferent to the welfare of the children," he said.

"The children were not old enough to endure such treatment. . . . These children were not told why they were there. They were impressed with the fear they were going to die.

"These children were put through an ordeal by terror."

Fred, Jim and Rick, prepared by the attorneys for the possibility of defeat, sat impassively as the judge, in effect, consigned them to die in prison.

Fred's parents and Mrs. Merry Schoenfeld stared in frozen silence in the courtroom, only half filled because most of the reporters had expected the judge to take the case under submission before making his ruling.

The three defense attorneys immediately gave verbal notice of appeal, and asked for a hearing on possible mitigating circumstances. The judge agreed to hear additional motions after the new year, even though the law, without exception, decreed a mandatory sentence.

It was over. The prisoners were taken back to their cells, and their shattered parents left the courtroom. Mr. and Mrs. Woods declined to talk with the reporters. Mrs. Schoenfeld was the only one to speak.

"I can't believe it," she said. "I'm stunned."

Jack Baugh remained for a time after the courtroom was cleared, unsure of his emotions.

At first he had been a little surprised at the verdict, but as the

271

judge cited other cases that defined bodily injury, he realized that Deegan's hands had been tied by the legislature. Although the law in the present case might seem draconian, it was the law and had to be obeyed. Deegan had done his homework. It was probably the hardest decision he had ever made.

Baugh thought about the number of convicted murderers he knew who were walking the streets after serving minimum terms. In his mind he saw the three young men in their white jail coveralls, not a lot older than his own children.

As he walked down the steps of the courthouse he heard the tinkling of a Salvation Army worker's Christmas bell.

He shuddered. I need a drink, he thought.

In many respects the Chowchilla case has all the elements of an American tragedy. It was a crime committed not by criminals but by three otherwise law-abiding young members of the upper middle class whose futures could have been as bright as they wanted to make them. It was a crime committed against twenty-seven people they did not know and probably never would have met, against whom they bore no malice.

It is difficult to speculate about what might have happened if Ray and the children had not escaped that Friday night.

The plot was at once sophisticated and childishly incomplete. That it worked as far as it did is almost unbelievable. It is clear the kidnappers didn't intend to hurt anyone, and that they planned to return their victims after receiving the ransom, probably in the same vans they had used to abduct them. The ransom demand was never delivered, but it's doubtful the state would have paid the $5 million in any case.

No one will ever know exactly how long the three would have held their prisoners if the authorities had refused to make the payoff, because the kidnappers didn't really know, themselves. Jim Schoenfeld told the detectives he and the others planned to return to the quarry with fresh batteries for the ventilator fans. But if they had waited until Saturday night or Sunday to do so, the original batteries would have failed, and it's possible they would have inadvertently perpetrated one of the largest nonpolitical mass

272

murders in history, the senseless massacre of twenty-six children and one adult by asphyxiation.

Fred, Jim, and Rick did not think about the consequences of their acts. In that, they may be symbolic of a generation frustrated by a lack of goals. They wanted for nothing in a material sense, and had grown up in a milieu where the pranks and misdemeanors of the children of good people are often tolerated and usually go unpunished. Their only contact with crime and violence and the police reaction to it was the unreal world created by movies and television. They were compelled not by the lofty dreams of human betterment fantasized in Jim's diary nor by Fred's desire to make films or live in a mansion, but by boredom. They set themselves a challenge, farfetched and grandiose enough that success in this single adventure would have cancelled all the failures that had come before.

The three, products of the times and their environment, lacking direction, simply allowed themselves to be swept along by events they had set in motion themselves. To that extent it was a tragedy: the kidnappers, their victims, and the thousands of others touched directly by the crime were caught up in the vortex of a horror over which they had no control. The motive of the three was that they had no motive.

They probably will regret it forever, perhaps not so much because they are sorry for the terror they caused, but because it didn't work and they had to go to jail. For them remorse was a function of getting caught.

One unmeasurable consequence of the Chowchilla kidnapping was the impact it had on nameless millions of middle-class parents whose initial reaction, that the victims could have been their children, was followed by the fearful realization that the kidnappers resembled their offspring as well.

Lee Roy Tatom was wrong. There will be those who always will remember.

The victims will never forget. Those who loved and trusted the kidnappers, their families and friends, will remember with sorrow and confusion. Still others, such as Baugh and Volpe and Bates,

273

will retrace perpetually the bizarre trail that led them to three totally improbable "master criminals."

Most of all, perhaps, Fred, Jim, and Rick will remember. These three, in many ways as immature as their victims, will recall how they planned it and how they executed it. But it is hard to tell whether or not they will ever appreciate the malignancy of what they did, or whether they themselves will ever really know why they had taken the children.